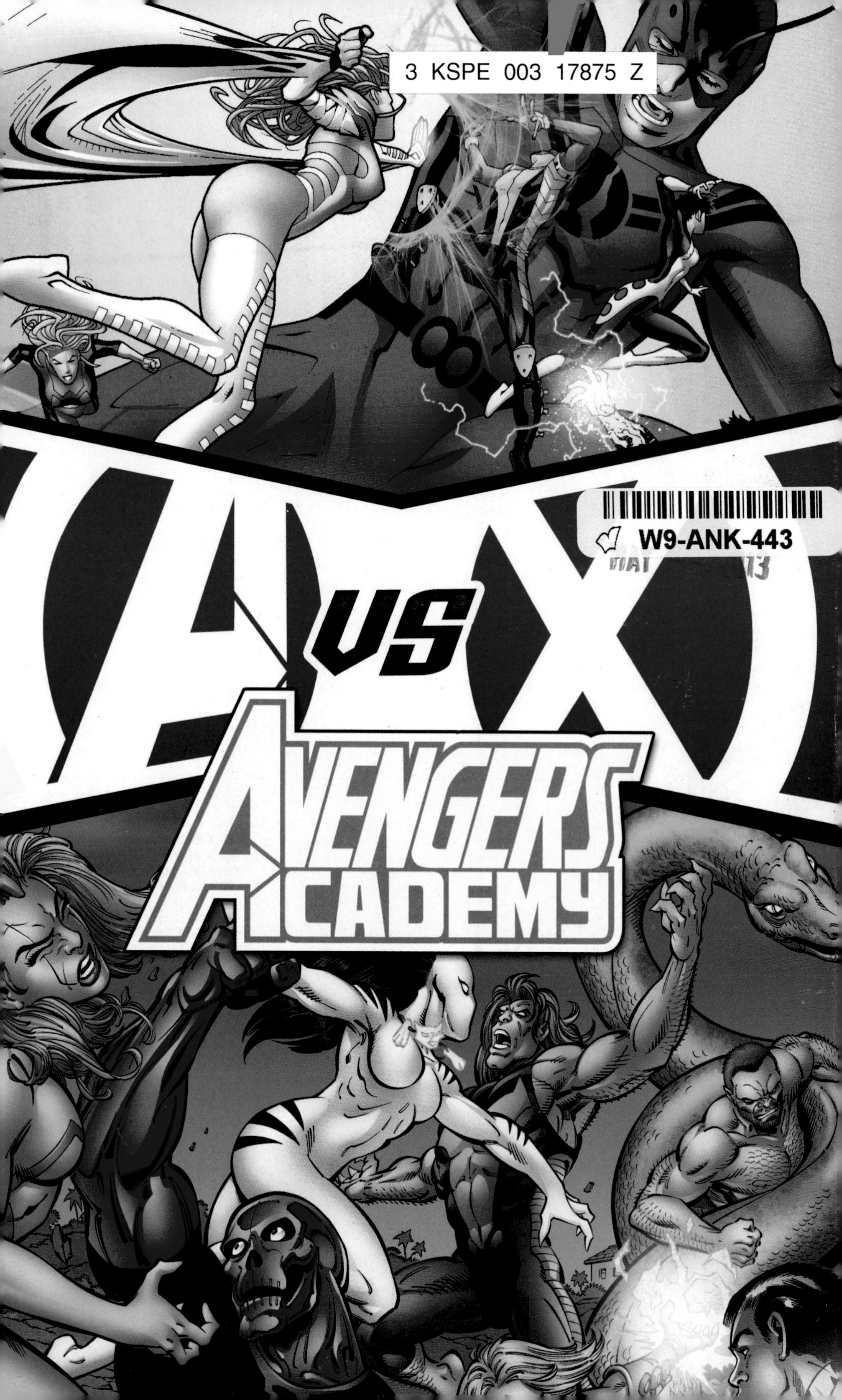
A VS X
AVENGERS ACADEMY

AVENGERS ACADEMY

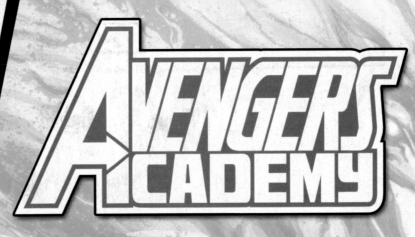

WRITER: **CHRISTOS GAGE**
PENCILERS: **TOM GRUMMETT** (#29-31)
& **TIMOTHY GREEN II** (#32-33)
INKERS: **CORY HAMSCHER** (#29-31) & **JEFF HUET** (#32-33)
COLORIST: **CHRIS SOTOMAYOR**
LETTERER: **VC'S JOE CARAMAGNA**
COVER ARTIST: **GIUSEPPE CAMUNCOLI**
WITH **JIM CHARALAMPIDIS**
ASSISTANT EDITORS: **JAKE THOMAS** & **JON MOISAN**
EDITOR: **BILL ROSEMANN**

COLLECTION EDITOR: **CORY LEVINE**
ASSISTANT EDITORS: **ALEX STARBUCK & NELSON RIBEIRO**
EDITORS, SPECIAL PROJECTS: **JENNIFER GRÜNWALD & MARK D. BEAZLEY**
SENIOR EDITOR, SPECIAL PROJECTS: **JEFF YOUNGQUIST**
SVP OF PRINT & DIGITAL PUBLISHING SALES: **DAVID GABRIEL**
BOOK DESIGN: **JEFF POWELL**

EDITOR IN CHIEF: **AXEL ALONSO** CHIEF CREATIVE OFFICER: **JOE QUESADA**
PUBLISHER: **DAN BUCKLEY** EXECUTIVE PRODUCER: **ALAN FINE**

AVENGERS VS. X-MEN: AVENGERS ACADEMY. Contains material originally published in magazine form as AVENGERS ACADEMY #29-33. First printing 2013. ISBN# 978-0-7851-6581-1. Published by MARVEL WORLDWIDE, INC., a subsidiary of MARVEL ENTERTAINMENT, LLC. OFFICE OF PUBLICATION: 135 West 50th Street, New York, NY 10020. **Printed in the U.S.A.** ALAN FINE, EVP - Office of the President, Marvel Worldwide, Inc. and EVP & CMO Marvel Characters B.V.; DAN BUCKLEY, Publisher & President - Print, Animation & Digital Divisions; JOE QUESADA, Chief Creative Officer; TOM BREVOORT, SVP of Publishing; DAVID BOGART, SVP of Operations & Procurement, Publishing; RUWAN JAYATILLEKE, SVP & Associate Publisher, Publishing; C.B. CEBULSKI, SVP of Creator & Content Development; DAVID GABRIEL, SVP of Print & Digital Publishing Sales; JIM O'KEEFE, VP of Operations & Logistics; DAN CARR, Executive Director of Publishing Technology; SUSAN CRESPI, Editorial Operations Manager; ALEX MORALES, Publishing Operations Manager; STAN LEE, Chairman Emeritus. For information regarding advertising in Marvel Comics or on Marvel.com, please contact Niza Disla, Director of Marvel Partnerships, at ndisla@marvel.com. For Marvel subscription inquiries, please call 800-217-9158. **Manufactured between 1/24/2013 and 2/26/2013 by QUAD/GRAPHICS, VERSAILLES, KY, USA.**

10 9 8 7 6 5 4 3 2 1

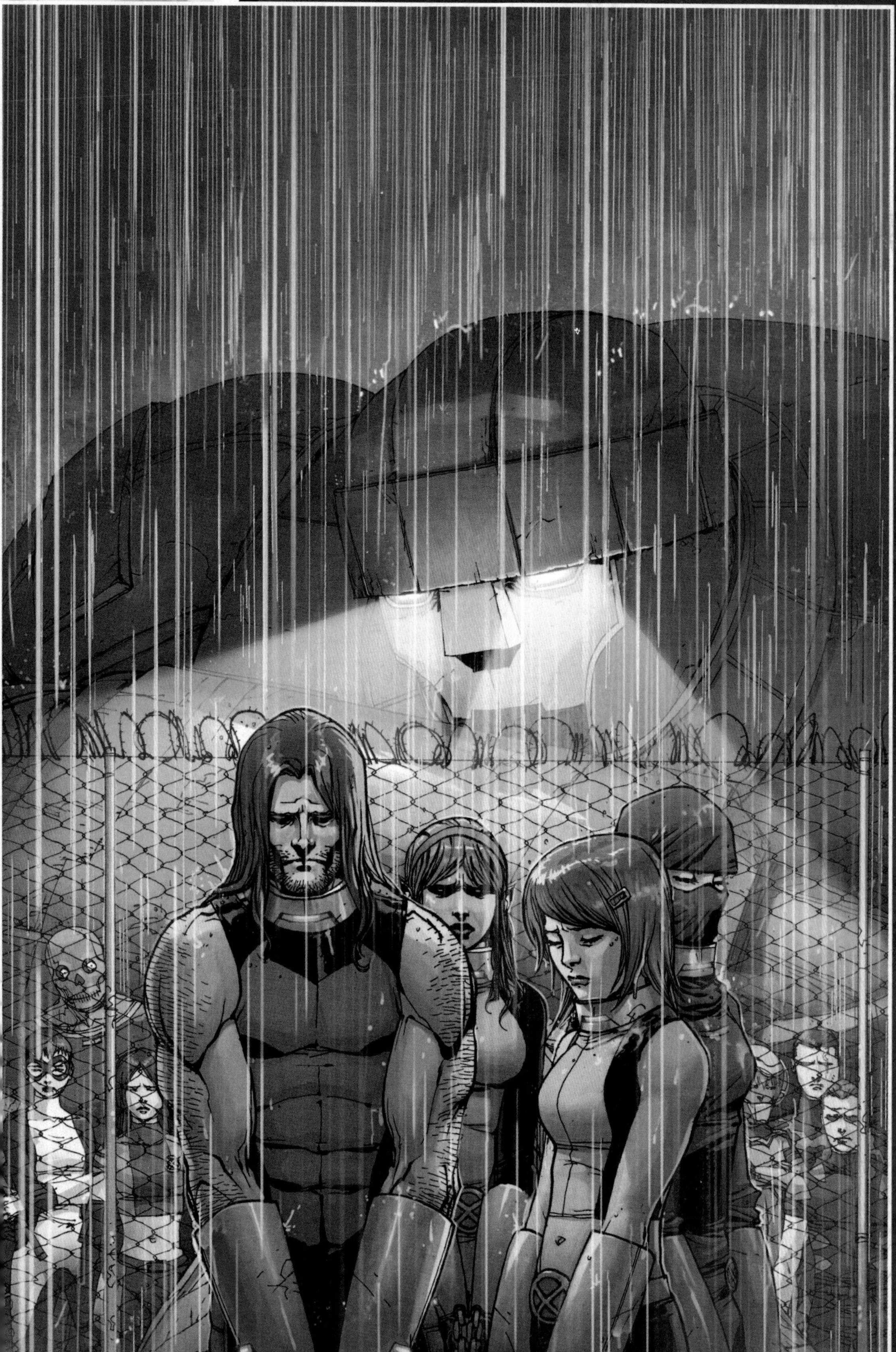

ISSUE #29

AND THERE CAME A DAY, A DAY UNLIKE ANY OTHER, WHEN EARTH'S MIGHTIEST HEROES OPENED THEIR DOORS TO TEACH THE NEXT GENERATION! ON THAT DAY, THE AVENGERS ACADEMY WAS BORN, TO TRAIN YOUNG ADULTS TO FIGHT THE FOES NO SINGLE SUPER HERO COULD WITHSTAND!

AVENGERS ACADEMY

STUDENTS

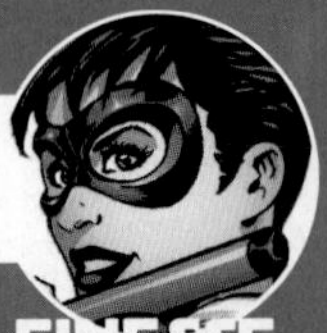

FINESSE — PHOTOGRAPHIC FIGHTER. ALL HEAD, NO HEART.

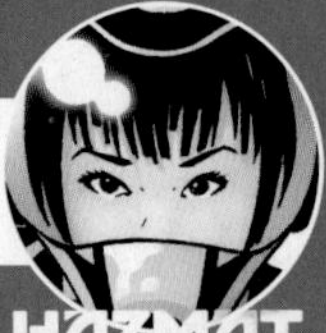

HAZMAT — HUMAN TOXIC SPILL. CAUSTIC PERSONALITY.

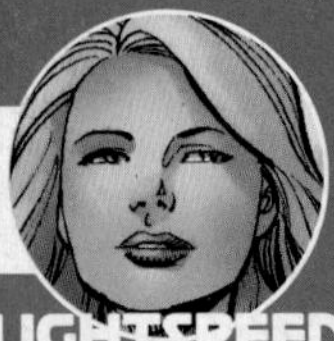

LIGHTSPEED — ABLE TO FLY, LOOKING TO BE MORE GROUNDED.

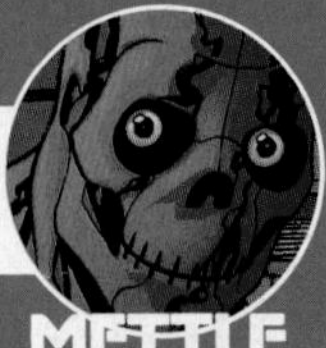

METTLE — STEEL-SKINNED POWERHOUSE. ARMORED SHELL PROTECTING INNER FEELINGS.

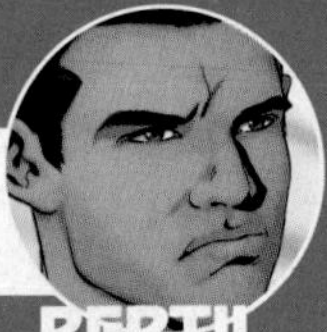

REPTIL — DINOSAUR MORPHER. FUTURE HERO OR NAIVE OPTIMIST?

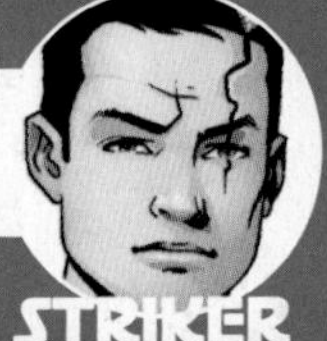

STRIKER — ELECTRIC DYNAMO. SELF-PROMOTES THROUGH SHOCK TACTICS.

GIANT-MAN RECENTLY RELOCATED THE ACADEMY TO THE NEWLY REFURBISHED AND REINFORCED WEST COAST AVENGERS COMPOUND AND OPENED THE SCHOOL'S DOORS FOR NEW STUDENTS, INCLUDING THE FEMALE CLONE OF WOLVERINE, **X-23**.

THE AVENGERS AND THE X-MEN HAVE GONE TO BATTLE AGAINST EACH OTHER OVER THE FATE OF THE MUTANT MESSIAH **HOPE** AND HER SUSCEPTIBILITY TO THE ONCOMING, POTENTIALLY CATACLYSMIC PHOENIX FORCE. WHAT DOES THIS MEAN FOR A SCHOOL RUN BY THE AVENGERS BUT CONTAINING MANY MUTANTS?

IS WAR COMING TO THE AVENGERS ACADEMY?

NOTE: THIS STORY HAPPENS AFTER THE EVENTS OF AVX #2...BUT YOU ALREADY READ THAT, RIGHT?

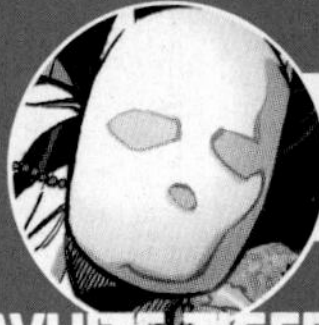

WHITE TIGER — POWERED BY MYSTICAL AMULET, FUELED BY FAMILY PRIDE.

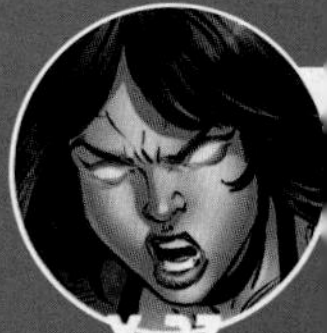

X-23 — FEMALE CLONE OF WOLVERINE SEARCHING FOR HER SOUL.

STAFF

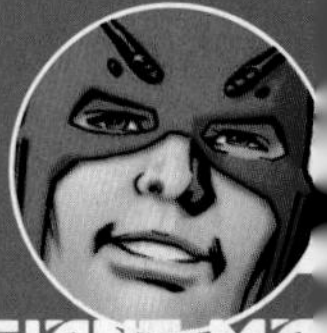

GIANT-MA — SIZE-CHANGING SCIENTIST SUPREME.

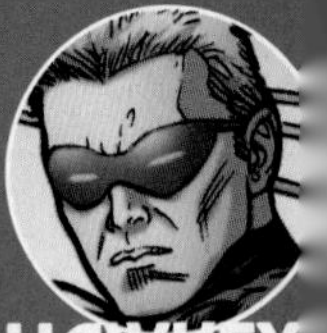

HAWKEY — CANNOT MISS, NOW AIMING AT TEACHING.

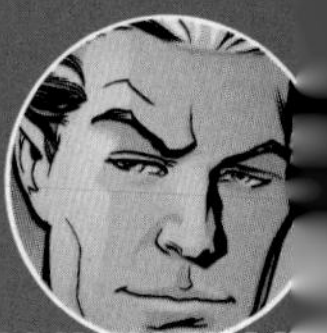

QUICKSILV — SURLY SPEEDSTER.

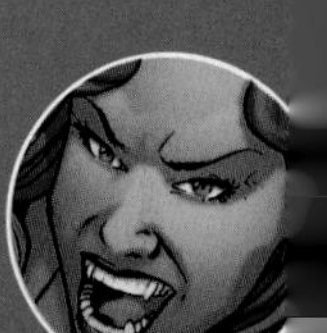

TIGRA — CAT WOMAN. ENHANCED STRENGTH, AGILITY AND ATTITUDE.

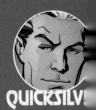

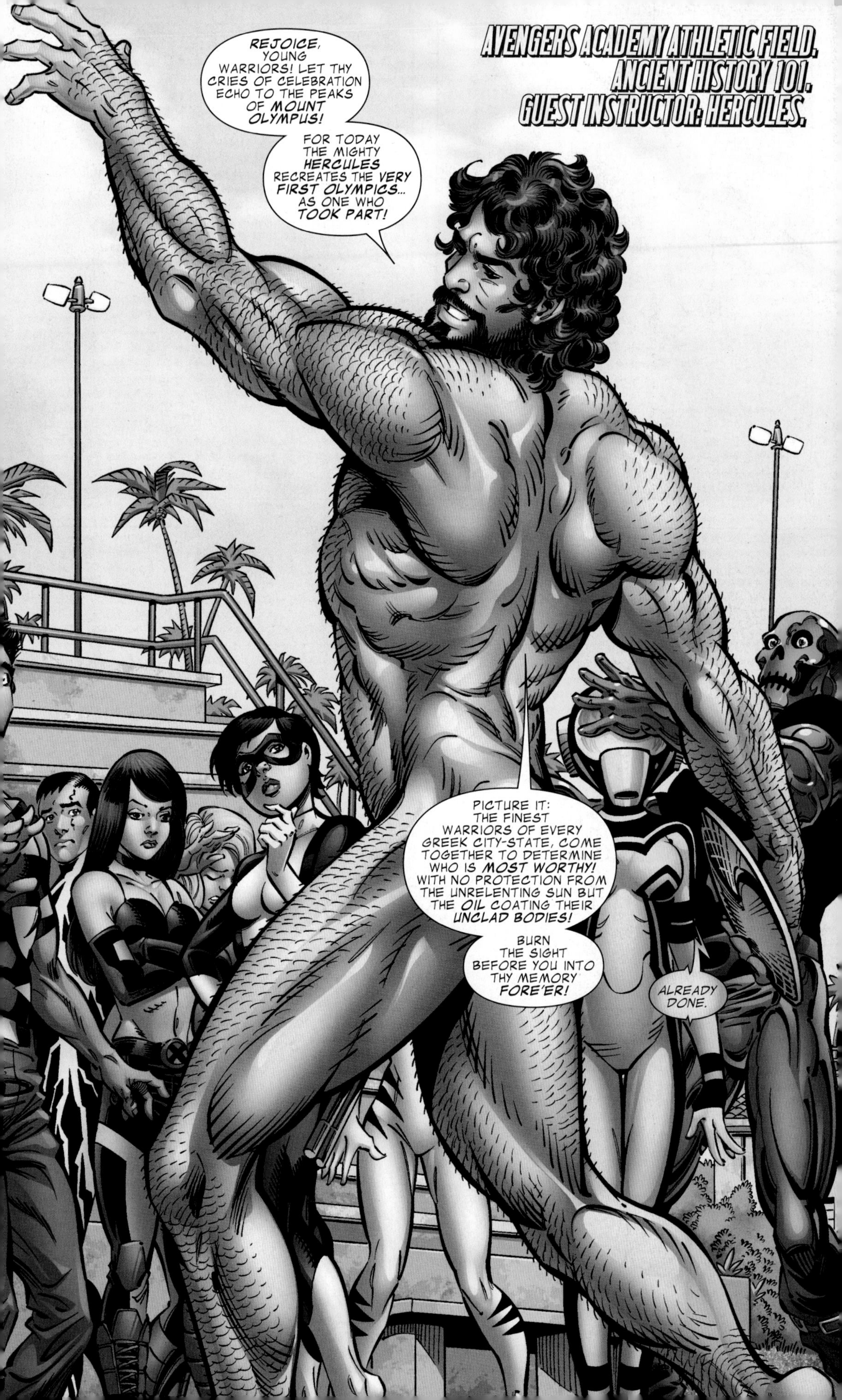
AVENGERS ACADEMY ATHLETIC FIELD. ANCIENT HISTORY 101. GUEST INSTRUCTOR: HERCULES.
REJOICE, YOUNG WARRIORS! LET THY CRIES OF CELEBRATION ECHO TO THE PEAKS OF MOUNT OLYMPUS!
FOR TODAY THE MIGHTY HERCULES RECREATES THE VERY FIRST OLYMPICS... AS ONE WHO TOOK PART!
PICTURE IT: THE FINEST WARRIORS OF EVERY GREEK CITY-STATE, COME TOGETHER TO DETERMINE WHO IS MOST WORTHY! WITH NO PROTECTION FROM THE UNRELENTING SUN BUT THE OIL COATING THEIR UNCLAD BODIES!
BURN THE SIGHT BEFORE YOU INTO THY MEMORY FORE'ER!
ALREADY DONE.

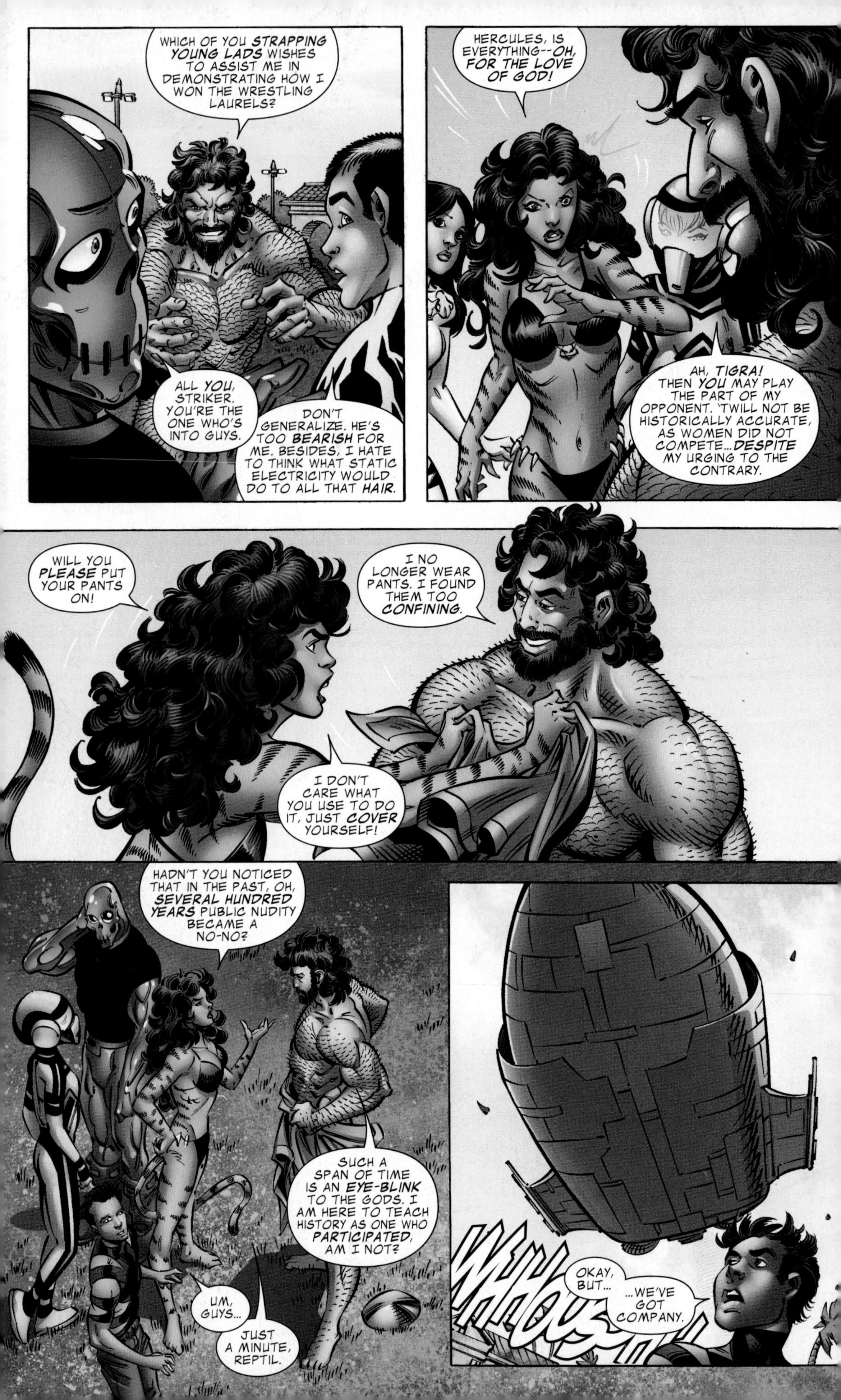
WHICH OF YOU STRAPPING YOUNG LADS WISHES TO ASSIST ME IN DEMONSTRATING HOW I WON THE WRESTLING LAURELS?
ALL YOU, STRIKER. YOU'RE THE ONE WHO'S INTO GUYS.
DON'T GENERALIZE. HE'S TOO BEARISH FOR ME. BESIDES, I HATE TO THINK WHAT STATIC ELECTRICITY WOULD DO TO ALL THAT HAIR.
HERCULES, IS EVERYTHING--OH, FOR THE LOVE OF GOD!
AH, TIGRA! THEN YOU MAY PLAY THE PART OF MY OPPONENT. 'TWILL NOT BE HISTORICALLY ACCURATE, AS WOMEN DID NOT COMPETE...DESPITE MY URGING TO THE CONTRARY.
WILL YOU PLEASE PUT YOUR PANTS ON!
I NO LONGER WEAR PANTS. I FOUND THEM TOO CONFINING.
I DON'T CARE WHAT YOU USE TO DO IT, JUST COVER YOURSELF!
HADN'T YOU NOTICED THAT IN THE PAST, OH, SEVERAL HUNDRED YEARS PUBLIC NUDITY BECAME A NO-NO?
SUCH A SPAN OF TIME IS AN EYE-BLINK TO THE GODS. I AM HERE TO TEACH HISTORY AS ONE WHO PARTICIPATED, AM I NOT?
UM, GUYS...
JUST A MINUTE, REPTIL.
OKAY, BUT...
...WE'VE GOT COMPANY.

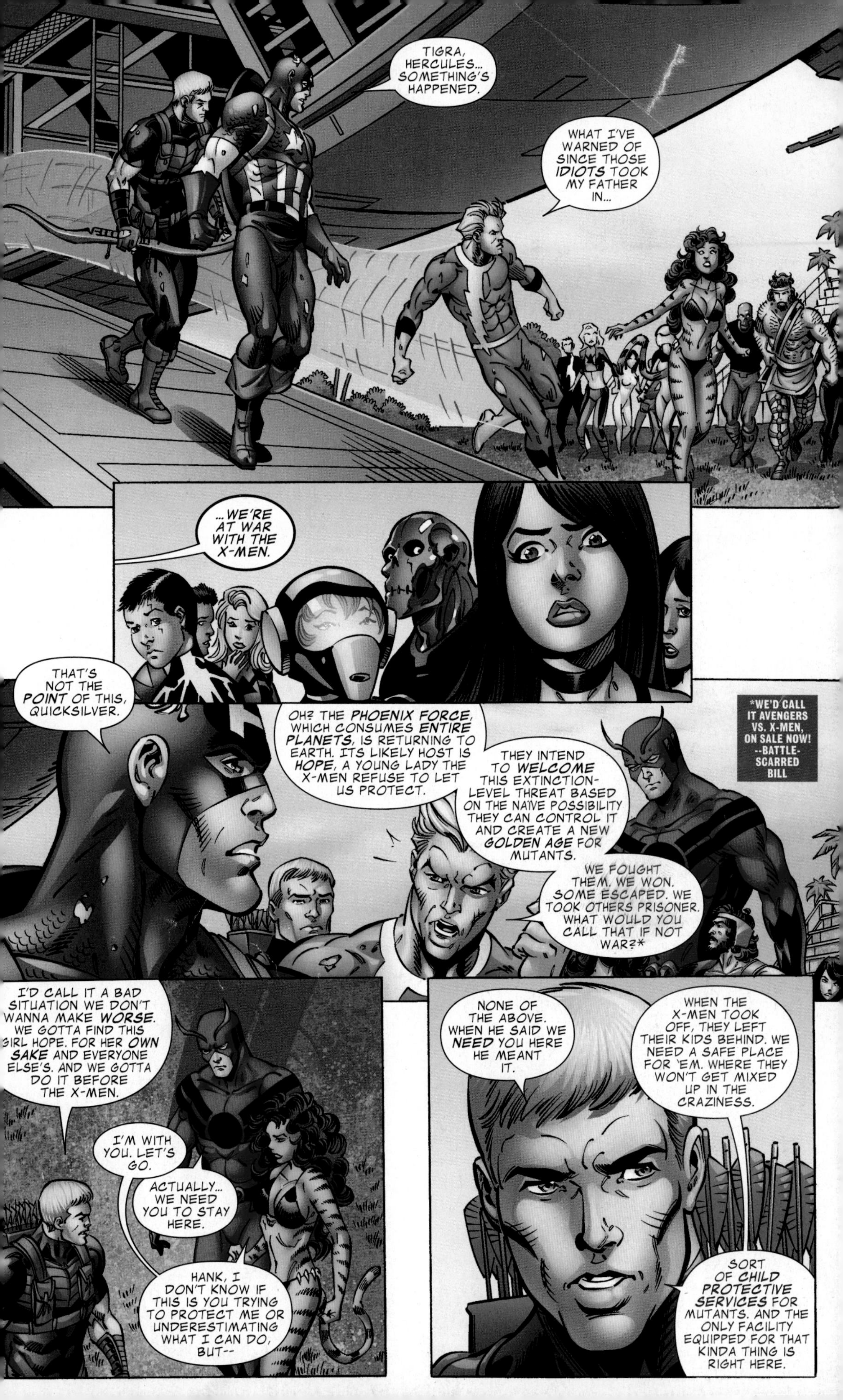
TIGRA, HERCULES... SOMETHING'S HAPPENED.
WHAT I'VE WARNED OF SINCE THOSE IDIOTS TOOK MY FATHER IN...
...WE'RE AT WAR WITH THE X-MEN.
THAT'S NOT THE POINT OF THIS, QUICKSILVER.
OH? THE PHOENIX FORCE, WHICH CONSUMES ENTIRE PLANETS, IS RETURNING TO EARTH. ITS LIKELY HOST IS HOPE, A YOUNG LADY THE X-MEN REFUSE TO LET US PROTECT.
THEY INTEND TO WELCOME THIS EXTINCTION-LEVEL THREAT BASED ON THE NAÏVE POSSIBILITY THEY CAN CONTROL IT AND CREATE A NEW GOLDEN AGE FOR MUTANTS.
WE FOUGHT THEM. WE WON. SOME ESCAPED. WE TOOK OTHERS PRISONER. WHAT WOULD YOU CALL THAT IF NOT WAR?*
*WE'D CALL IT AVENGERS VS. X-MEN, ON SALE NOW! --BATTLE-SCARRED BILL
I'D CALL IT A BAD SITUATION WE DON'T WANNA MAKE WORSE. WE GOTTA FIND THIS GIRL HOPE. FOR HER OWN SAKE AND EVERYONE ELSE'S. AND WE GOTTA DO IT BEFORE THE X-MEN.
I'M WITH YOU. LET'S GO.
ACTUALLY... WE NEED YOU TO STAY HERE.
HANK, I DON'T KNOW IF THIS IS YOU TRYING TO PROTECT ME OR UNDERESTIMATING WHAT I CAN DO, BUT--
NONE OF THE ABOVE. WHEN HE SAID WE NEED YOU HERE HE MEANT IT.
WHEN THE X-MEN TOOK OFF, THEY LEFT THEIR KIDS BEHIND. WE NEED A SAFE PLACE FOR 'EM. WHERE THEY WON'T GET MIXED UP IN THE CRAZINESS.
SORT OF CHILD PROTECTIVE SERVICES FOR MUTANTS. AND THE ONLY FACILITY EQUIPPED FOR THAT KINDA THING IS RIGHT HERE.

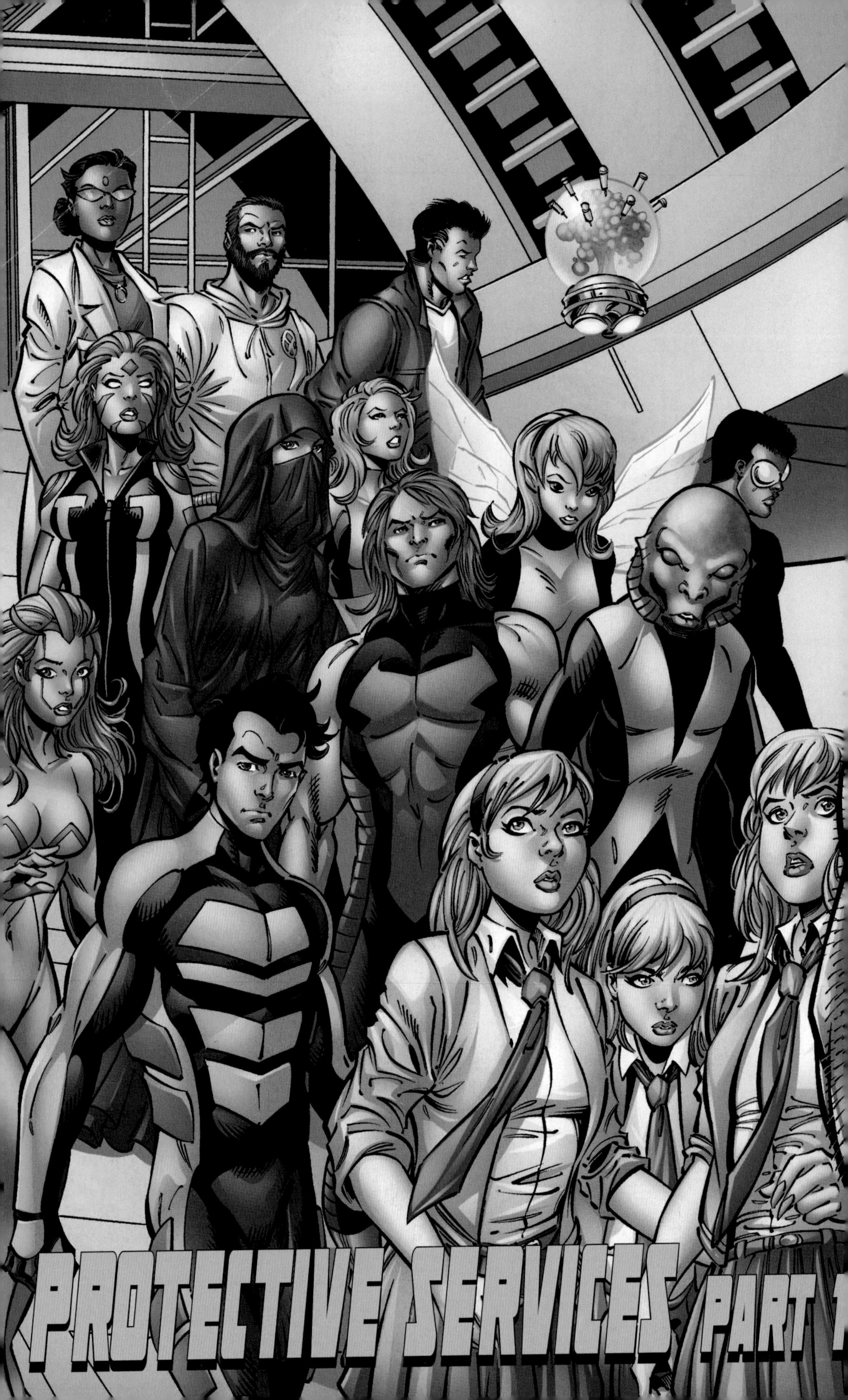
PROTECTIVE SERVICES PART 1

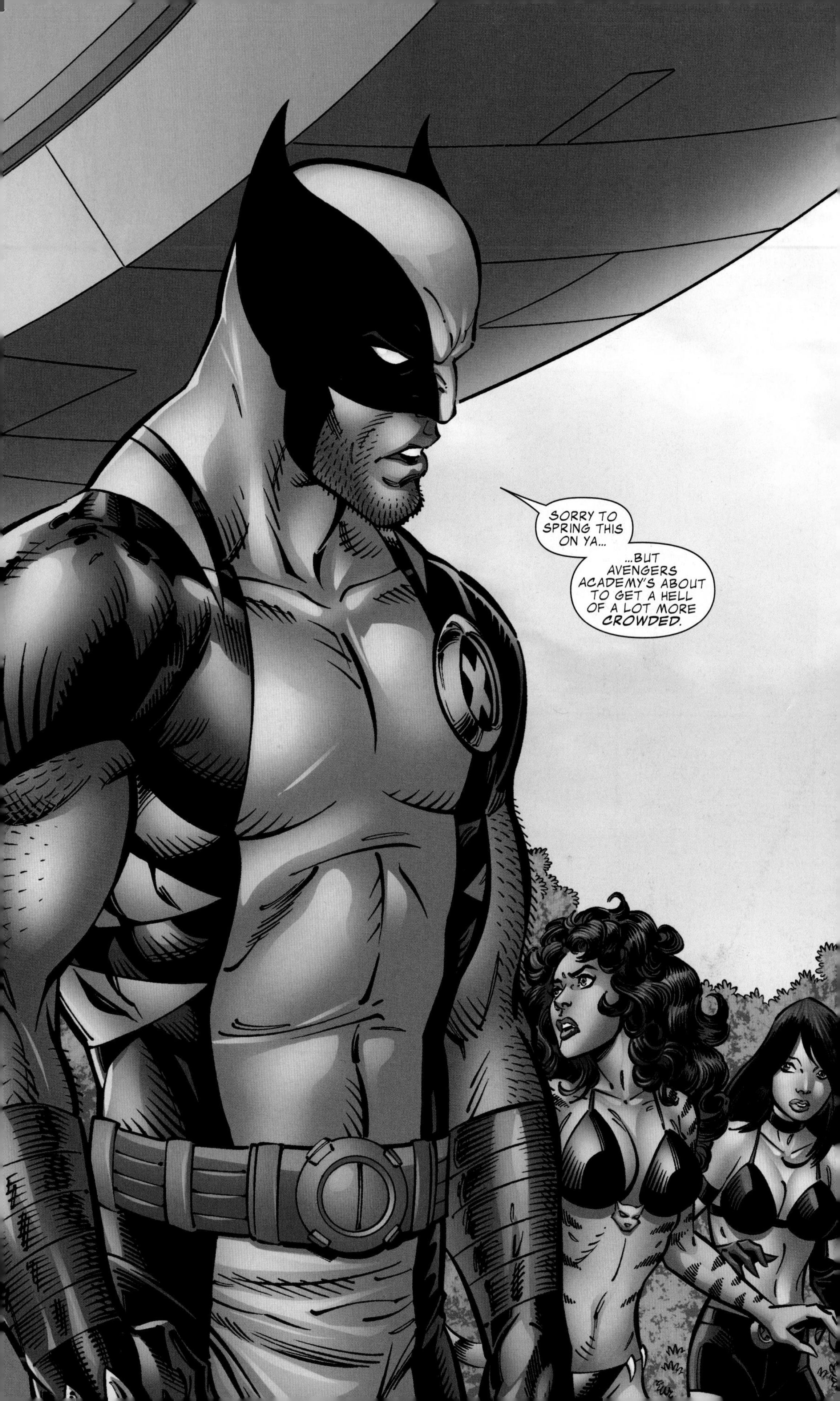
SORRY TO SPRING THIS ON YA...
...BUT AVENGERS ACADEMY'S ABOUT TO GET A HELL OF A LOT MORE *CROWDED*.

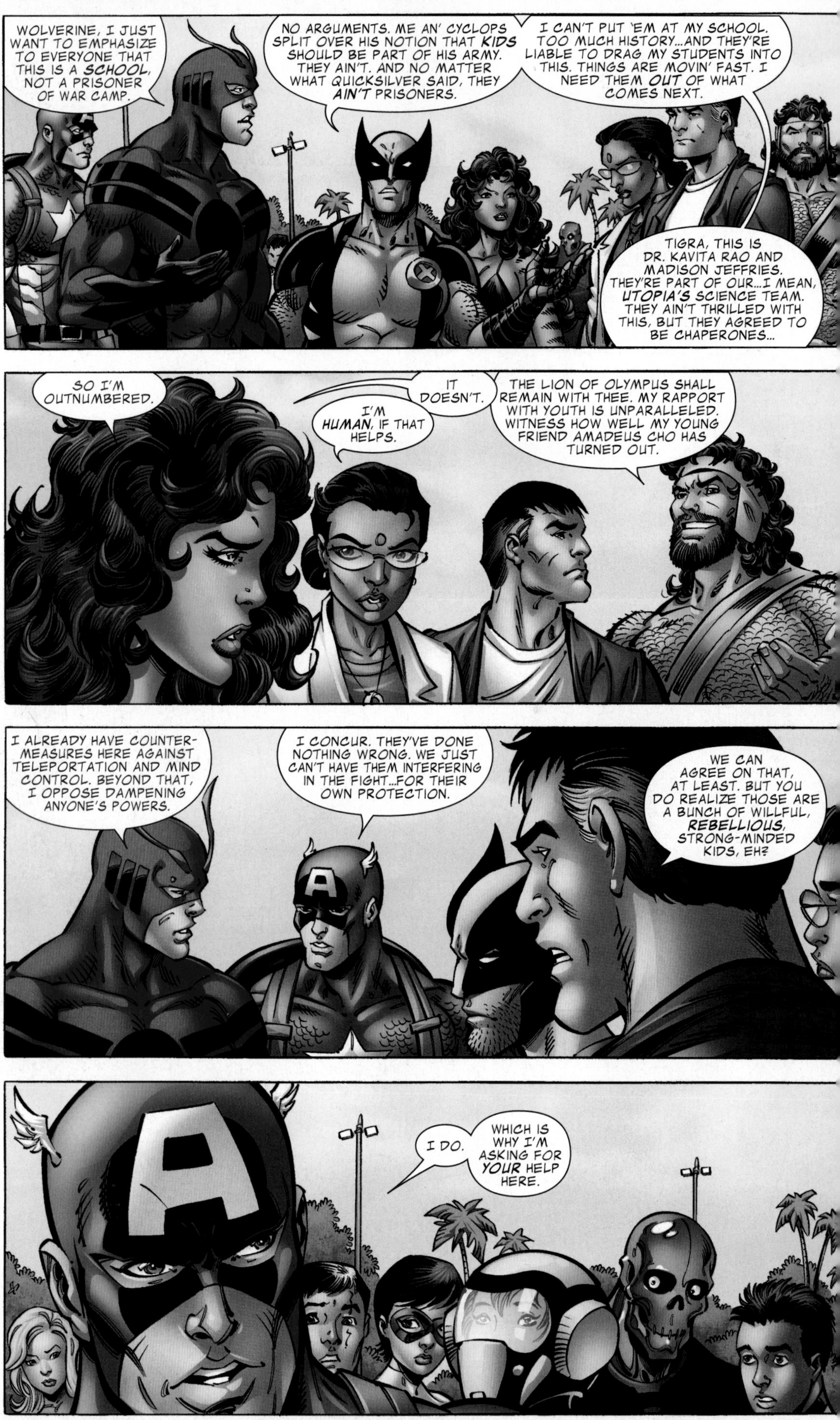

WOLVERINE, I JUST WANT TO EMPHASIZE TO EVERYONE THAT THIS IS A *SCHOOL*, NOT A PRISONER OF WAR CAMP.
NO ARGUMENTS. ME AN' CYCLOPS SPLIT OVER HIS NOTION THAT *KIDS* SHOULD BE PART OF HIS ARMY. THEY AIN'T. AND NO MATTER WHAT QUICKSILVER SAID, THEY *AIN'T* PRISONERS.
I CAN'T PUT 'EM AT MY *SCHOOL*. TOO MUCH HISTORY...AND THEY'RE LIABLE TO DRAG MY STUDENTS INTO THIS. THINGS ARE MOVIN' FAST. I NEED THEM *OUT* OF WHAT COMES NEXT.
TIGRA, THIS IS DR. KAVITA RAO AND MADISON JEFFRIES. THEY'RE PART OF OUR...I MEAN, *UTOPIA'S* SCIENCE TEAM. THEY AIN'T THRILLED WITH THIS, BUT THEY AGREED TO BE CHAPERONES...
SO I'M OUTNUMBERED.
I'M *HUMAN*, IF THAT HELPS.
IT DOESN'T.
THE LION OF OLYMPUS SHALL REMAIN WITH THEE. MY RAPPORT WITH YOUTH IS UNPARALLELED. WITNESS HOW WELL MY YOUNG FRIEND AMADEUS CHO HAS TURNED OUT.
I ALREADY HAVE COUNTER-MEASURES HERE AGAINST TELEPORTATION AND MIND CONTROL. BEYOND THAT, I OPPOSE DAMPENING ANYONE'S POWERS.
I CONCUR. THEY'VE DONE NOTHING WRONG. WE JUST CAN'T HAVE THEM INTERFERING IN THE FIGHT...FOR THEIR OWN PROTECTION.
WE CAN AGREE ON THAT, AT LEAST. BUT YOU DO REALIZE THOSE ARE A BUNCH OF WILLFUL, *REBELLIOUS*, STRONG-MINDED KIDS, EH?
I DO.
WHICH IS WHY I'M ASKING FOR *YOUR* HELP HERE.

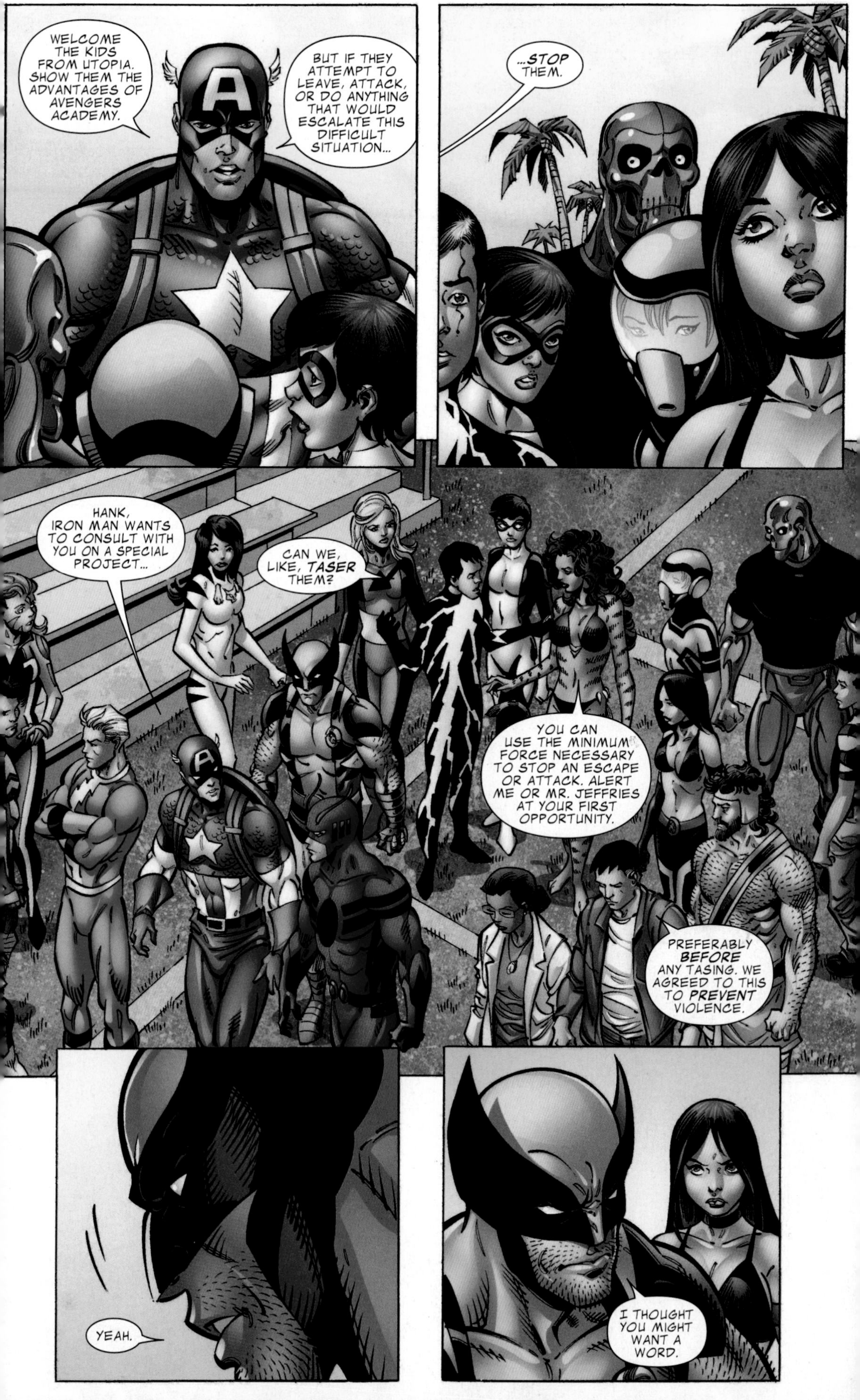
WELCOME THE KIDS FROM UTOPIA. SHOW THEM THE ADVANTAGES OF AVENGERS ACADEMY.
BUT IF THEY ATTEMPT TO LEAVE, ATTACK, OR DO ANYTHING THAT WOULD ESCALATE THIS DIFFICULT SITUATION...
...STOP THEM.
HANK, IRON MAN WANTS TO CONSULT WITH YOU ON A SPECIAL PROJECT...
CAN WE, LIKE, TASER THEM?
YOU CAN USE THE MINIMUM FORCE NECESSARY TO STOP AN ESCAPE OR ATTACK. ALERT ME OR MR. JEFFRIES AT YOUR FIRST OPPORTUNITY.
PREFERABLY BEFORE ANY TASING. WE AGREED TO THIS TO PREVENT VIOLENCE.
YEAH.
I THOUGHT YOU MIGHT WANT A WORD.

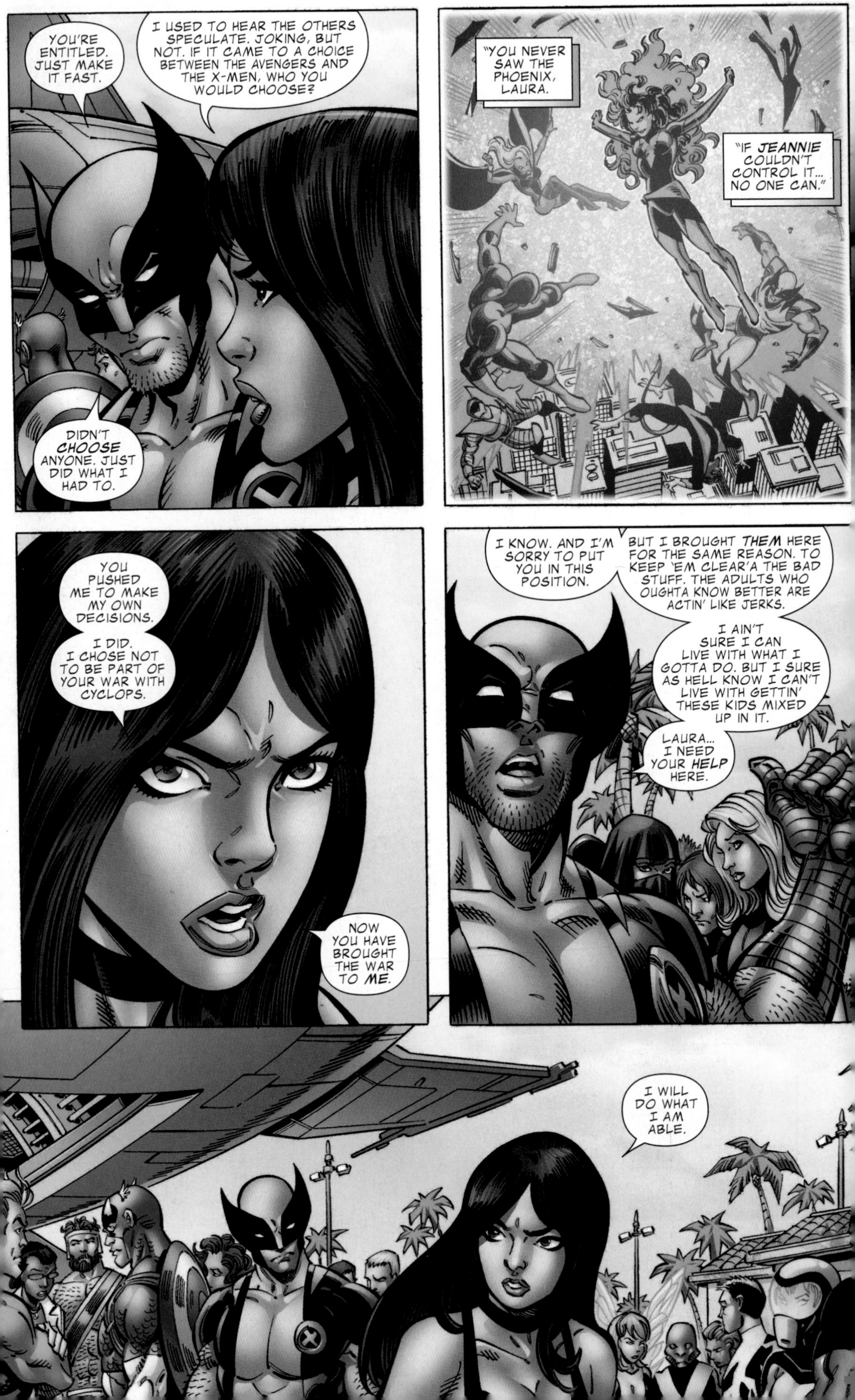
YOU'RE ENTITLED. JUST MAKE IT FAST.
I USED TO HEAR THE OTHERS SPECULATE. JOKING, BUT NOT. IF IT CAME TO A CHOICE BETWEEN THE AVENGERS AND THE X-MEN, WHO YOU WOULD CHOOSE?
DIDN'T CHOOSE ANYONE. JUST DID WHAT I HAD TO.
"YOU NEVER SAW THE PHOENIX, LAURA.
"IF JEANNIE COULDN'T CONTROL IT... NO ONE CAN."
YOU PUSHED ME TO MAKE MY OWN DECISIONS.
I DID. I CHOSE NOT TO BE PART OF YOUR WAR WITH CYCLOPS.
NOW YOU HAVE BROUGHT THE WAR TO ME.
I KNOW. AND I'M SORRY TO PUT YOU IN THIS POSITION.
BUT I BROUGHT THEM HERE FOR THE SAME REASON. TO KEEP 'EM CLEAR'A THE BAD STUFF. THE ADULTS WHO OUGHTA KNOW BETTER ARE ACTIN' LIKE JERKS.
I AIN'T SURE I CAN LIVE WITH WHAT I GOTTA DO. BUT I SURE AS HELL KNOW I CAN'T LIVE WITH GETTIN' THESE KIDS MIXED UP IN IT.
LAURA... I NEED YOUR HELP HERE.
I WILL DO WHAT I AM ABLE.

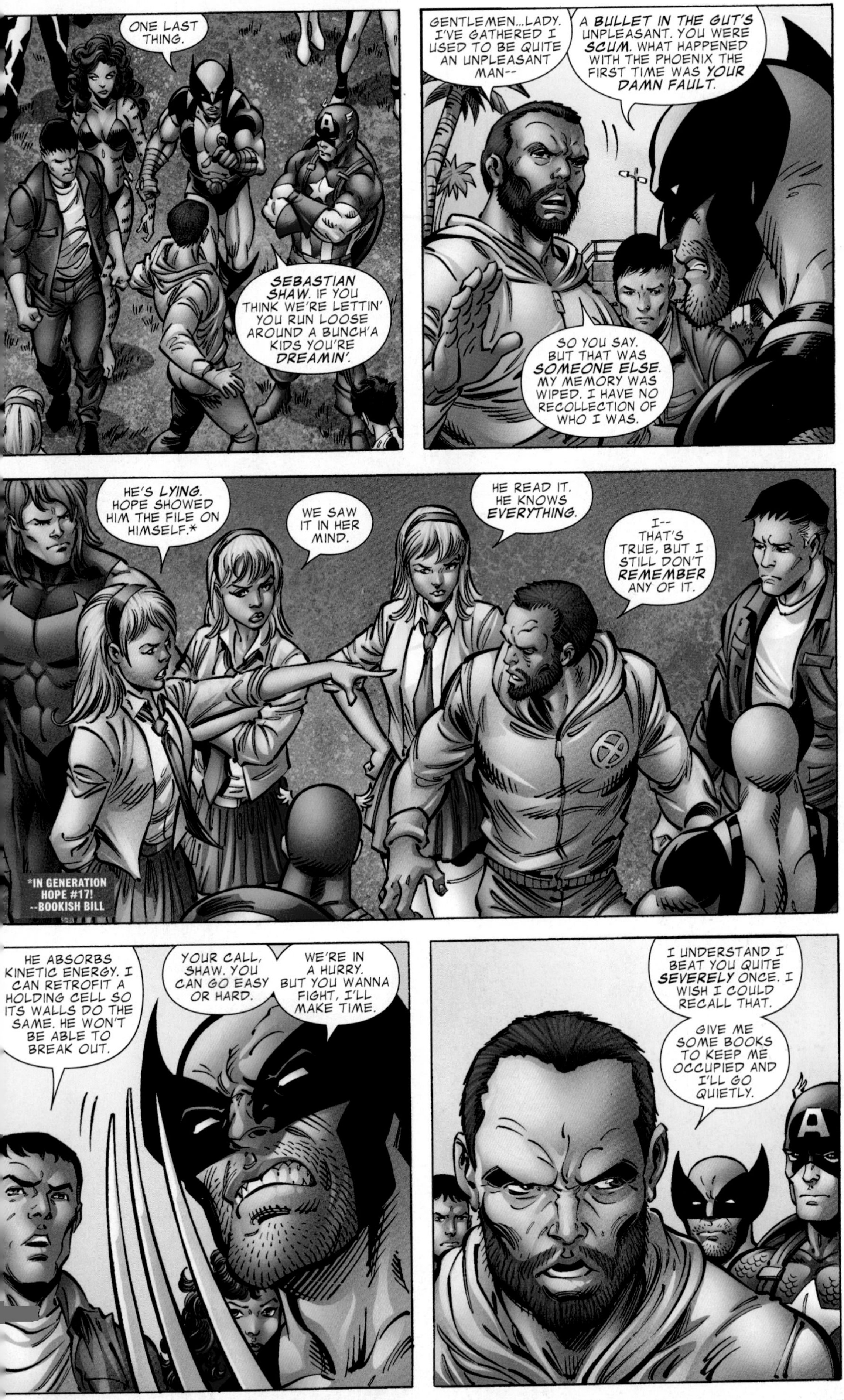

ONE LAST THING.
SEBASTIAN SHAW. IF YOU THINK WE'RE LETTIN' YOU RUN LOOSE AROUND A BUNCH'A KIDS YOU'RE DREAMIN'.
GENTLEMEN...LADY. I'VE GATHERED I USED TO BE QUITE AN UNPLEASANT MAN--
A BULLET IN THE GUT'S UNPLEASANT. YOU WERE SCUM. WHAT HAPPENED WITH THE PHOENIX THE FIRST TIME WAS YOUR DAMN FAULT.
SO YOU SAY. BUT THAT WAS SOMEONE ELSE. MY MEMORY WAS WIPED. I HAVE NO RECOLLECTION OF WHO I WAS.
HE'S LYING. HOPE SHOWED HIM THE FILE ON HIMSELF.*
WE SAW IT IN HER MIND.
HE READ IT. HE KNOWS EVERYTHING.
I-- THAT'S TRUE, BUT I STILL DON'T REMEMBER ANY OF IT.
*IN GENERATION HOPE #17! --BOOKISH BILL
HE ABSORBS KINETIC ENERGY. I CAN RETROFIT A HOLDING CELL SO ITS WALLS DO THE SAME. HE WON'T BE ABLE TO BREAK OUT.
YOUR CALL, SHAW. YOU CAN GO EASY OR HARD.
WE'RE IN A HURRY. BUT YOU WANNA FIGHT, I'LL MAKE TIME.
I UNDERSTAND I BEAT YOU QUITE SEVERELY ONCE. I WISH I COULD RECALL THAT.
GIVE ME SOME BOOKS TO KEEP ME OCCUPIED AND I'LL GO QUIETLY.

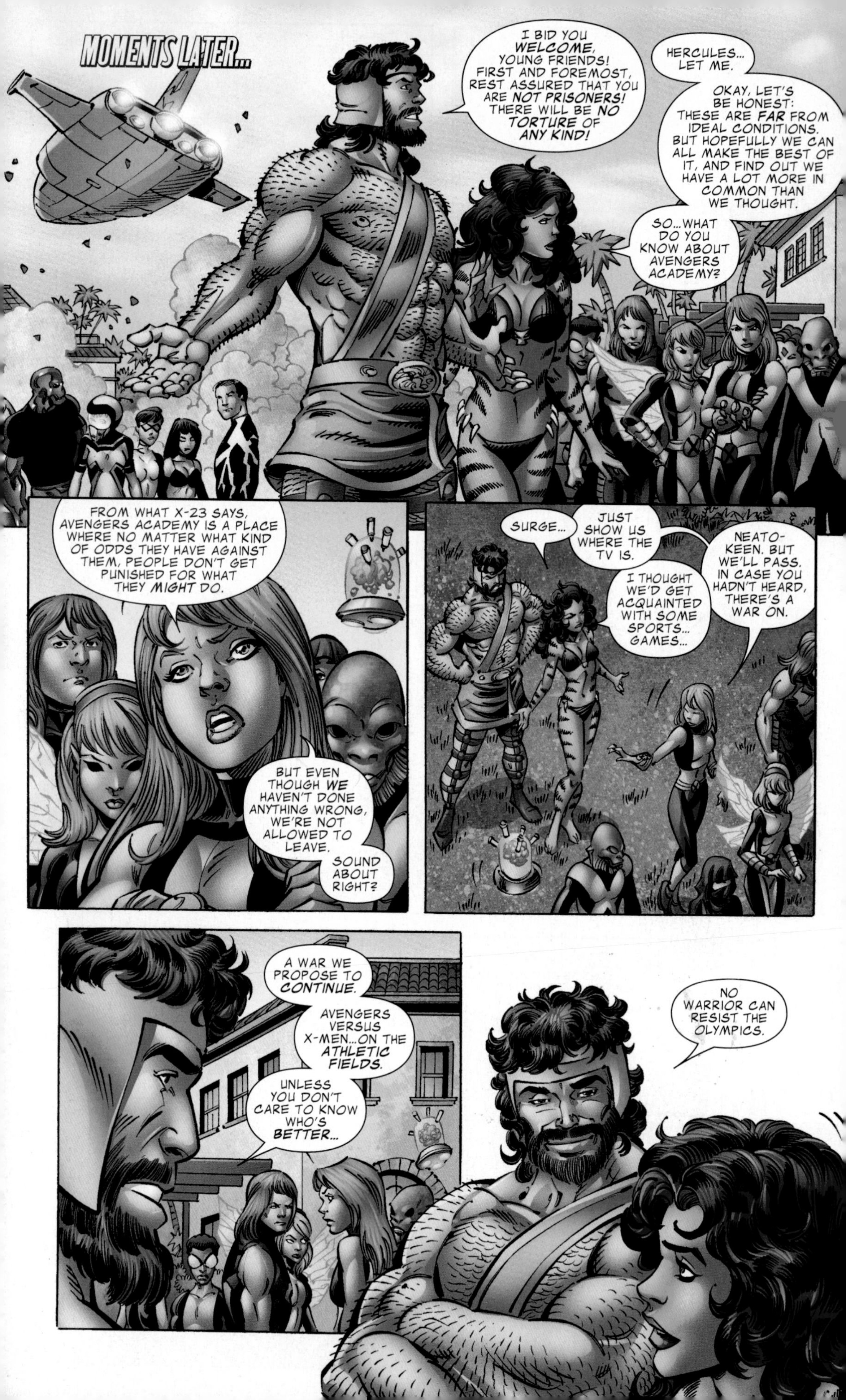
MOMENTS LATER...
I BID YOU WELCOME, YOUNG FRIENDS! FIRST AND FOREMOST, REST ASSURED THAT YOU ARE NOT PRISONERS! THERE WILL BE NO TORTURE OF ANY KIND!
HERCULES... LET ME.
OKAY, LET'S BE HONEST: THESE ARE FAR FROM IDEAL CONDITIONS. BUT HOPEFULLY WE CAN ALL MAKE THE BEST OF IT, AND FIND OUT WE HAVE A LOT MORE IN COMMON THAN WE THOUGHT.
SO...WHAT DO YOU KNOW ABOUT AVENGERS ACADEMY?
FROM WHAT X-23 SAYS, AVENGERS ACADEMY IS A PLACE WHERE NO MATTER WHAT KIND OF ODDS THEY HAVE AGAINST THEM, PEOPLE DON'T GET PUNISHED FOR WHAT THEY MIGHT DO.
BUT EVEN THOUGH WE HAVEN'T DONE ANYTHING WRONG, WE'RE NOT ALLOWED TO LEAVE.
SOUND ABOUT RIGHT?
SURGE...
JUST SHOW US WHERE THE TV IS.
I THOUGHT WE'D GET ACQUAINTED WITH SOME SPORTS... GAMES...
NEATO-KEEN. BUT WE'LL PASS. IN CASE YOU HADN'T HEARD, THERE'S A WAR ON.
A WAR WE PROPOSE TO CONTINUE.
AVENGERS VERSUS X-MEN...ON THE ATHLETIC FIELDS.
UNLESS YOU DON'T CARE TO KNOW WHO'S BETTER...
NO WARRIOR CAN RESIST THE OLYMPICS.

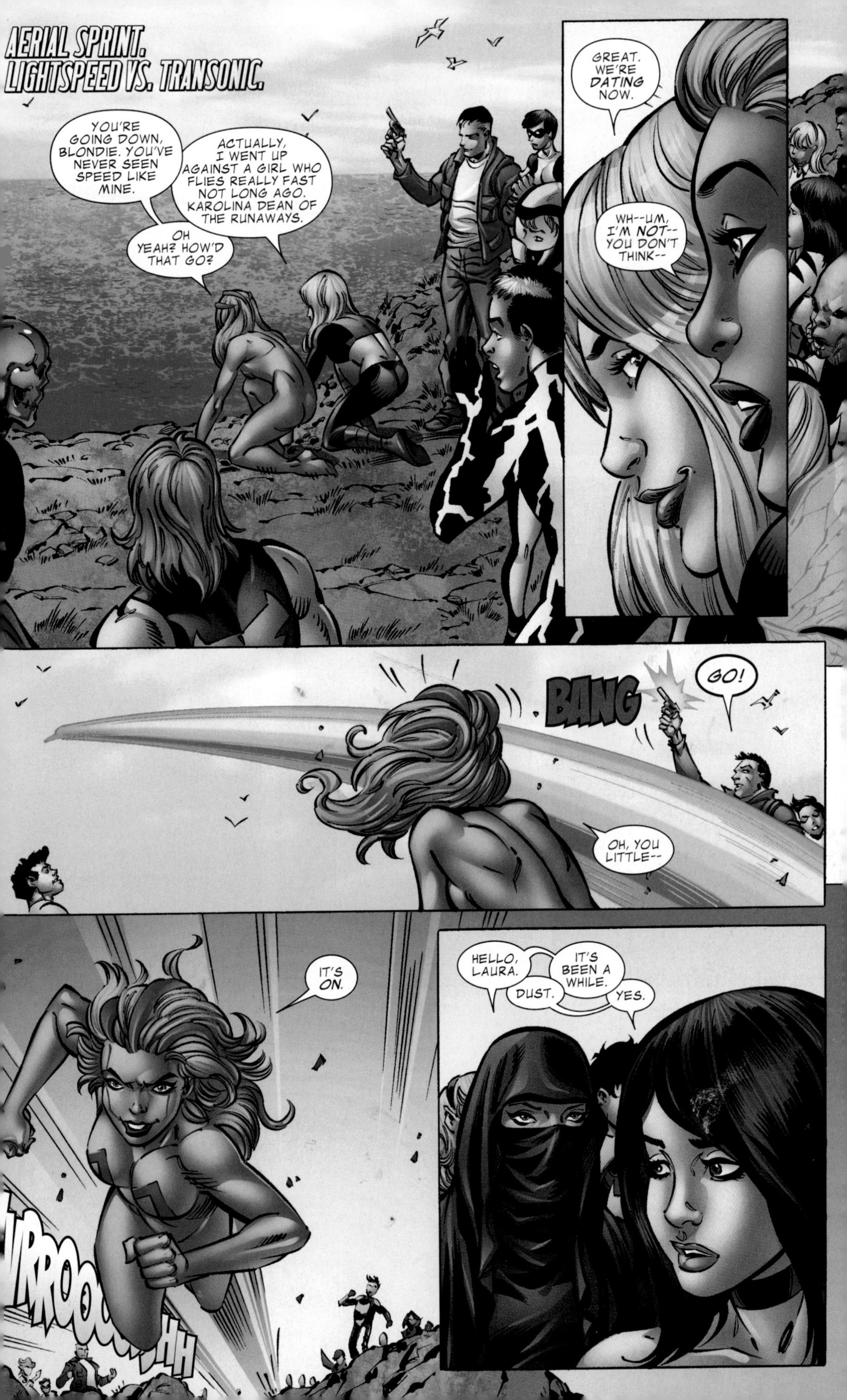
AERIAL SPRINT. LIGHTSPEED VS. TRANSONIC.
YOU'RE GOING DOWN, BLONDIE. YOU'VE NEVER SEEN SPEED LIKE MINE.
ACTUALLY, I WENT UP AGAINST A GIRL WHO FLIES REALLY FAST NOT LONG AGO. KAROLINA DEAN OF THE RUNAWAYS.
OH YEAH? HOW'D THAT GO?
GREAT. WE'RE DATING NOW.
WH--UM, I'M NOT-- YOU DON'T THINK--
BANG
GO!
OH, YOU LITTLE--
IT'S ON.
VRROOOOOSHH
HELLO, LAURA.
DUST.
IT'S BEEN A WHILE.
YES.

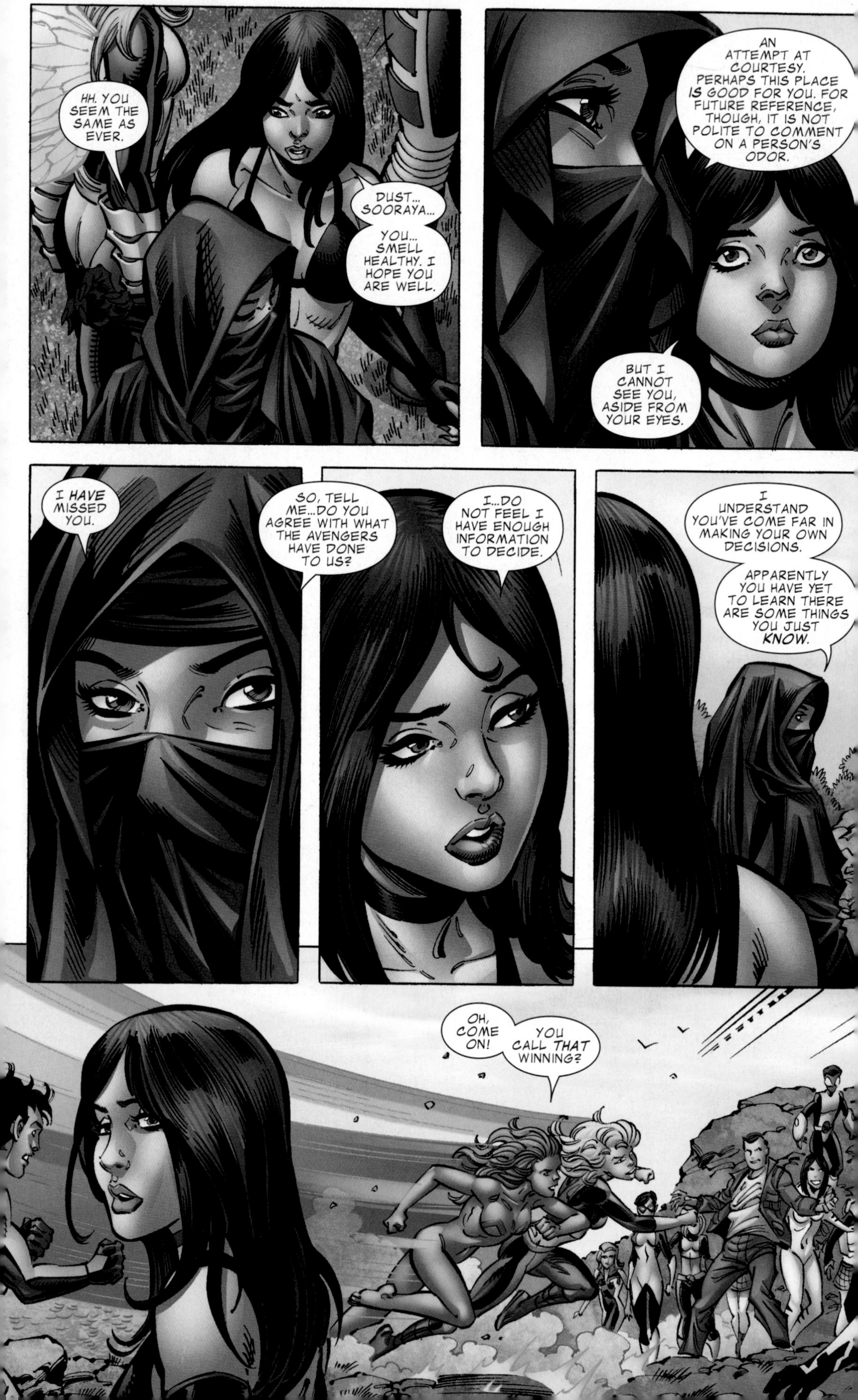
HH. YOU SEEM THE SAME AS EVER.
DUST... SOORAYA...
YOU... SMELL HEALTHY. I HOPE YOU ARE WELL.
AN ATTEMPT AT COURTESY. PERHAPS THIS PLACE IS GOOD FOR YOU. FOR FUTURE REFERENCE, THOUGH, IT IS NOT POLITE TO COMMENT ON A PERSON'S ODOR.
BUT I CANNOT SEE YOU, ASIDE FROM YOUR EYES.
I HAVE MISSED YOU.
SO, TELL ME...DO YOU AGREE WITH WHAT THE AVENGERS HAVE DONE TO US?
I...DO NOT FEEL I HAVE ENOUGH INFORMATION TO DECIDE.
I UNDERSTAND YOU'VE COME FAR IN MAKING YOUR OWN DECISIONS.
APPARENTLY YOU HAVE YET TO LEARN THERE ARE SOME THINGS YOU JUST KNOW.
OH, COME ON!
YOU CALL THAT WINNING?

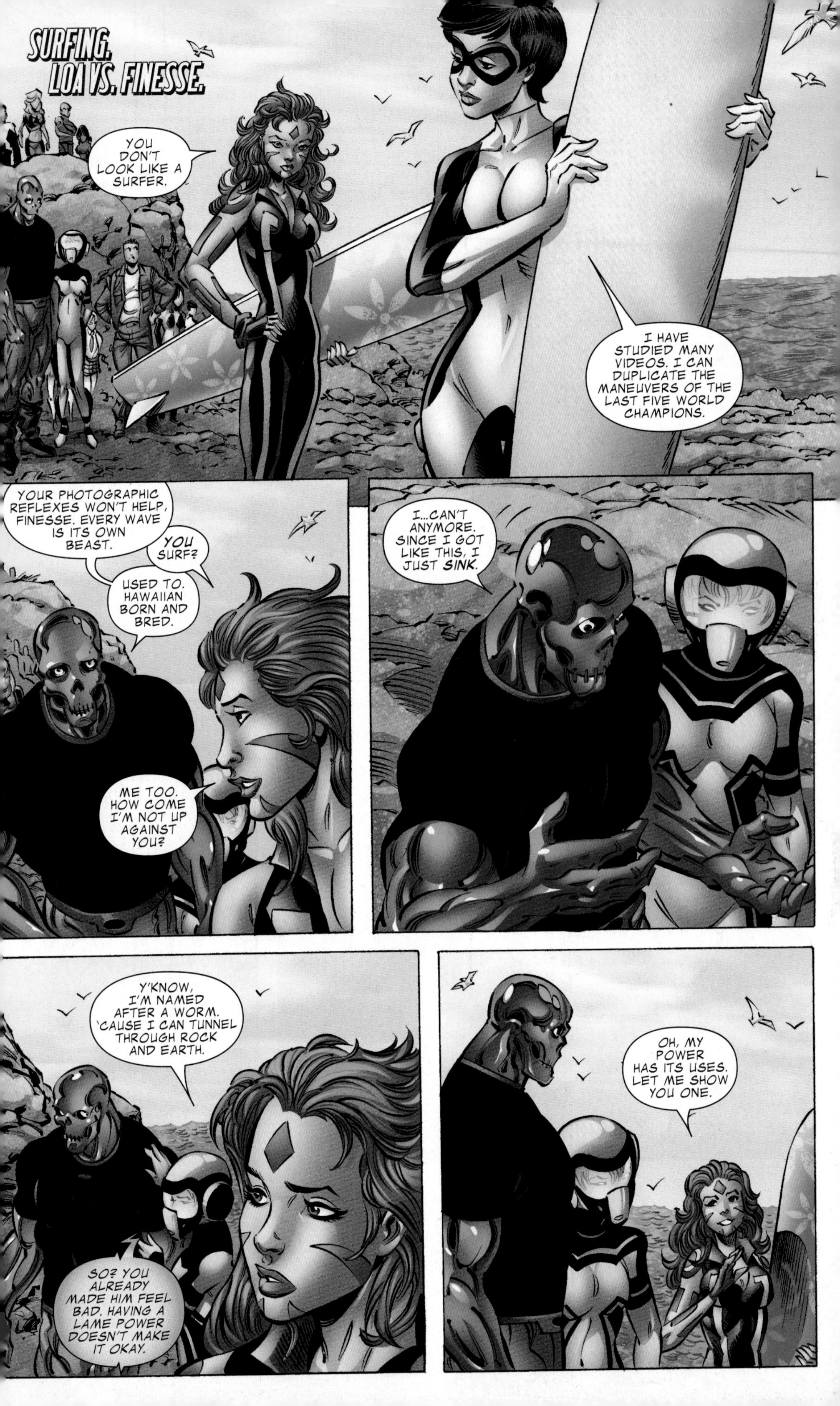
SURFING. LOA VS. FINESSE.
YOU DON'T LOOK LIKE A SURFER.
I HAVE STUDIED MANY VIDEOS. I CAN DUPLICATE THE MANEUVERS OF THE LAST FIVE WORLD CHAMPIONS.
YOUR PHOTOGRAPHIC REFLEXES WON'T HELP, FINESSE. EVERY WAVE IS ITS OWN BEAST.
YOU SURF?
USED TO. HAWAIIAN BORN AND BRED.
ME TOO. HOW COME I'M NOT UP AGAINST YOU?
I...CAN'T ANYMORE. SINCE I GOT LIKE THIS, I JUST SINK.
Y'KNOW, I'M NAMED AFTER A WORM. 'CAUSE I CAN TUNNEL THROUGH ROCK AND EARTH.
SO? YOU ALREADY MADE HIM FEEL BAD. HAVING A LAME POWER DOESN'T MAKE IT OKAY.
OH, MY POWER HAS ITS USES. LET ME SHOW YOU ONE.

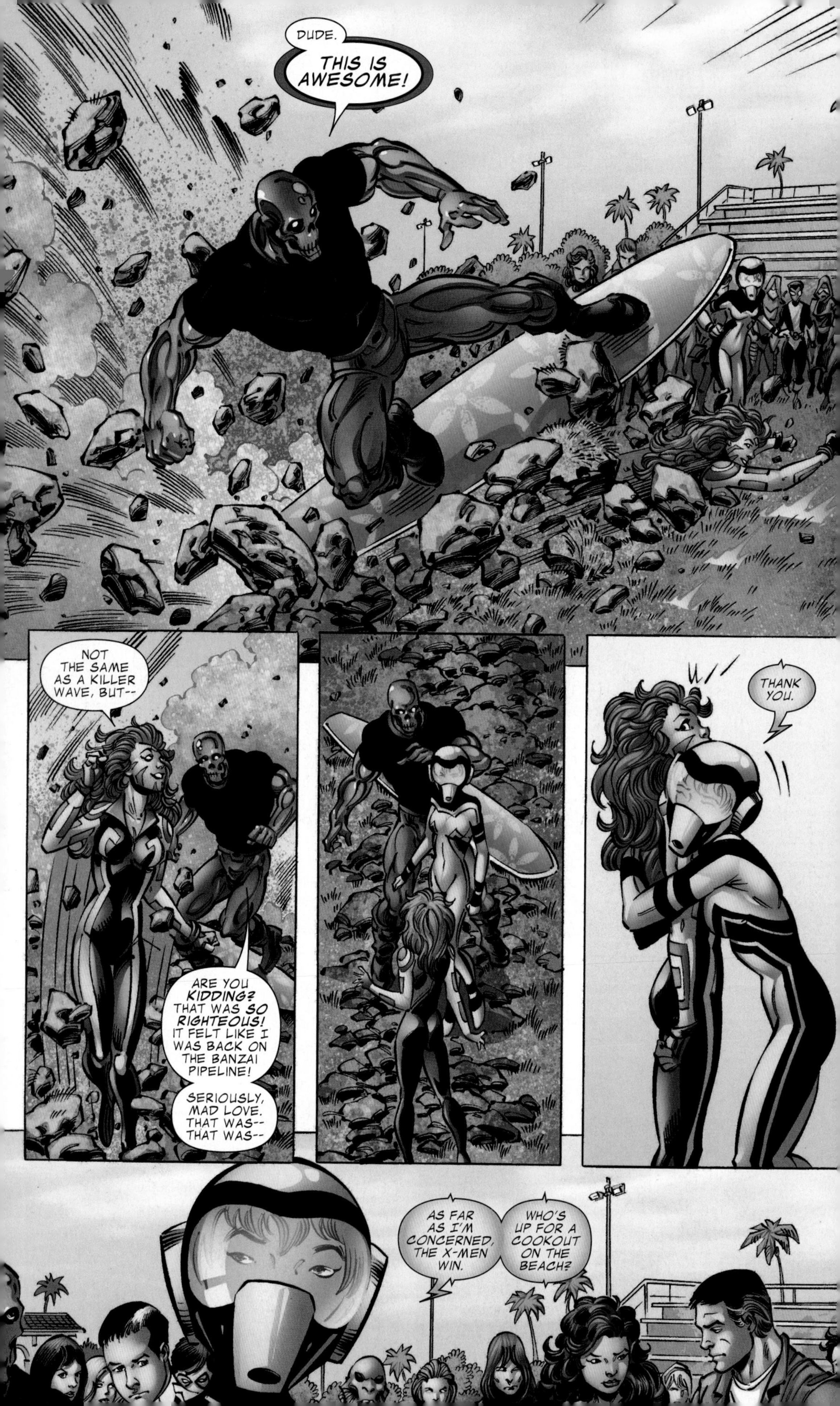

DUDE.
THIS IS AWESOME!
NOT THE SAME AS A KILLER WAVE, BUT--
ARE YOU KIDDING? THAT WAS SO RIGHTEOUS! IT FELT LIKE I WAS BACK ON THE BANZAI PIPELINE!
SERIOUSLY, MAD LOVE. THAT WAS-- THAT WAS--
THANK YOU.
AS FAR AS I'M CONCERNED, THE X-MEN WIN.
WHO'S UP FOR A COOKOUT ON THE BEACH?

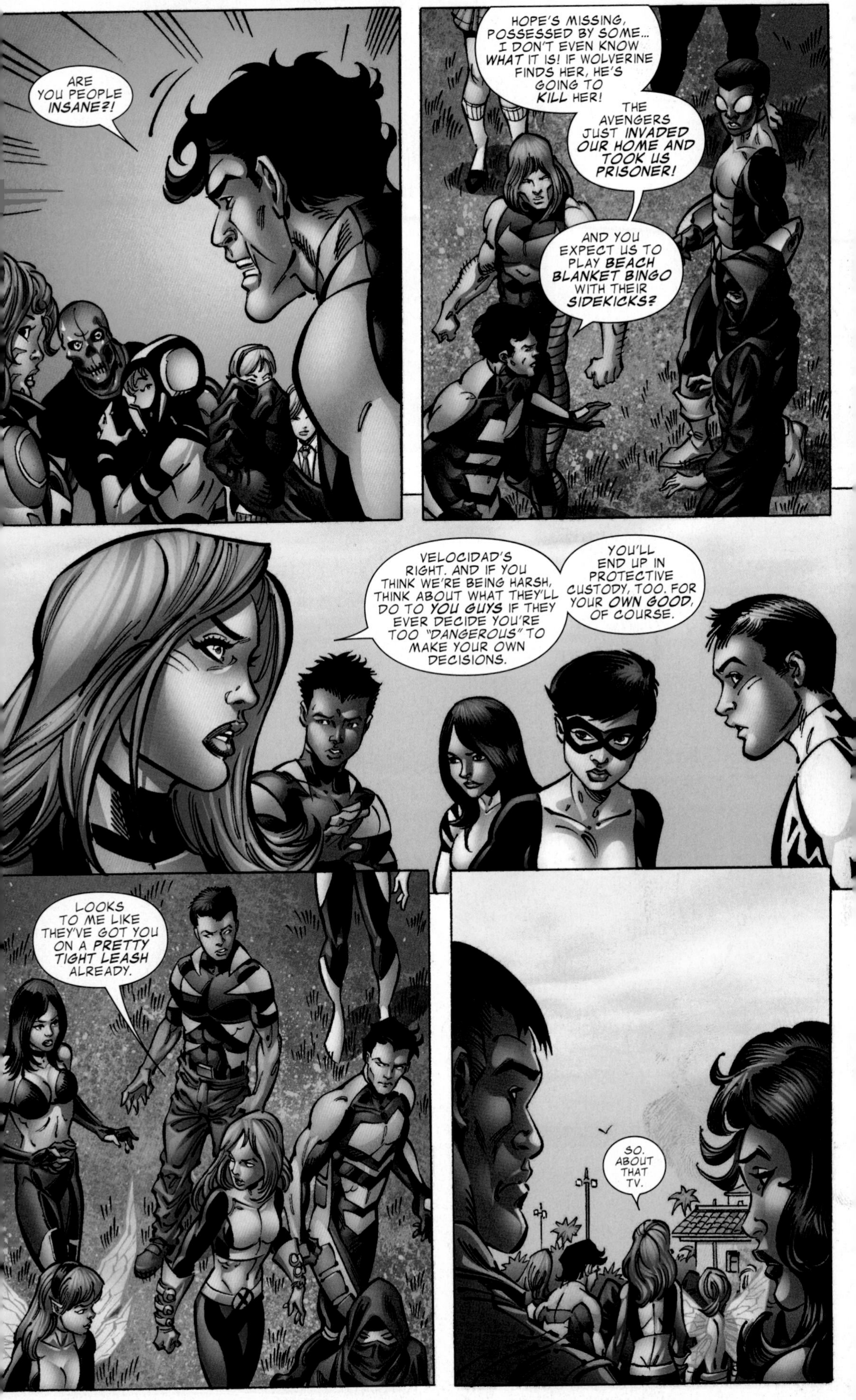

ARE YOU PEOPLE INSANE?!
HOPE'S MISSING, POSSESSED BY SOME... I DON'T EVEN KNOW WHAT IT IS! IF WOLVERINE FINDS HER, HE'S GOING TO KILL HER!
THE AVENGERS JUST INVADED OUR HOME AND TOOK US PRISONER!
AND YOU EXPECT US TO PLAY BEACH BLANKET BINGO WITH THEIR SIDEKICKS?
VELOCIDAD'S RIGHT. AND IF YOU THINK WE'RE BEING HARSH, THINK ABOUT WHAT THEY'LL DO TO YOU GUYS IF THEY EVER DECIDE YOU'RE TOO "DANGEROUS" TO MAKE YOUR OWN DECISIONS.
YOU'LL END UP IN PROTECTIVE CUSTODY, TOO. FOR YOUR OWN GOOD, OF COURSE.
LOOKS TO ME LIKE THEY'VE GOT YOU ON A PRETTY TIGHT LEASH ALREADY.
SO. ABOUT THAT TV.

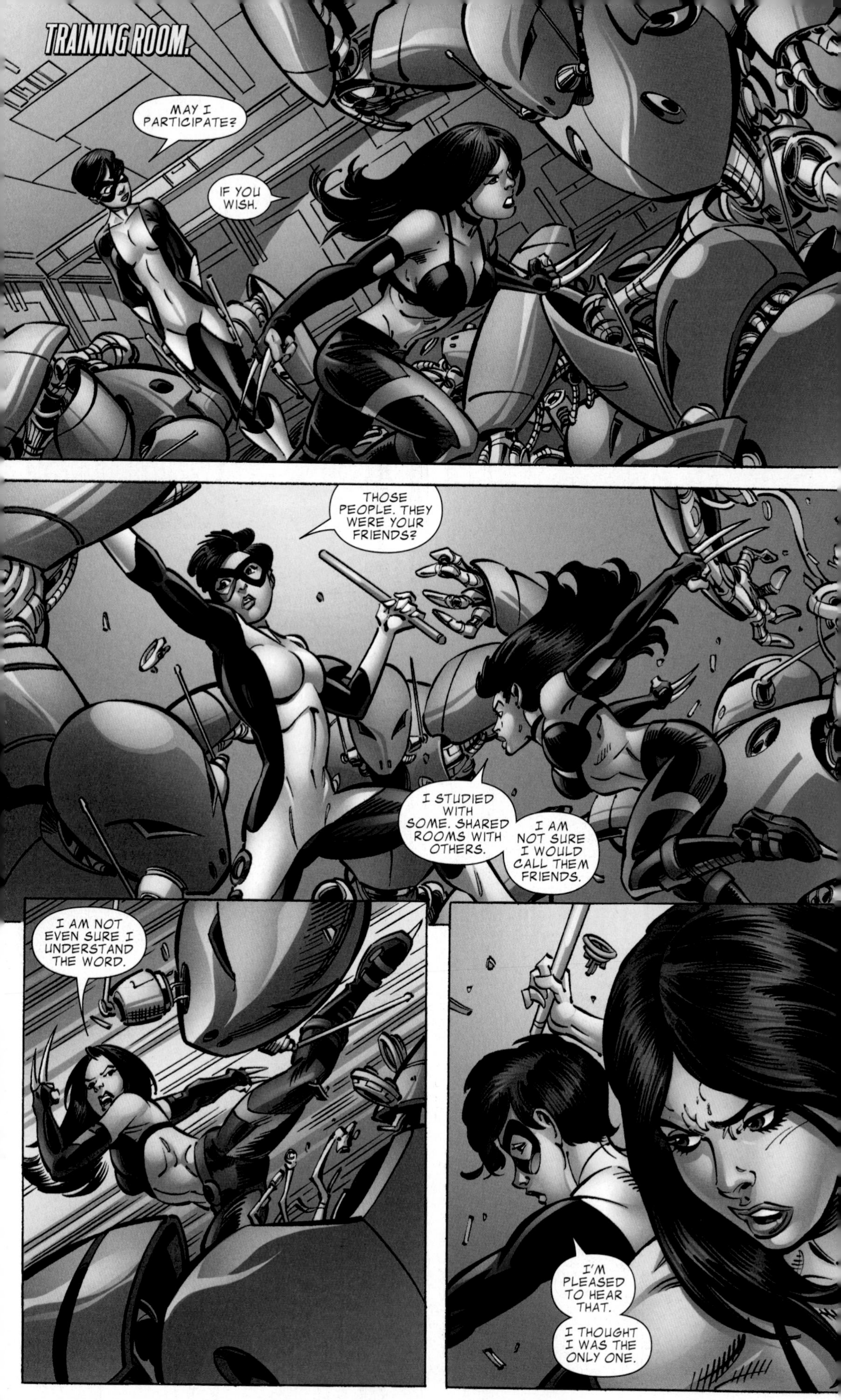
TRAINING ROOM.
MAY I PARTICIPATE?
IF YOU WISH.
THOSE PEOPLE. THEY WERE YOUR FRIENDS?
I STUDIED WITH SOME. SHARED ROOMS WITH OTHERS.
I AM NOT SURE I WOULD CALL THEM FRIENDS.
I AM NOT EVEN SURE I UNDERSTAND THE WORD.
I'M PLEASED TO HEAR THAT.
I THOUGHT I WAS THE ONLY ONE.

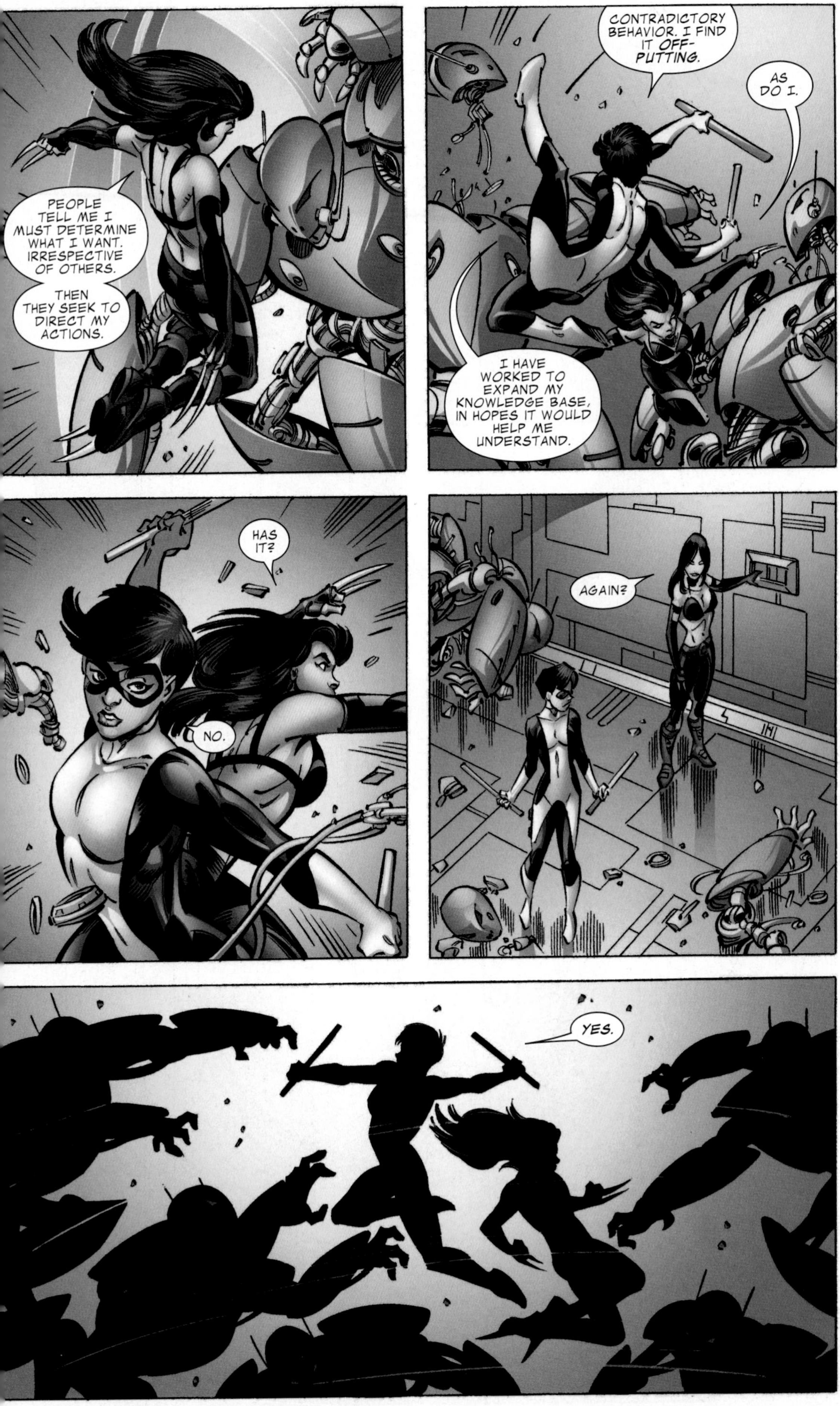

PEOPLE TELL ME I MUST DETERMINE WHAT I WANT. IRRESPECTIVE OF OTHERS.
THEN THEY SEEK TO DIRECT MY ACTIONS.
CONTRADICTORY BEHAVIOR. I FIND IT OFF-PUTTING.
AS DO I.
I HAVE WORKED TO EXPAND MY KNOWLEDGE BASE, IN HOPES IT WOULD HELP ME UNDERSTAND.
HAS IT?
NO.
AGAIN?
YES.

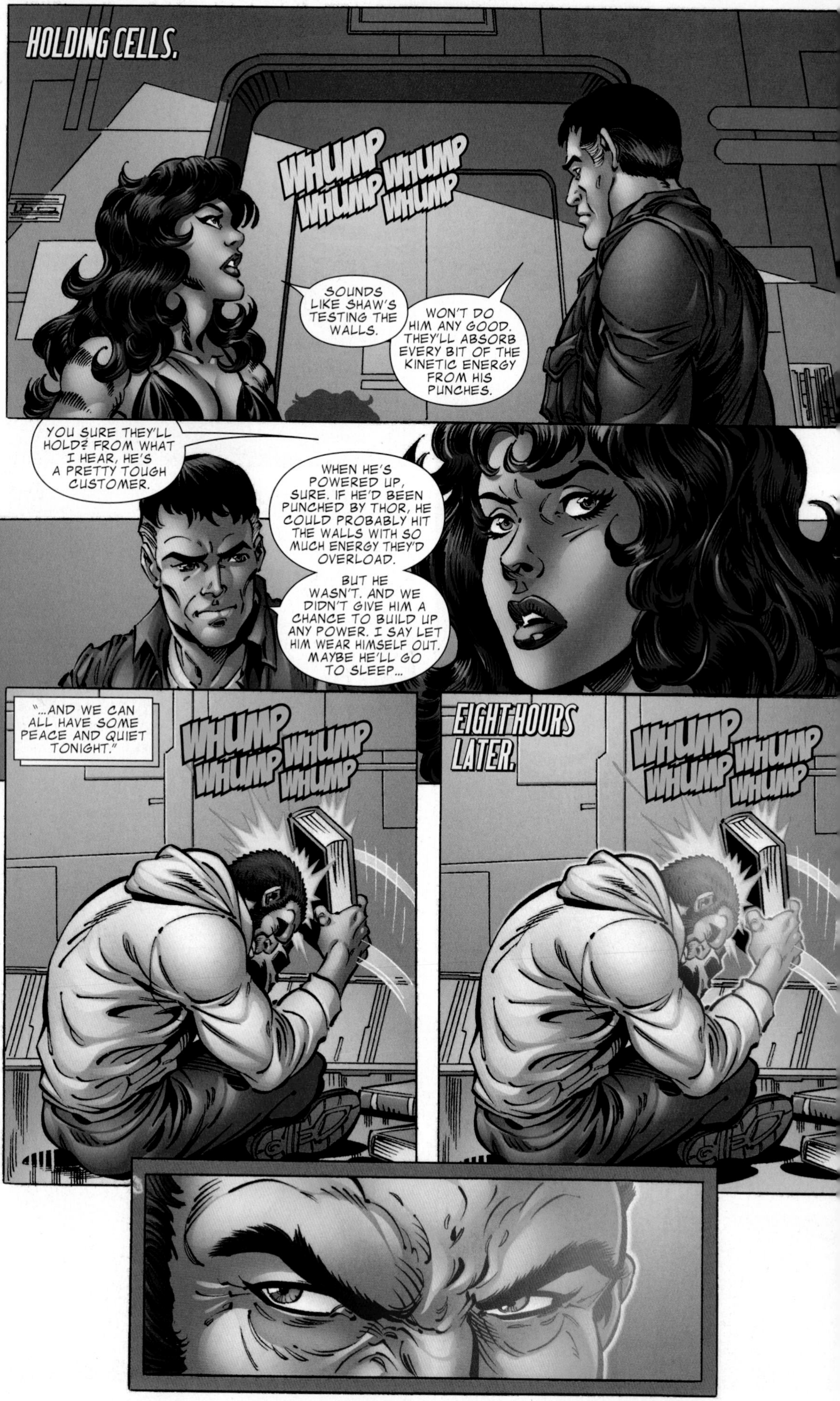
HOLDING CELLS.
WHUMP WHUMP WHUMP WHUMP
SOUNDS LIKE SHAW'S TESTING THE WALLS.
WON'T DO HIM ANY GOOD. THEY'LL ABSORB EVERY BIT OF THE KINETIC ENERGY FROM HIS PUNCHES.
YOU SURE THEY'LL HOLD? FROM WHAT I HEAR, HE'S A PRETTY TOUGH CUSTOMER.
WHEN HE'S POWERED UP, SURE. IF HE'D BEEN PUNCHED BY THOR, HE COULD PROBABLY HIT THE WALLS WITH SO MUCH ENERGY THEY'D OVERLOAD.
BUT HE WASN'T. AND WE DIDN'T GIVE HIM A CHANCE TO BUILD UP ANY POWER. I SAY LET HIM WEAR HIMSELF OUT. MAYBE HE'LL GO TO SLEEP...
"...AND WE CAN ALL HAVE SOME PEACE AND QUIET TONIGHT."
WHUMP WHUMP WHUMP WHUMP
EIGHT HOURS LATER.
WHUMP WHUMP WHUMP WHUMP

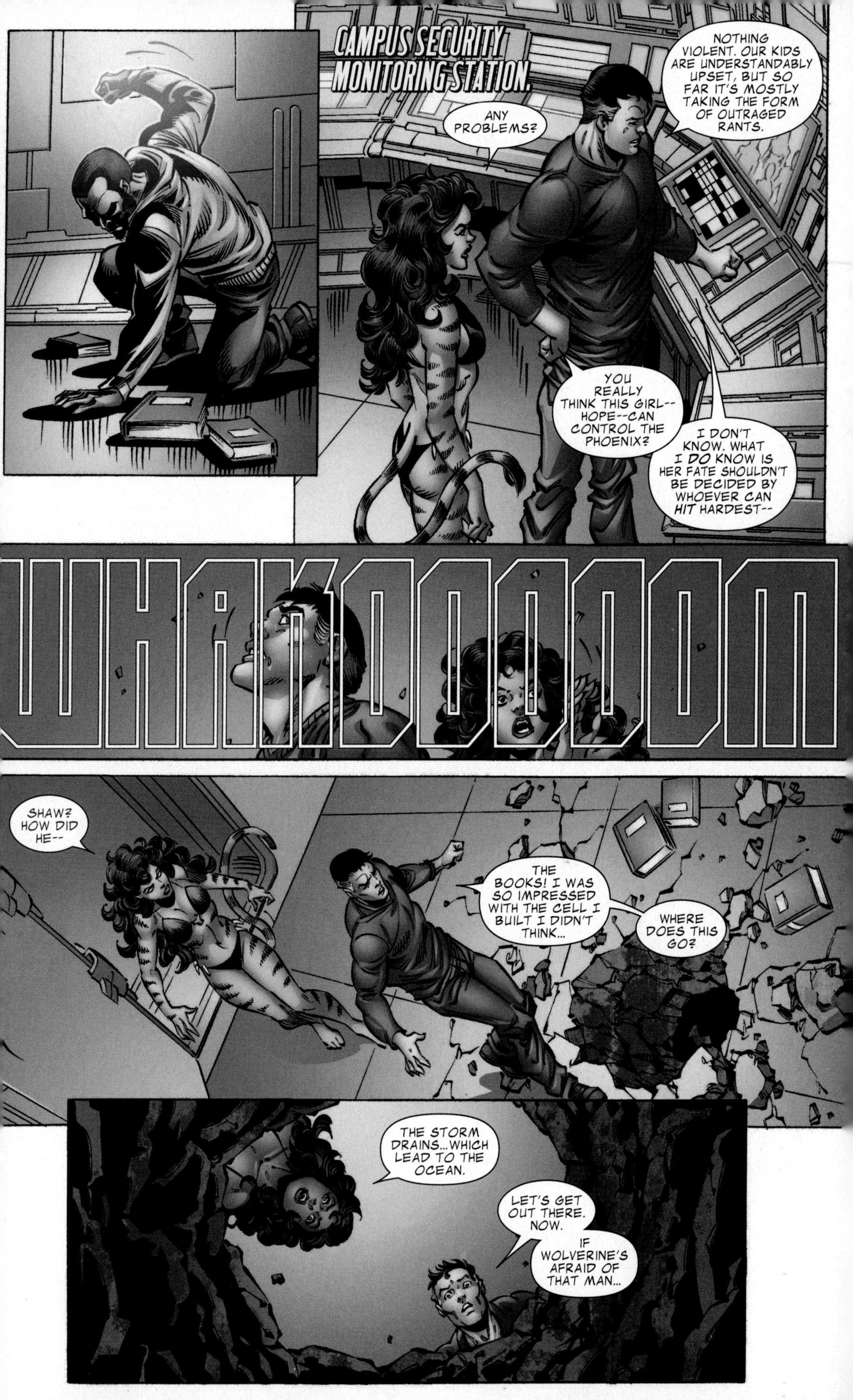
CAMPUS SECURITY MONITORING STATION.
ANY PROBLEMS?
NOTHING VIOLENT. OUR KIDS ARE UNDERSTANDABLY UPSET, BUT SO FAR IT'S MOSTLY TAKING THE FORM OF OUTRAGED RANTS.
YOU REALLY THINK THIS GIRL-- HOPE--CAN CONTROL THE PHOENIX?
I DON'T KNOW. WHAT I DO KNOW IS HER FATE SHOULDN'T BE DECIDED BY WHOEVER CAN HIT HARDEST--
WHAKOOOOOOM
SHAW? HOW DID HE--
THE BOOKS! I WAS SO IMPRESSED WITH THE CELL I BUILT I DIDN'T THINK...
WHERE DOES THIS GO?
THE STORM DRAINS...WHICH LEAD TO THE OCEAN.
LET'S GET OUT THERE. NOW.
IF WOLVERINE'S AFRAID OF THAT MAN...

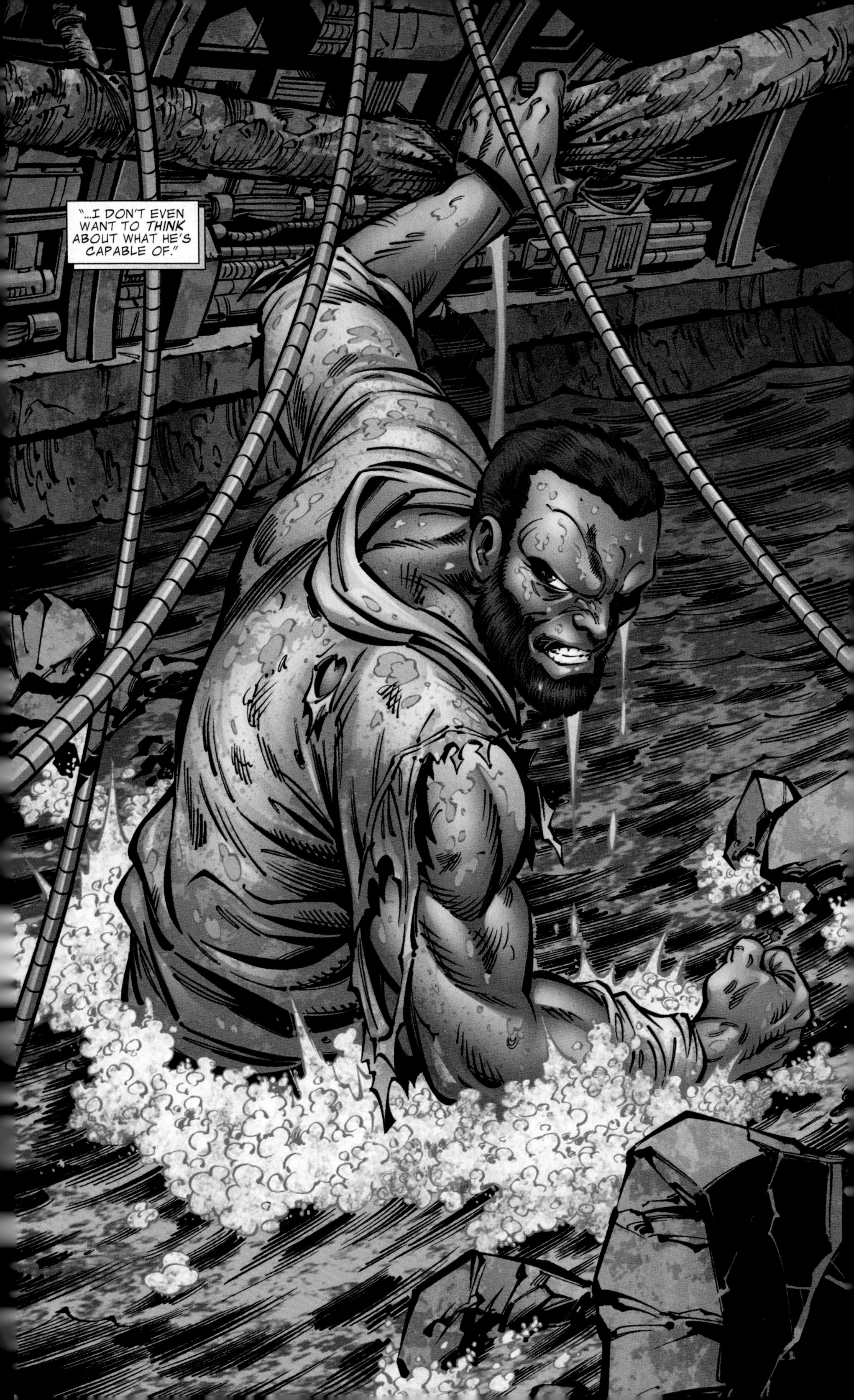
"...I DON'T EVEN WANT TO THINK ABOUT WHAT HE'S CAPABLE OF."

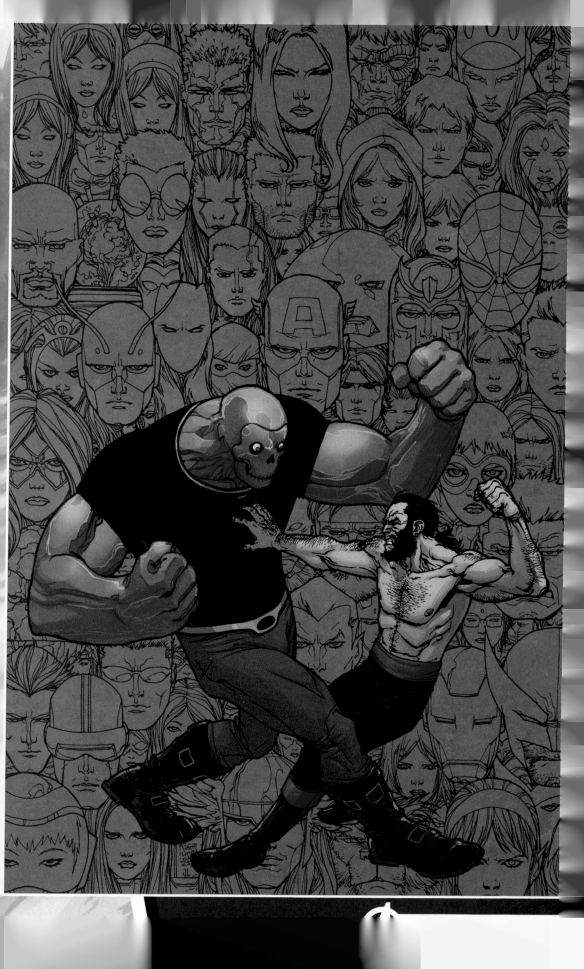

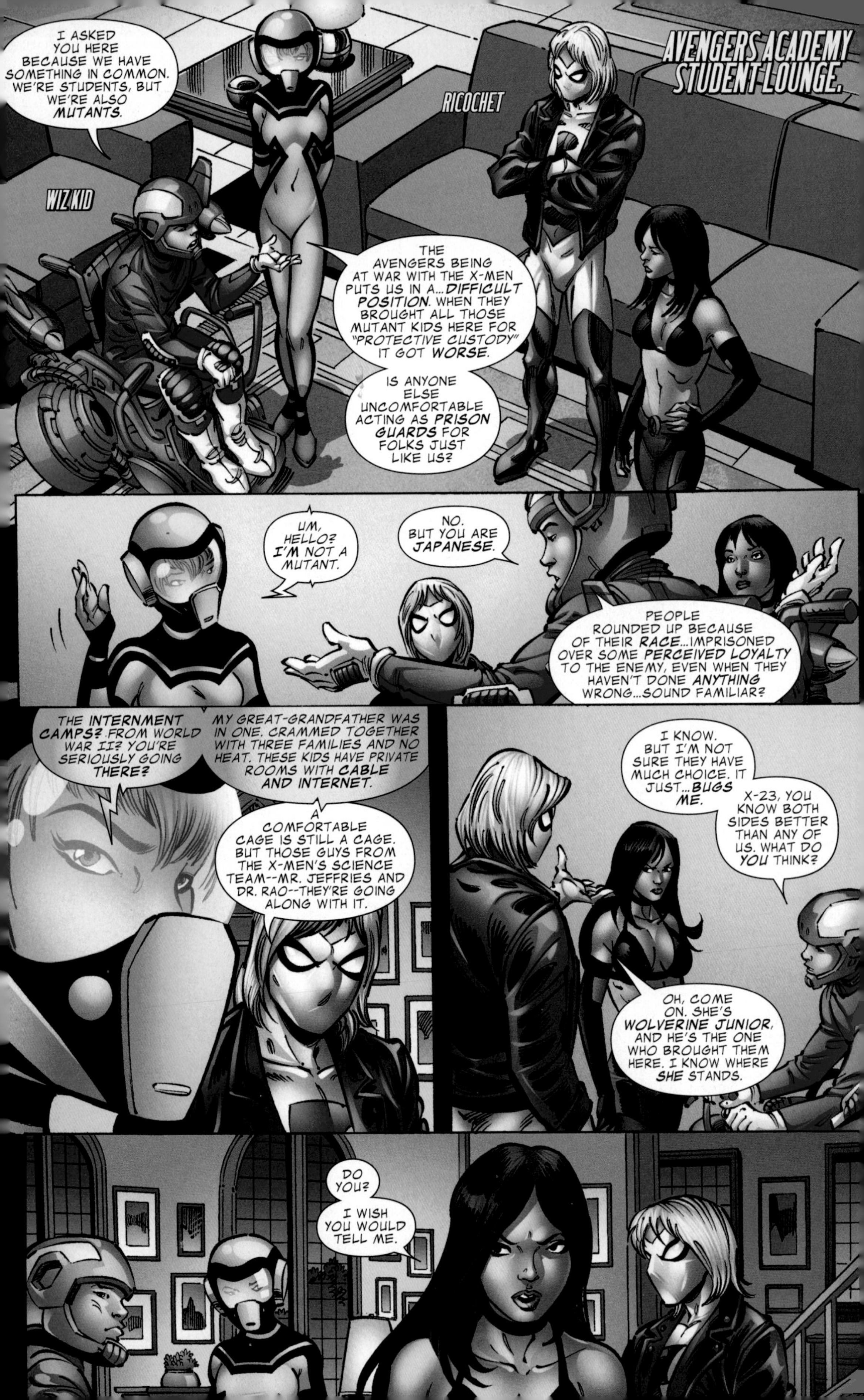
AVENGERS ACADEMY STUDENT LOUNGE.
I ASKED YOU HERE BECAUSE WE HAVE SOMETHING IN COMMON. WE'RE STUDENTS, BUT WE'RE ALSO MUTANTS.
RICOCHET
WIZ KID
THE AVENGERS BEING AT WAR WITH THE X-MEN PUTS US IN A...DIFFICULT POSITION. WHEN THEY BROUGHT ALL THOSE MUTANT KIDS HERE FOR "PROTECTIVE CUSTODY" IT GOT WORSE.
IS ANYONE ELSE UNCOMFORTABLE ACTING AS PRISON GUARDS FOR FOLKS JUST LIKE US?
UM, HELLO? I'M NOT A MUTANT.
NO. BUT YOU ARE JAPANESE.
PEOPLE ROUNDED UP BECAUSE OF THEIR RACE...IMPRISONED OVER SOME PERCEIVED LOYALTY TO THE ENEMY, EVEN WHEN THEY HAVEN'T DONE ANYTHING WRONG...SOUND FAMILIAR?
THE INTERNMENT CAMPS? FROM WORLD WAR II? YOU'RE SERIOUSLY GOING THERE?
MY GREAT-GRANDFATHER WAS IN ONE. CRAMMED TOGETHER WITH THREE FAMILIES AND NO HEAT. THESE KIDS HAVE PRIVATE ROOMS WITH CABLE AND INTERNET.
A COMFORTABLE CAGE IS STILL A CAGE. BUT THOSE GUYS FROM THE X-MEN'S SCIENCE TEAM--MR. JEFFRIES AND DR. RAO--THEY'RE GOING ALONG WITH IT.
I KNOW. BUT I'M NOT SURE THEY HAVE MUCH CHOICE. IT JUST...BUGS ME.
X-23, YOU KNOW BOTH SIDES BETTER THAN ANY OF US. WHAT DO YOU THINK?
OH, COME ON. SHE'S WOLVERINE JUNIOR, AND HE'S THE ONE WHO BROUGHT THEM HERE. I KNOW WHERE SHE STANDS.
DO YOU?
I WISH YOU WOULD TELL ME.

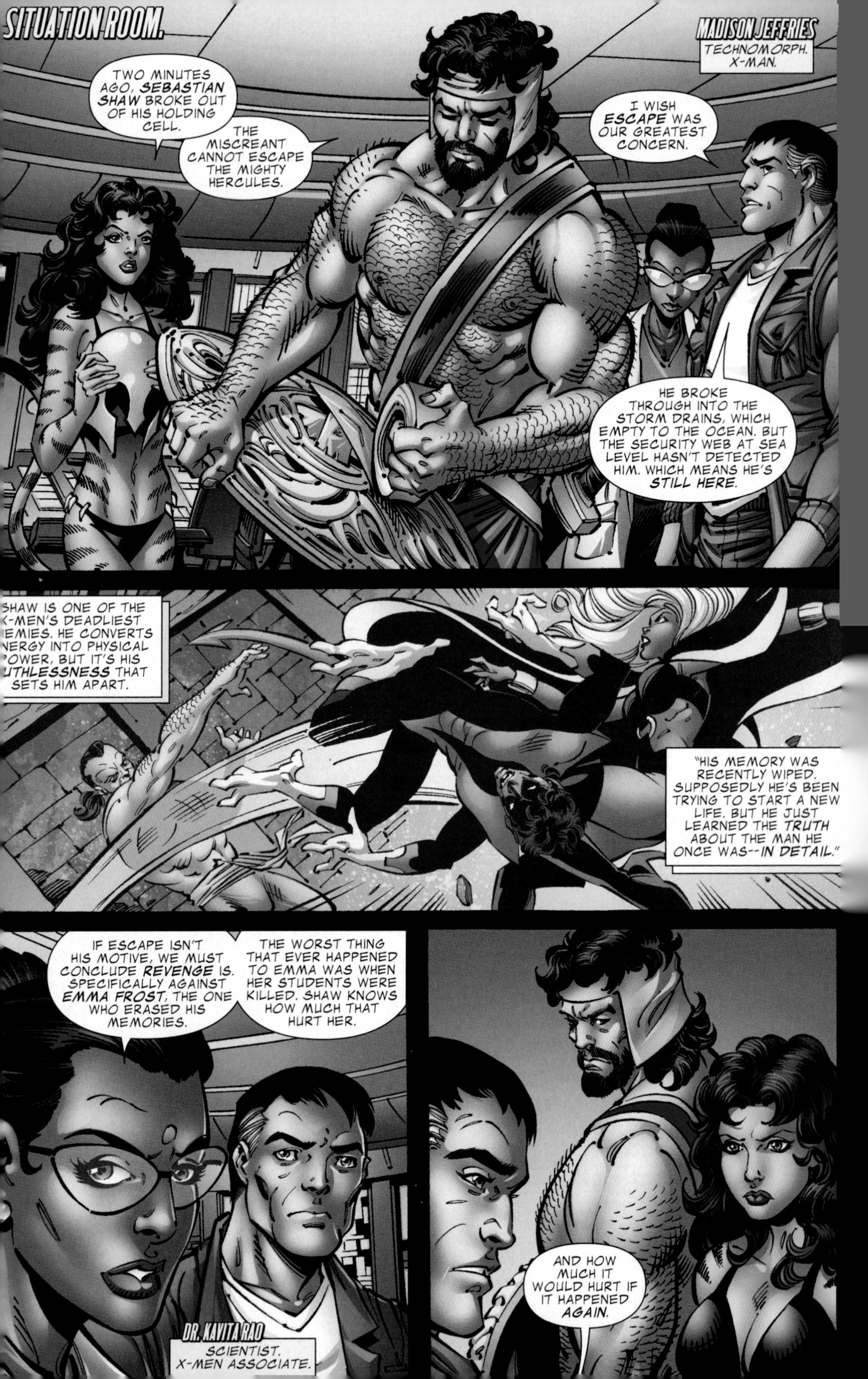
SITUATION ROOM.
MADISON JEFFRIES
TECHNOMORPH. X-MAN.
TWO MINUTES AGO, SEBASTIAN SHAW BROKE OUT OF HIS HOLDING CELL.
THE MISCREANT CANNOT ESCAPE THE MIGHTY HERCULES.
I WISH ESCAPE WAS OUR GREATEST CONCERN.
HE BROKE THROUGH INTO THE STORM DRAINS, WHICH EMPTY TO THE OCEAN. BUT THE SECURITY WEB AT SEA LEVEL HASN'T DETECTED HIM. WHICH MEANS HE'S STILL HERE.
SHAW IS ONE OF THE X-MEN'S DEADLIEST EMIES. HE CONVERTS NERGY INTO PHYSICAL POWER, BUT IT'S HIS UTHLESSNESS THAT SETS HIM APART.
"HIS MEMORY WAS RECENTLY WIPED. SUPPOSEDLY HE'S BEEN TRYING TO START A NEW LIFE. BUT HE JUST LEARNED THE TRUTH ABOUT THE MAN HE ONCE WAS--IN DETAIL."
IF ESCAPE ISN'T HIS MOTIVE, WE MUST CONCLUDE REVENGE IS. SPECIFICALLY AGAINST EMMA FROST, THE ONE WHO ERASED HIS MEMORIES.
THE WORST THING THAT EVER HAPPENED TO EMMA WAS WHEN HER STUDENTS WERE KILLED. SHAW KNOWS HOW MUCH THAT HURT HER.
DR. KAVITA RAO
SCIENTIST. X-MEN ASSOCIATE.
AND HOW MUCH IT WOULD HURT IF IT HAPPENED AGAIN.

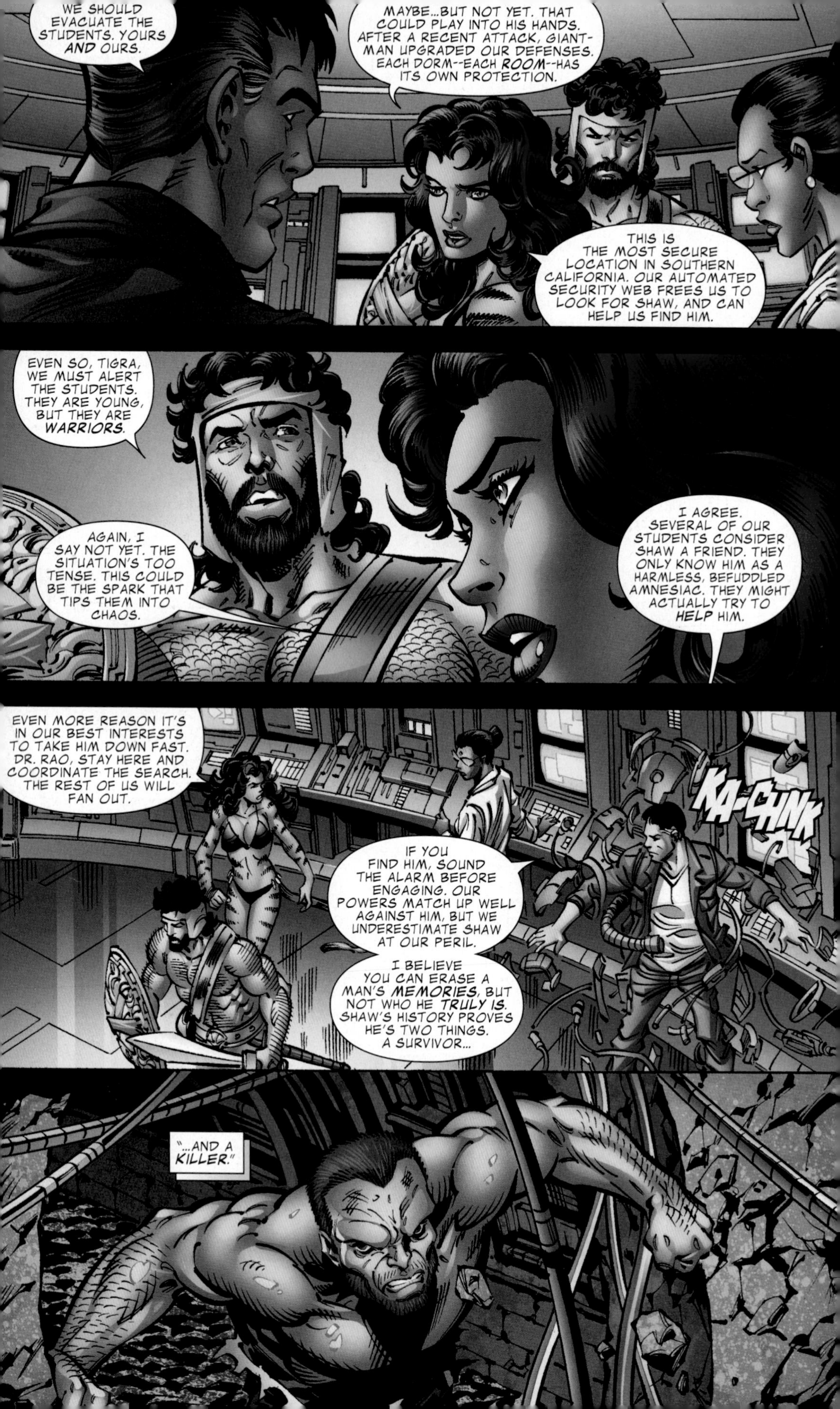
WE SHOULD EVACUATE THE STUDENTS. YOURS AND OURS.
MAYBE...BUT NOT YET. THAT COULD PLAY INTO HIS HANDS. AFTER A RECENT ATTACK, GIANT-MAN UPGRADED OUR DEFENSES. EACH DORM--EACH ROOM--HAS ITS OWN PROTECTION.
THIS IS THE MOST SECURE LOCATION IN SOUTHERN CALIFORNIA. OUR AUTOMATED SECURITY WEB FREES US TO LOOK FOR SHAW, AND CAN HELP US FIND HIM.
EVEN SO, TIGRA, WE MUST ALERT THE STUDENTS. THEY ARE YOUNG, BUT THEY ARE WARRIORS.
AGAIN, I SAY NOT YET. THE SITUATION'S TOO TENSE. THIS COULD BE THE SPARK THAT TIPS THEM INTO CHAOS.
I AGREE. SEVERAL OF OUR STUDENTS CONSIDER SHAW A FRIEND. THEY ONLY KNOW HIM AS A HARMLESS, BEFUDDLED AMNESIAC. THEY MIGHT ACTUALLY TRY TO HELP HIM.
EVEN MORE REASON IT'S IN OUR BEST INTERESTS TO TAKE HIM DOWN FAST. DR. RAO, STAY HERE AND COORDINATE THE SEARCH. THE REST OF US WILL FAN OUT.
KA-CHNK
IF YOU FIND HIM, SOUND THE ALARM BEFORE ENGAGING. OUR POWERS MATCH UP WELL AGAINST HIM, BUT WE UNDERESTIMATE SHAW AT OUR PERIL.
I BELIEVE YOU CAN ERASE A MAN'S MEMORIES, BUT NOT WHO HE TRULY IS. SHAW'S HISTORY PROVES HE'S TWO THINGS. A SURVIVOR...
"...AND A KILLER."

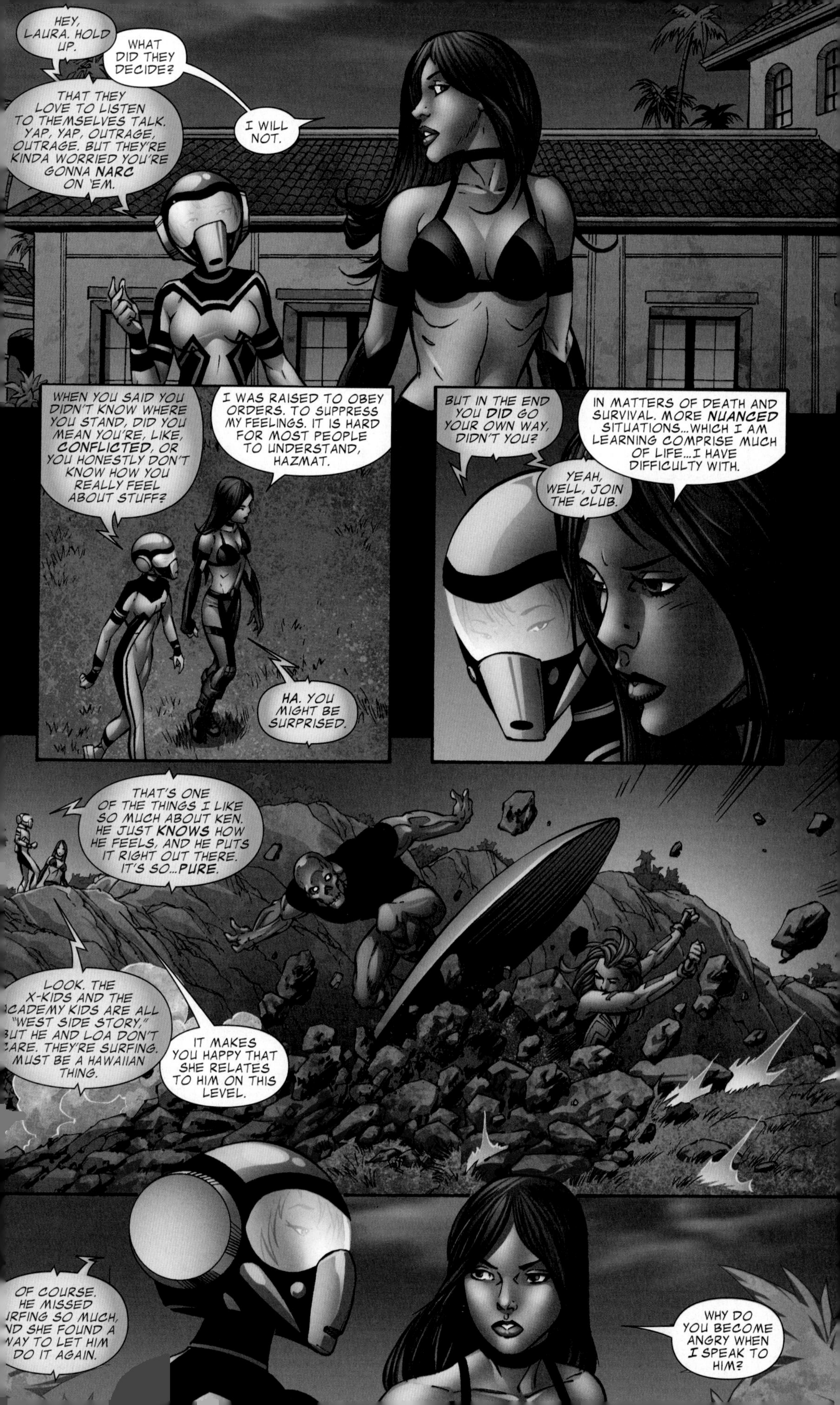
HEY, LAURA. HOLD UP.
WHAT DID THEY DECIDE?
THAT THEY LOVE TO LISTEN TO THEMSELVES TALK. YAP, YAP, OUTRAGE, OUTRAGE. BUT THEY'RE KINDA WORRIED YOU'RE GONNA NARC ON 'EM.
I WILL NOT.
WHEN YOU SAID YOU DIDN'T KNOW WHERE YOU STAND, DID YOU MEAN YOU'RE, LIKE, CONFLICTED, OR YOU HONESTLY DON'T KNOW HOW YOU REALLY FEEL ABOUT STUFF?
I WAS RAISED TO OBEY ORDERS. TO SUPPRESS MY FEELINGS. IT IS HARD FOR MOST PEOPLE TO UNDERSTAND, HAZMAT.
HA. YOU MIGHT BE SURPRISED.
BUT IN THE END YOU DID GO YOUR OWN WAY, DIDN'T YOU?
IN MATTERS OF DEATH AND SURVIVAL. MORE NUANCED SITUATIONS...WHICH I AM LEARNING COMPRISE MUCH OF LIFE...I HAVE DIFFICULTY WITH.
YEAH, WELL, JOIN THE CLUB.
THAT'S ONE OF THE THINGS I LIKE SO MUCH ABOUT KEN. HE JUST KNOWS HOW HE FEELS, AND HE PUTS IT RIGHT OUT THERE. IT'S SO...PURE.
LOOK. THE X-KIDS AND THE ACADEMY KIDS ARE ALL "WEST SIDE STORY," BUT HE AND LOA DON'T CARE. THEY'RE SURFING. MUST BE A HAWAIIAN THING.
IT MAKES YOU HAPPY THAT SHE RELATES TO HIM ON THIS LEVEL.
OF COURSE. HE MISSED SURFING SO MUCH, AND SHE FOUND A WAY TO LET HIM DO IT AGAIN.
WHY DO YOU BECOME ANGRY WHEN I SPEAK TO HIM?

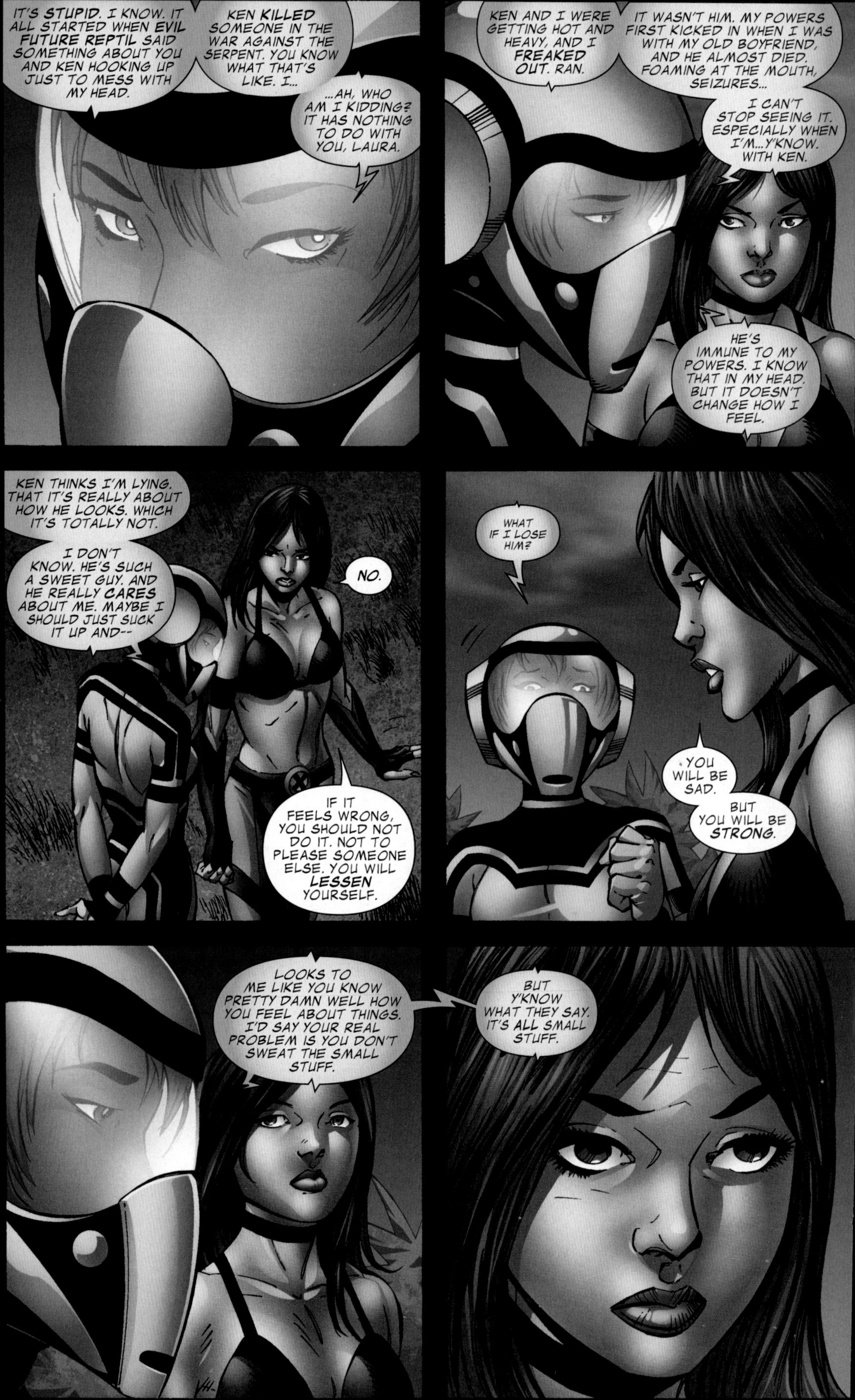
IT'S STUPID. I KNOW. IT ALL STARTED WHEN EVIL FUTURE REPTIL SAID SOMETHING ABOUT YOU AND KEN HOOKING UP JUST TO MESS WITH MY HEAD.
KEN KILLED SOMEONE IN THE WAR AGAINST THE SERPENT. YOU KNOW WHAT THAT'S LIKE. I...
...AH, WHO AM I KIDDING? IT HAS NOTHING TO DO WITH YOU, LAURA.
KEN AND I WERE GETTING HOT AND HEAVY, AND I FREAKED OUT. RAN.
IT WASN'T HIM. MY POWERS FIRST KICKED IN WHEN I WAS WITH MY OLD BOYFRIEND, AND HE ALMOST DIED. FOAMING AT THE MOUTH, SEIZURES...
I CAN'T STOP SEEING IT. ESPECIALLY WHEN I'M...Y'KNOW. WITH KEN.
HE'S IMMUNE TO MY POWERS. I KNOW THAT IN MY HEAD. BUT IT DOESN'T CHANGE HOW I FEEL.
KEN THINKS I'M LYING. THAT IT'S REALLY ABOUT HOW HE LOOKS. WHICH IT'S TOTALLY NOT.
I DON'T KNOW. HE'S SUCH A SWEET GUY. AND HE REALLY CARES ABOUT ME. MAYBE I SHOULD JUST SUCK IT UP AND--
NO.
IF IT FEELS WRONG, YOU SHOULD NOT DO IT. NOT TO PLEASE SOMEONE ELSE. YOU WILL LESSEN YOURSELF.
WHAT IF I LOSE HIM?
YOU WILL BE SAD.
BUT YOU WILL BE STRONG.
LOOKS TO ME LIKE YOU KNOW PRETTY DAMN WELL HOW YOU FEEL ABOUT THINGS. I'D SAY YOUR REAL PROBLEM IS YOU DON'T SWEAT THE SMALL STUFF.
BUT Y'KNOW WHAT THEY SAY. IT'S ALL SMALL STUFF.

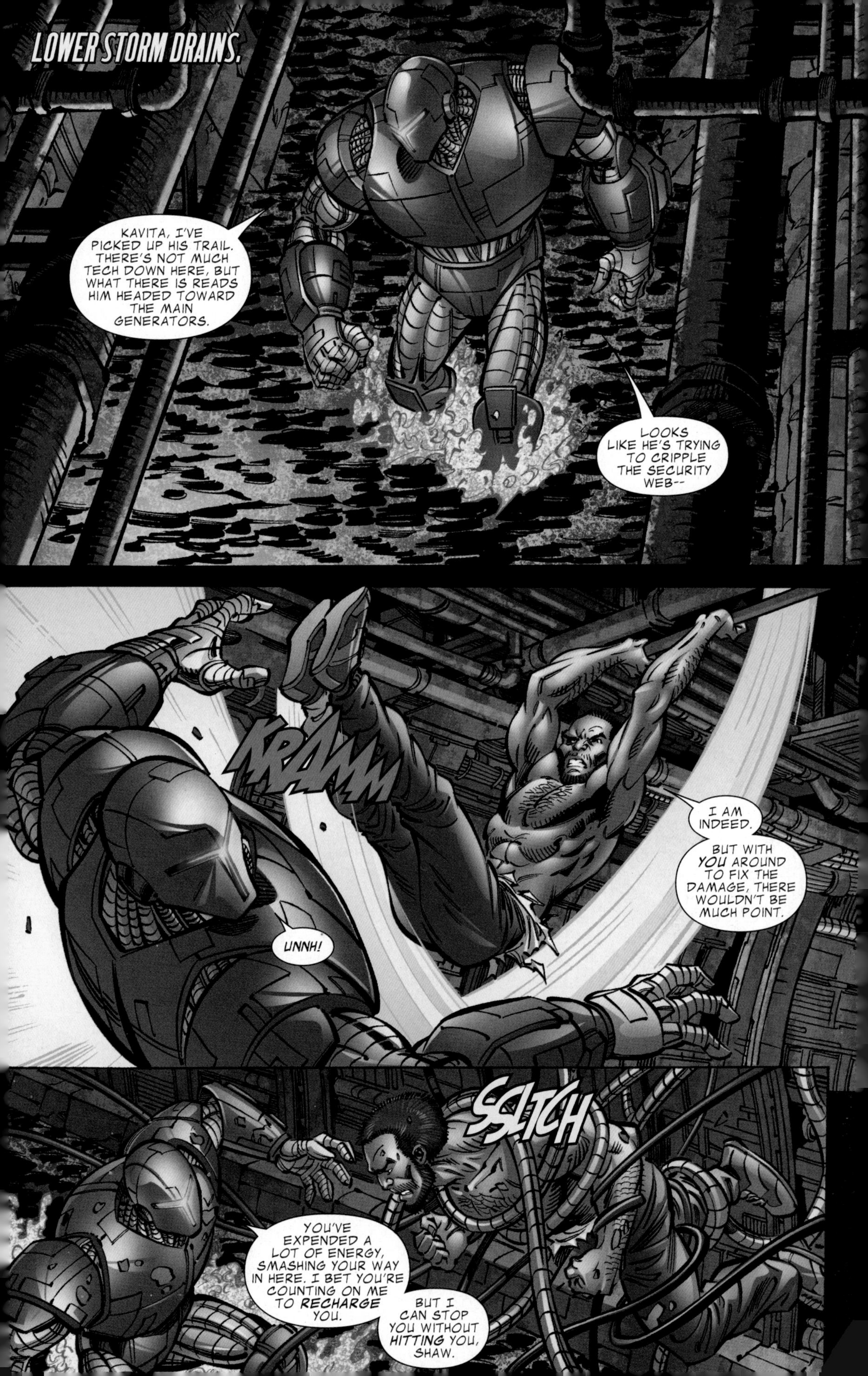
LOWER STORM DRAINS.
KAVITA, I'VE PICKED UP HIS TRAIL. THERE'S NOT MUCH TECH DOWN HERE, BUT WHAT THERE IS READS HIM HEADED TOWARD THE MAIN GENERATORS.
LOOKS LIKE HE'S TRYING TO CRIPPLE THE SECURITY WEB--
KRAMM
I AM INDEED.
BUT WITH YOU AROUND TO FIX THE DAMAGE, THERE WOULDN'T BE MUCH POINT.
UNNH!
SSLTCH
YOU'VE EXPENDED A LOT OF ENERGY, SMASHING YOUR WAY IN HERE. I BET YOU'RE COUNTING ON ME TO RECHARGE YOU.
BUT I CAN STOP YOU WITHOUT HITTING YOU, SHAW.

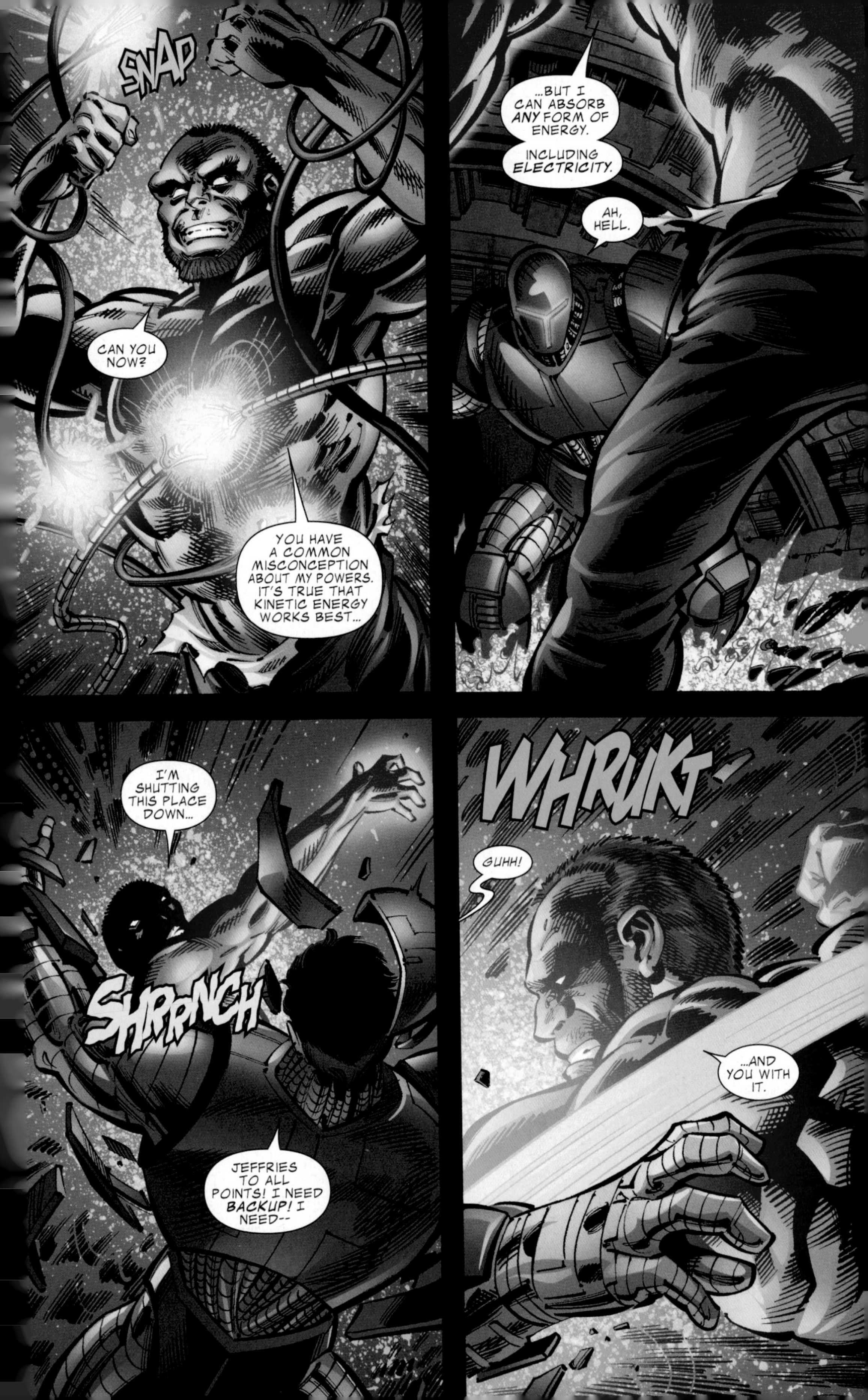
SNAP
CAN YOU NOW?
YOU HAVE A COMMON MISCONCEPTION ABOUT MY POWERS. IT'S TRUE THAT KINETIC ENERGY WORKS BEST...
...BUT I CAN ABSORB ANY FORM OF ENERGY.
INCLUDING ELECTRICITY.
AH, HELL.
I'M SHUTTING THIS PLACE DOWN...
SHRRNCH
JEFFRIES TO ALL POINTS! I NEED BACKUP! I NEED--
WHRUKT
GUHH!
...AND YOU WITH IT.

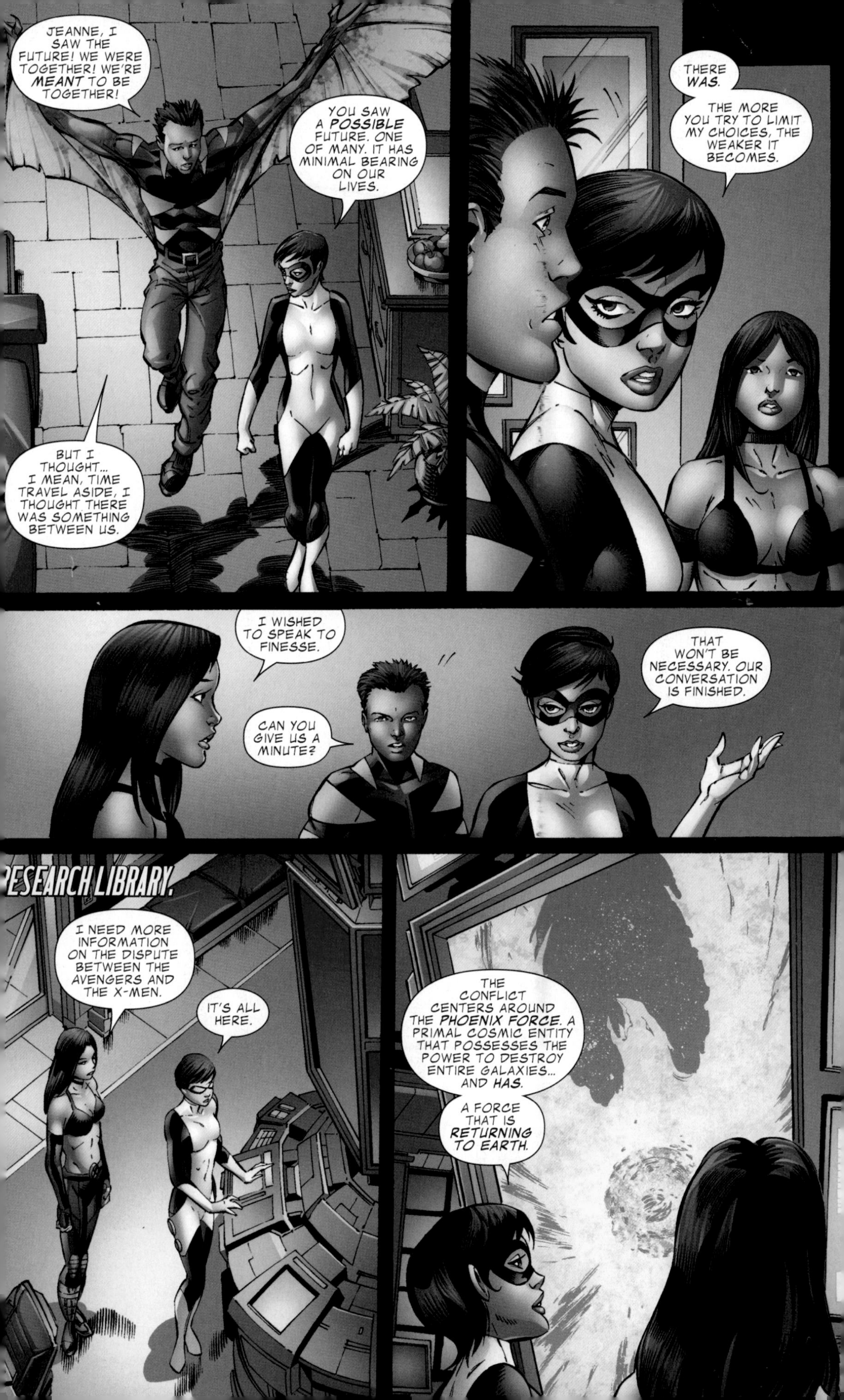
JEANNE, I SAW THE FUTURE! WE WERE TOGETHER! WE'RE MEANT TO BE TOGETHER!
YOU SAW A POSSIBLE FUTURE. ONE OF MANY. IT HAS MINIMAL BEARING ON OUR LIVES.
BUT I THOUGHT... I MEAN, TIME TRAVEL ASIDE, I THOUGHT THERE WAS SOMETHING BETWEEN US.
THERE WAS.
THE MORE YOU TRY TO LIMIT MY CHOICES, THE WEAKER IT BECOMES.
I WISHED TO SPEAK TO FINESSE.
CAN YOU GIVE US A MINUTE?
THAT WON'T BE NECESSARY. OUR CONVERSATION IS FINISHED.
ESEARCH LIBRARY.
I NEED MORE INFORMATION ON THE DISPUTE BETWEEN THE AVENGERS AND THE X-MEN.
IT'S ALL HERE.
THE CONFLICT CENTERS AROUND THE PHOENIX FORCE. A PRIMAL COSMIC ENTITY THAT POSSESSES THE POWER TO DESTROY ENTIRE GALAXIES... AND HAS.
A FORCE THAT IS RETURNING TO EARTH.

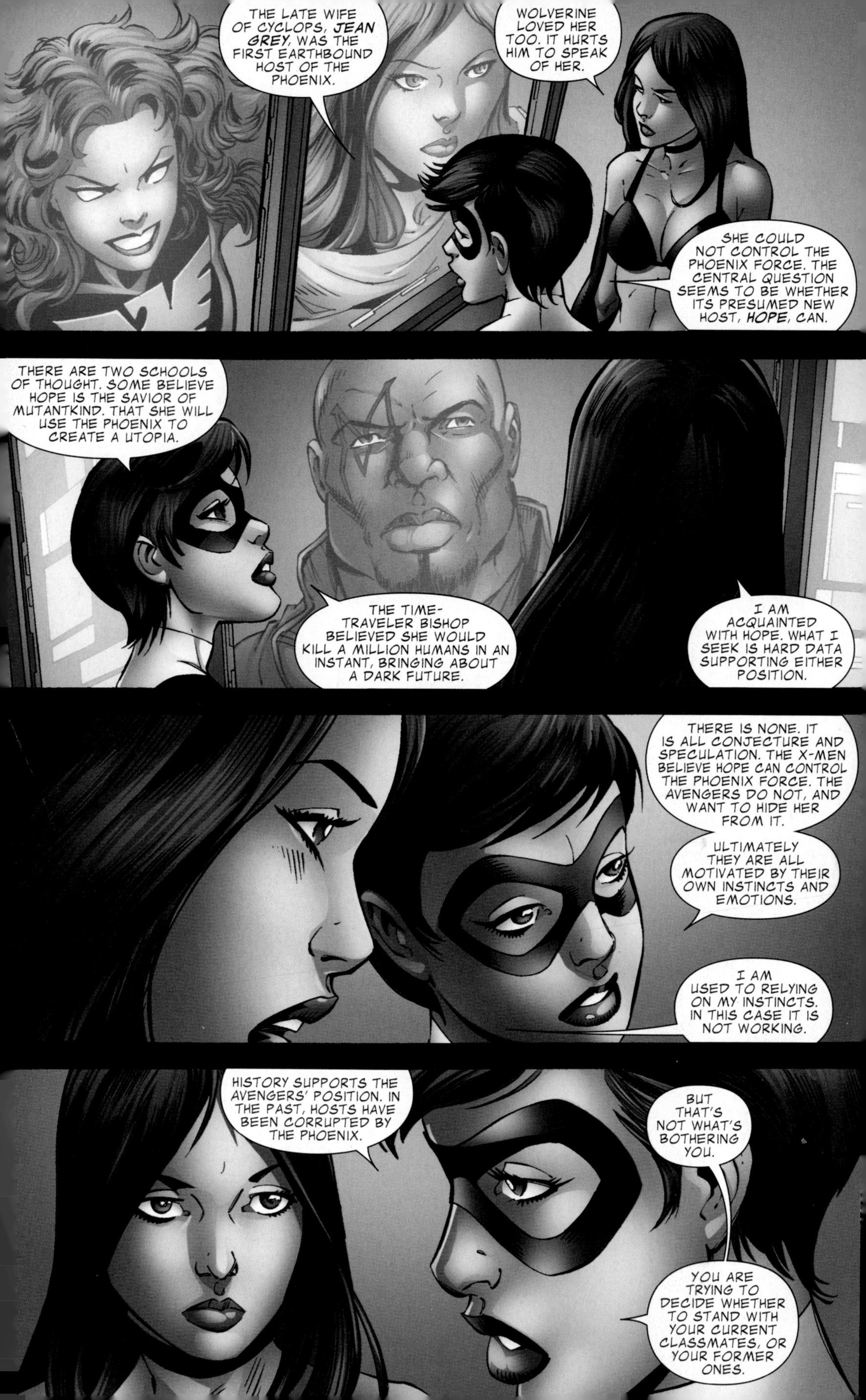
THE LATE WIFE OF CYCLOPS, JEAN GREY, WAS THE FIRST EARTHBOUND HOST OF THE PHOENIX.
WOLVERINE LOVED HER TOO. IT HURTS HIM TO SPEAK OF HER.
SHE COULD NOT CONTROL THE PHOENIX FORCE. THE CENTRAL QUESTION SEEMS TO BE WHETHER ITS PRESUMED NEW HOST, HOPE, CAN.
THERE ARE TWO SCHOOLS OF THOUGHT. SOME BELIEVE HOPE IS THE SAVIOR OF MUTANTKIND. THAT SHE WILL USE THE PHOENIX TO CREATE A UTOPIA.
THE TIME-TRAVELER BISHOP BELIEVED SHE WOULD KILL A MILLION HUMANS IN AN INSTANT, BRINGING ABOUT A DARK FUTURE.
I AM ACQUAINTED WITH HOPE. WHAT I SEEK IS HARD DATA SUPPORTING EITHER POSITION.
THERE IS NONE. IT IS ALL CONJECTURE AND SPECULATION. THE X-MEN BELIEVE HOPE CAN CONTROL THE PHOENIX FORCE. THE AVENGERS DO NOT, AND WANT TO HIDE HER FROM IT.
ULTIMATELY THEY ARE ALL MOTIVATED BY THEIR OWN INSTINCTS AND EMOTIONS.
I AM USED TO RELYING ON MY INSTINCTS. IN THIS CASE IT IS NOT WORKING.
HISTORY SUPPORTS THE AVENGERS' POSITION. IN THE PAST, HOSTS HAVE BEEN CORRUPTED BY THE PHOENIX.
BUT THAT'S NOT WHAT'S BOTHERING YOU.
YOU ARE TRYING TO DECIDE WHETHER TO STAND WITH YOUR CURRENT CLASSMATES, OR YOUR FORMER ONES.

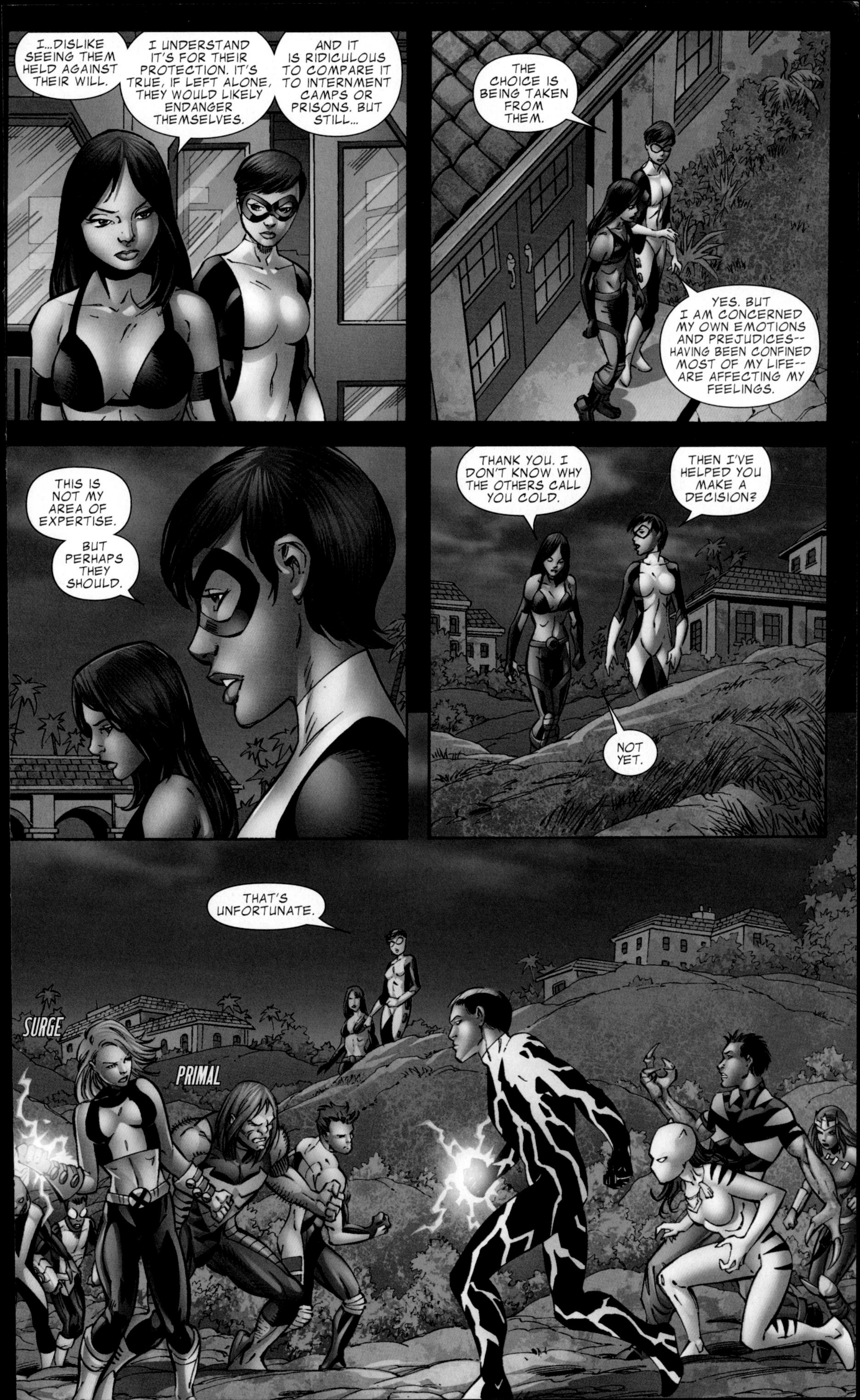
I...DISLIKE SEEING THEM HELD AGAINST THEIR WILL.
I UNDERSTAND IT'S FOR THEIR PROTECTION. IT'S TRUE, IF LEFT ALONE, THEY WOULD LIKELY ENDANGER THEMSELVES.
AND IT IS RIDICULOUS TO COMPARE IT TO INTERNMENT CAMPS OR PRISONS. BUT STILL...
THE CHOICE IS BEING TAKEN FROM THEM.
YES. BUT I AM CONCERNED MY OWN EMOTIONS AND PREJUDICES-- HAVING BEEN CONFINED MOST OF MY LIFE-- ARE AFFECTING MY FEELINGS.
THIS IS NOT MY AREA OF EXPERTISE.
BUT PERHAPS THEY SHOULD.
THANK YOU. I DON'T KNOW WHY THE OTHERS CALL YOU COLD.
THEN I'VE HELPED YOU MAKE A DECISION?
NOT YET.
THAT'S UNFORTUNATE.
SURGE
PRIMAL

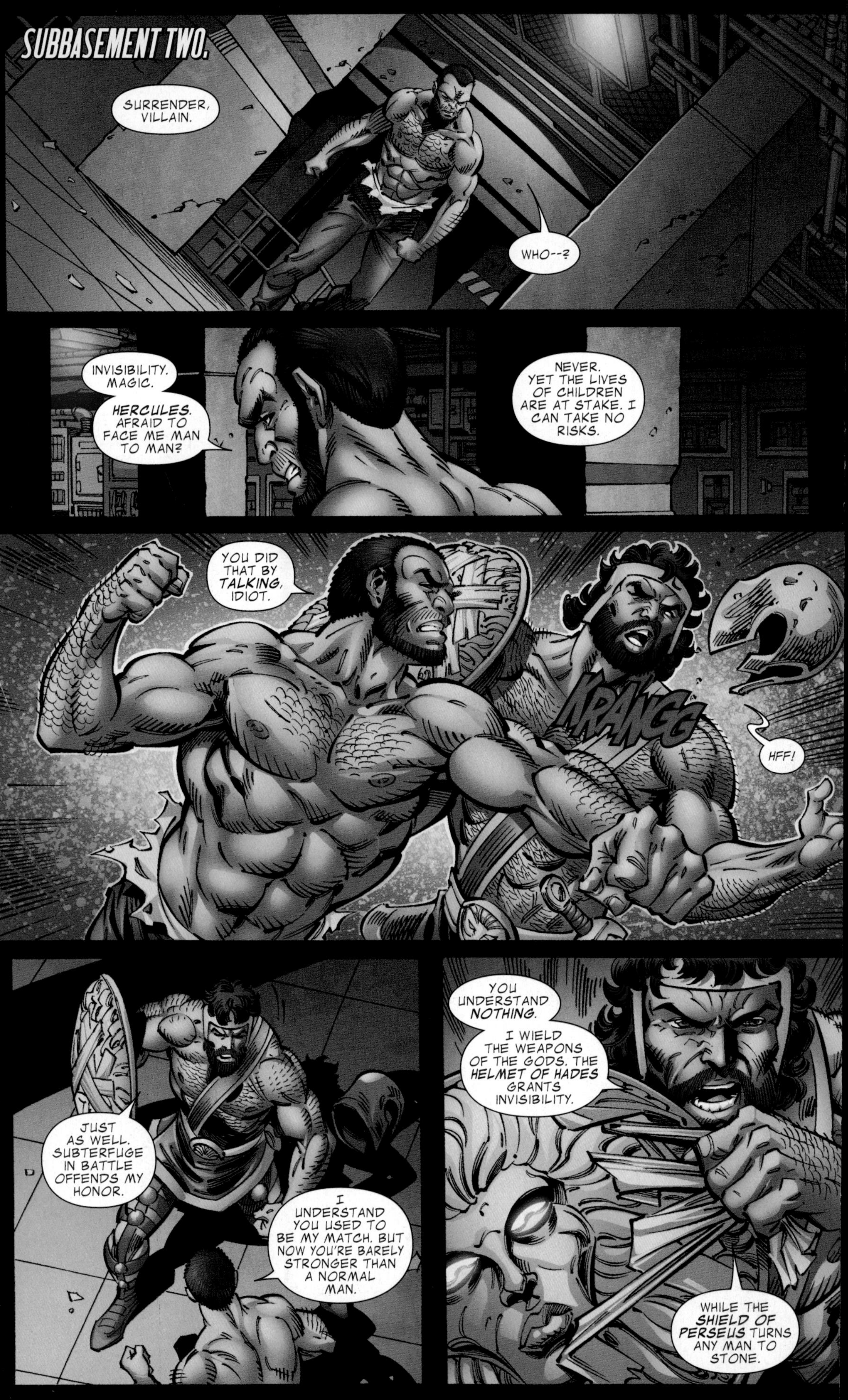
SUBBASEMENT TWO.
SURRENDER, VILLAIN.
WHO--?
INVISIBILITY. MAGIC.
HERCULES. AFRAID TO FACE ME MAN TO MAN?
NEVER. YET THE LIVES OF CHILDREN ARE AT STAKE. I CAN TAKE NO RISKS.
YOU DID THAT BY TALKING, IDIOT.
KRANGG
HFF!
JUST AS WELL. SUBTERFUGE IN BATTLE OFFENDS MY HONOR.
I UNDERSTAND YOU USED TO BE MY MATCH. BUT NOW YOU'RE BARELY STRONGER THAN A NORMAL MAN.
YOU UNDERSTAND NOTHING.
I WIELD THE WEAPONS OF THE GODS. THE HELMET OF HADES GRANTS INVISIBILITY.
WHILE THE SHIELD OF PERSEUS TURNS ANY MAN TO STONE.

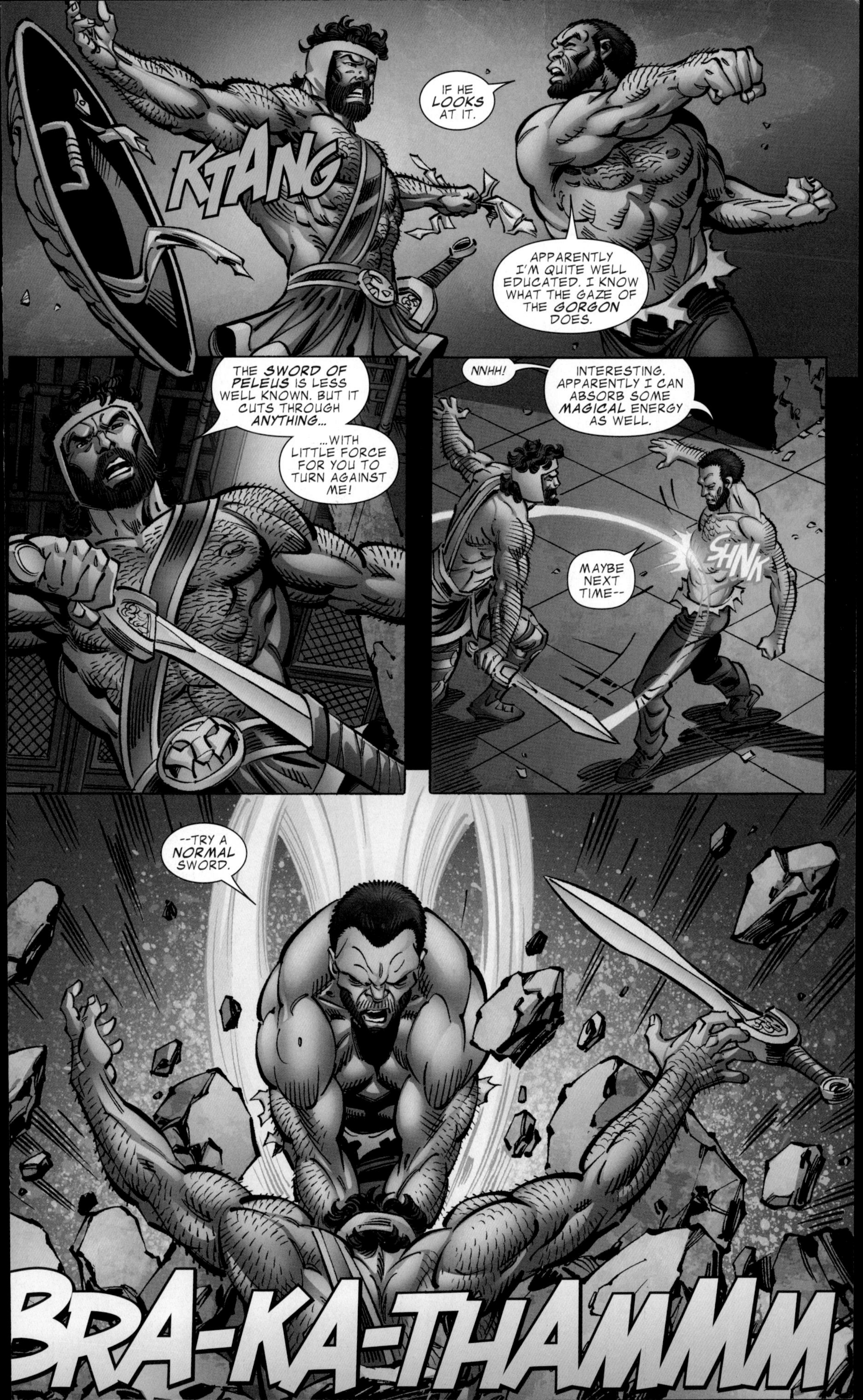
IF HE LOOKS AT IT.
KTANG
APPARENTLY I'M QUITE WELL EDUCATED. I KNOW WHAT THE GAZE OF THE GORGON DOES.
THE SWORD OF PELEUS IS LESS WELL KNOWN. BUT IT CUTS THROUGH ANYTHING...
...WITH LITTLE FORCE FOR YOU TO TURN AGAINST ME!
NNHH!
INTERESTING. APPARENTLY I CAN ABSORB SOME MAGICAL ENERGY AS WELL.
SHNK
MAYBE NEXT TIME--
--TRY A NORMAL SWORD.
BRA-KA-THAMMM

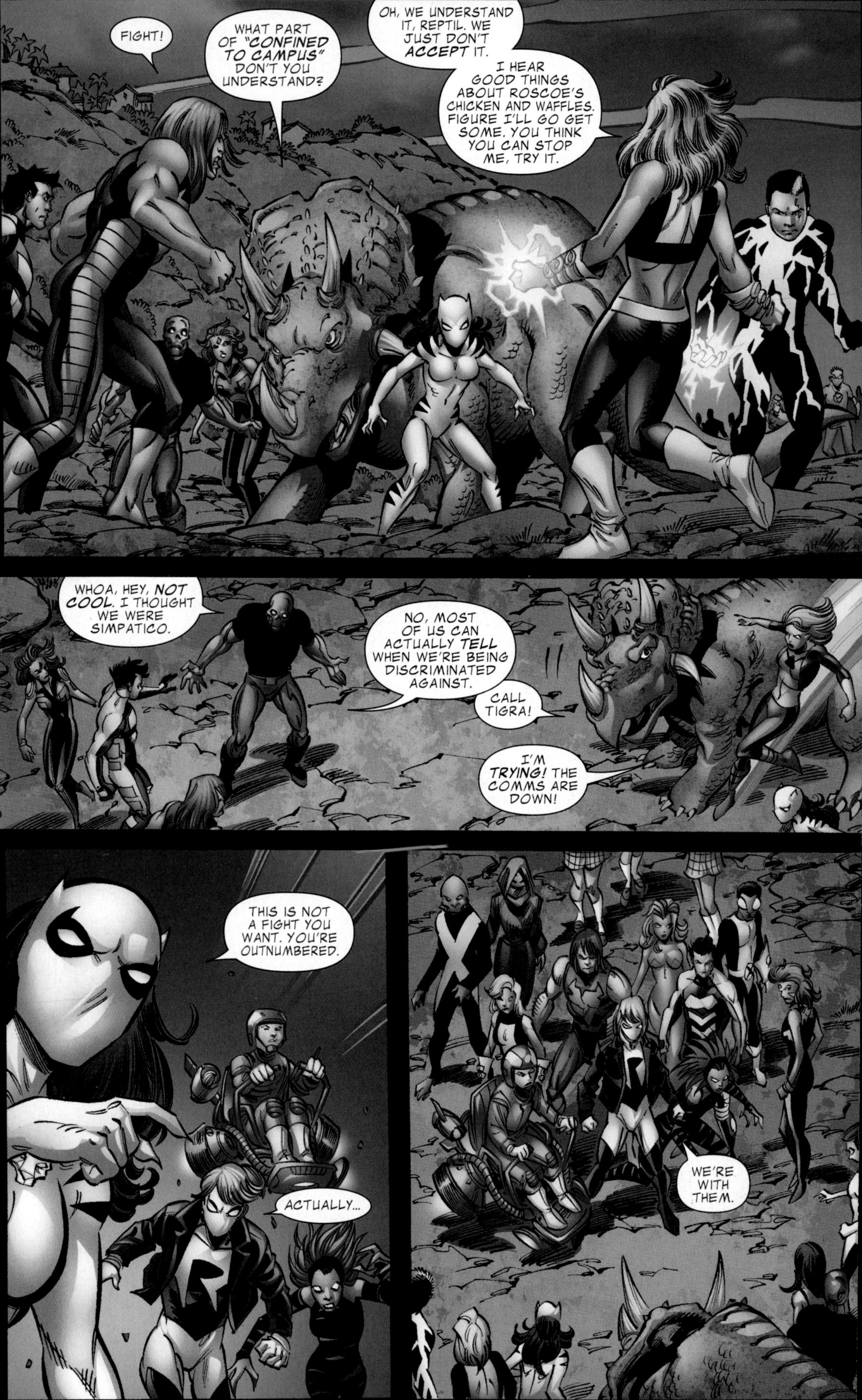
FIGHT!
WHAT PART OF "CONFINED TO CAMPUS" DON'T YOU UNDERSTAND?
OH, WE UNDERSTAND IT, REPTIL. WE JUST DON'T ACCEPT IT.
I HEAR GOOD THINGS ABOUT ROSCOE'S CHICKEN AND WAFFLES. FIGURE I'LL GO GET SOME. YOU THINK YOU CAN STOP ME, TRY IT.
WHOA, HEY, NOT COOL. I THOUGHT WE WERE SIMPATICO.
NO, MOST OF US CAN ACTUALLY TELL WHEN WE'RE BEING DISCRIMINATED AGAINST.
CALL TIGRA!
I'M TRYING! THE COMMS ARE DOWN!
THIS IS NOT A FIGHT YOU WANT. YOU'RE OUTNUMBERED.
ACTUALLY...
WE'RE WITH THEM.

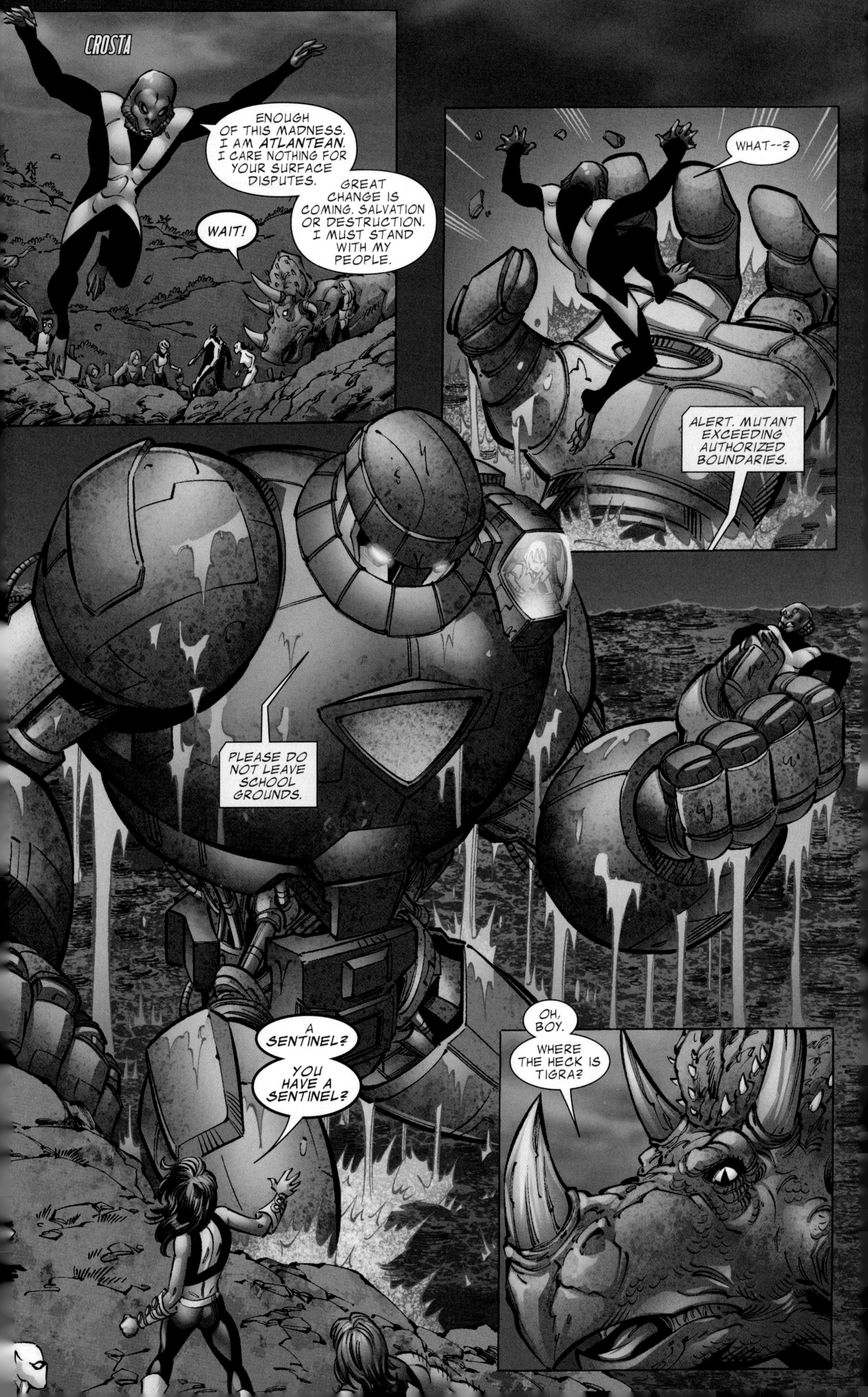
CROSTA
ENOUGH OF THIS MADNESS. I AM ATLANTEAN. I CARE NOTHING FOR YOUR SURFACE DISPUTES.
WAIT!
GREAT CHANGE IS COMING. SALVATION OR DESTRUCTION. I MUST STAND WITH MY PEOPLE.
WHAT--?
ALERT. MUTANT EXCEEDING AUTHORIZED BOUNDARIES.
PLEASE DO NOT LEAVE SCHOOL GROUNDS.
A SENTINEL?
YOU HAVE A SENTINEL?
OH, BOY.
WHERE THE HECK IS TIGRA?

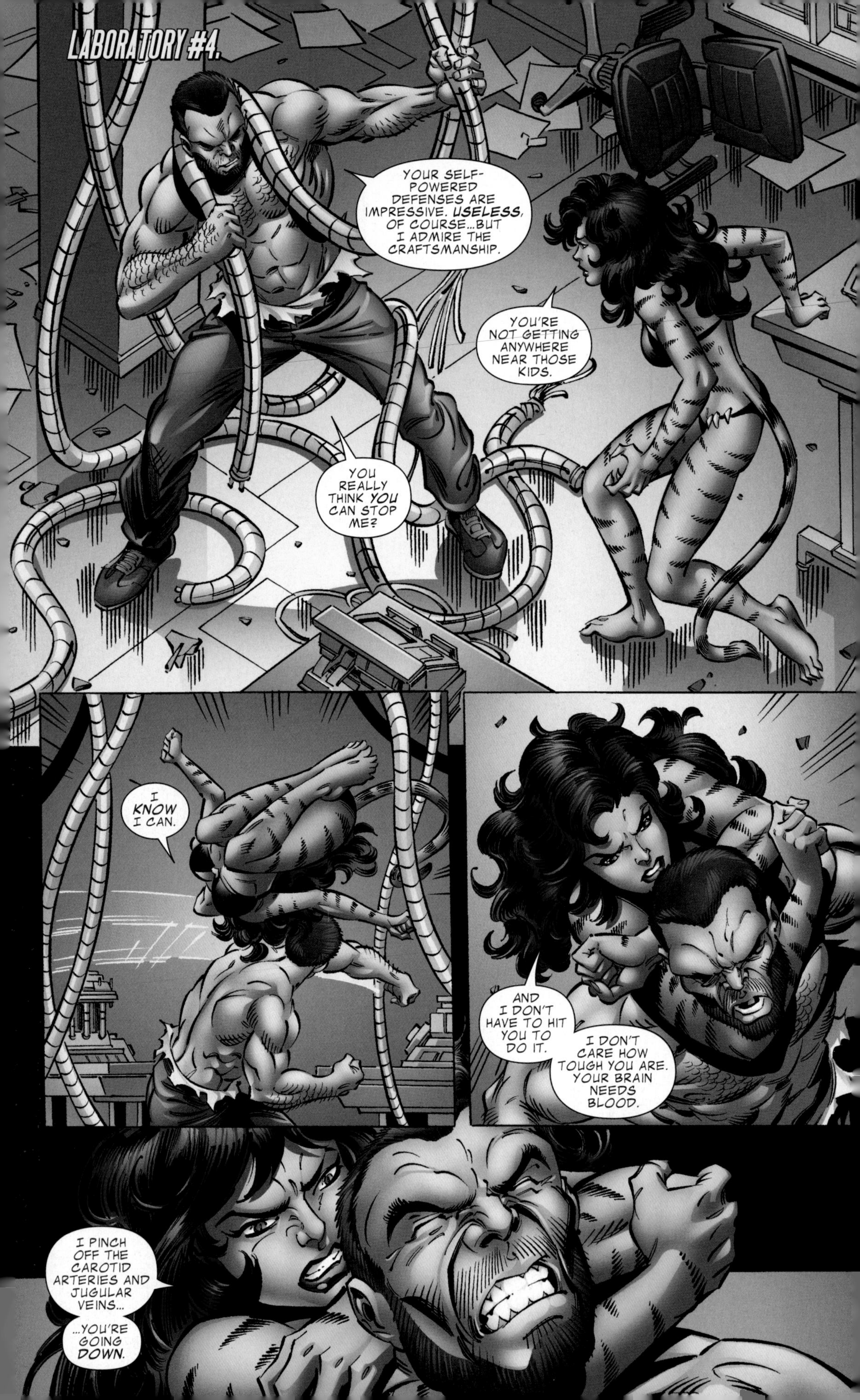
LABORATORY #4.
YOUR SELF-POWERED DEFENSES ARE IMPRESSIVE. USELESS, OF COURSE...BUT I ADMIRE THE CRAFTSMANSHIP.
YOU'RE NOT GETTING ANYWHERE NEAR THOSE KIDS.
YOU REALLY THINK YOU CAN STOP ME?
I KNOW I CAN.
AND I DON'T HAVE TO HIT YOU TO DO IT.
I DON'T CARE HOW TOUGH YOU ARE. YOUR BRAIN NEEDS BLOOD.
I PINCH OFF THE CAROTID ARTERIES AND JUGULAR VEINS...
...YOU'RE GOING DOWN.

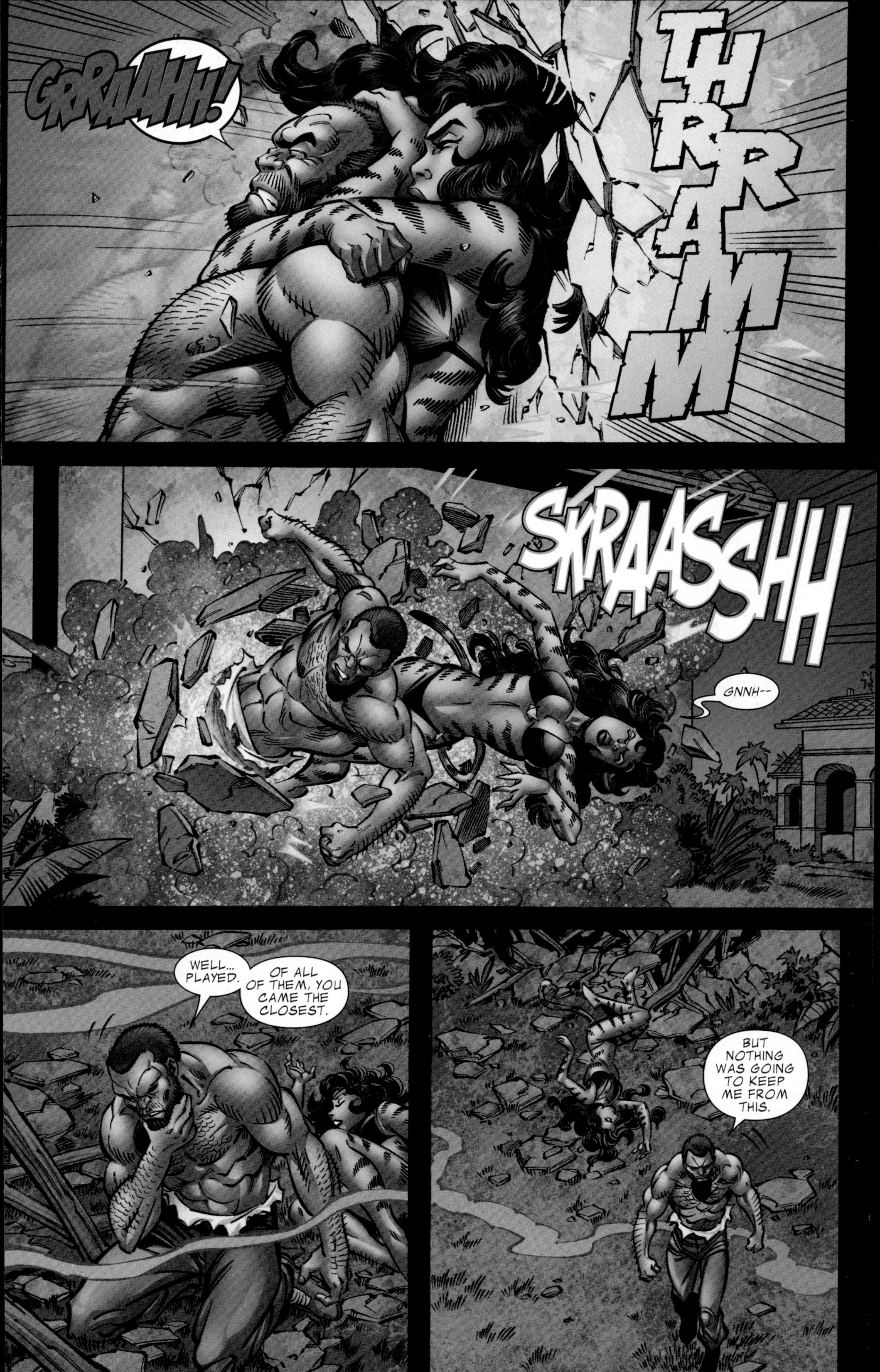
GRRAAHH!
THRRAMM
SKRAASSHH
GNNH--
WELL... PLAYED.
OF ALL OF THEM, YOU CAME THE CLOSEST.
BUT NOTHING WAS GOING TO KEEP ME FROM THIS.

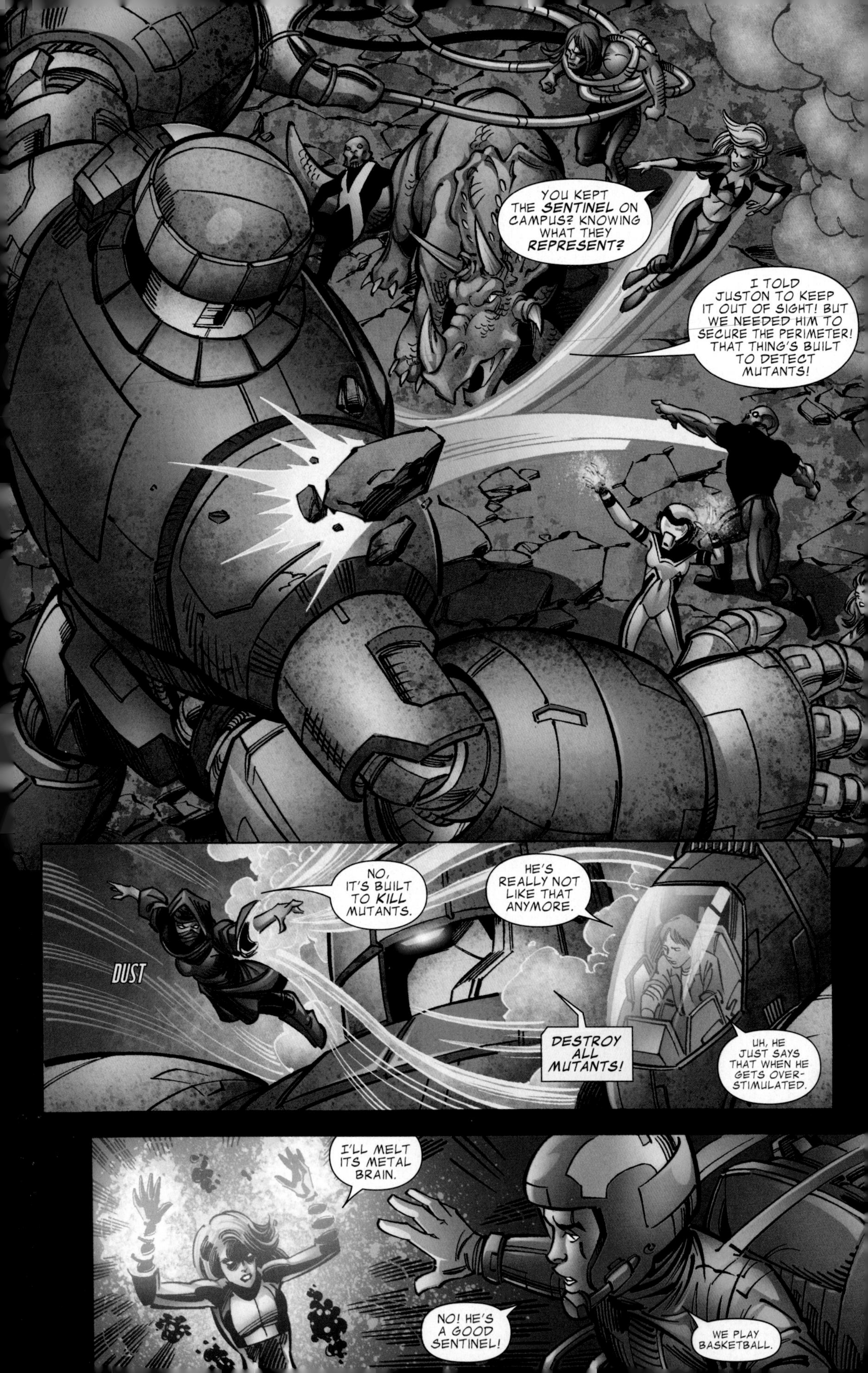
YOU KEPT THE SENTINEL ON CAMPUS? KNOWING WHAT THEY REPRESENT?
I TOLD JUSTON TO KEEP IT OUT OF SIGHT! BUT WE NEEDED HIM TO SECURE THE PERIMETER! THAT THING'S BUILT TO DETECT MUTANTS!
NO, IT'S BUILT TO KILL MUTANTS.
HE'S REALLY NOT LIKE THAT ANYMORE.
DUST
DESTROY ALL MUTANTS!
UH, HE JUST SAYS THAT WHEN HE GETS OVER-STIMULATED.
I'LL MELT ITS METAL BRAIN.
NO! HE'S A GOOD SENTINEL!
WE PLAY BASKETBALL.

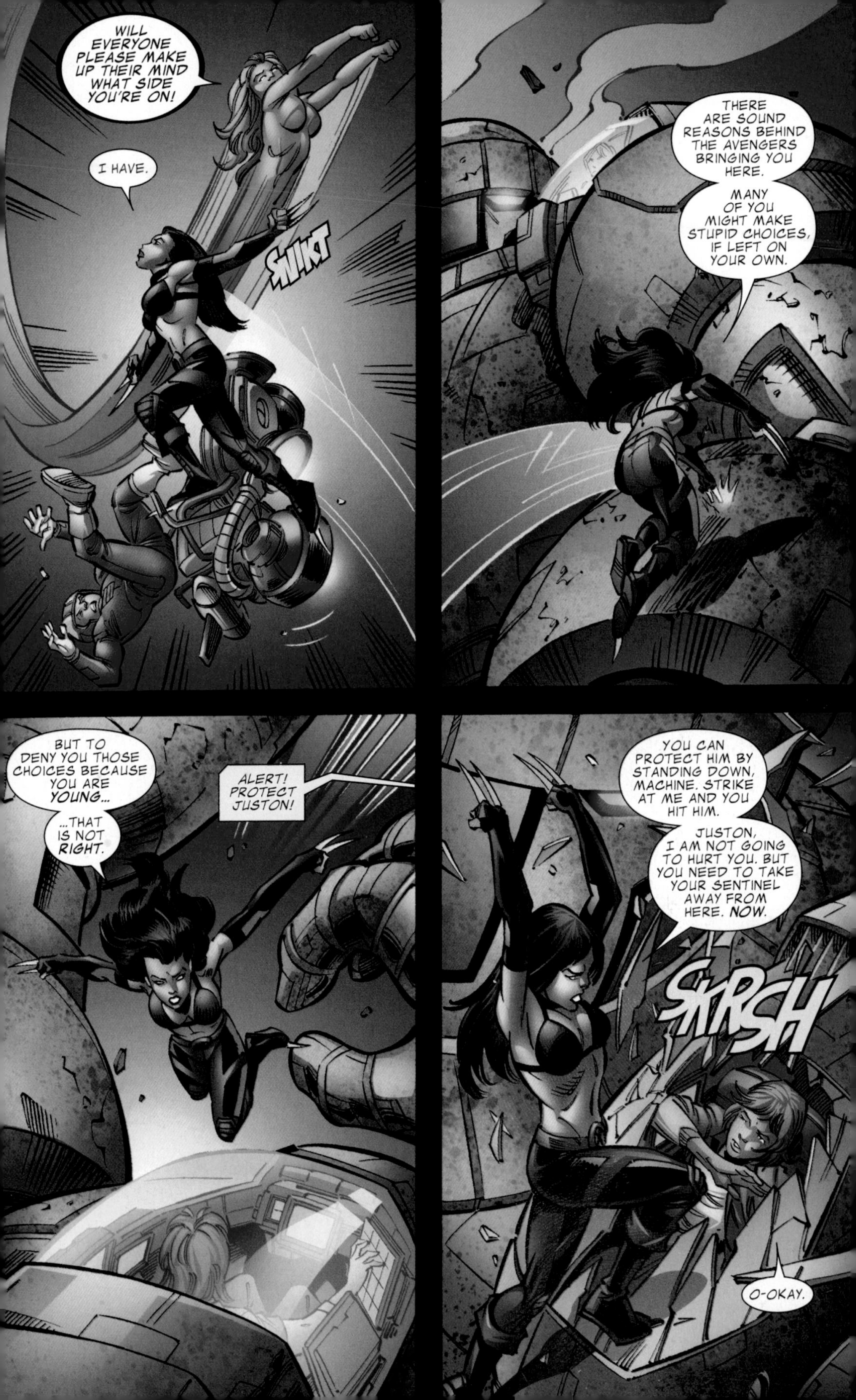
WILL EVERYONE PLEASE MAKE UP THEIR MIND WHAT SIDE YOU'RE ON!
I HAVE.
SNIKT
THERE ARE SOUND REASONS BEHIND THE AVENGERS BRINGING YOU HERE.
MANY OF YOU MIGHT MAKE STUPID CHOICES, IF LEFT ON YOUR OWN.
BUT TO DENY YOU THOSE CHOICES BECAUSE YOU ARE YOUNG...
...THAT IS NOT RIGHT.
ALERT! PROTECT JUSTON!
YOU CAN PROTECT HIM BY STANDING DOWN, MACHINE. STRIKE AT ME AND YOU HIT HIM.
JUSTON, I AM NOT GOING TO HURT YOU. BUT YOU NEED TO TAKE YOUR SENTINEL AWAY FROM HERE. NOW.
SKRSH
O-OKAY.

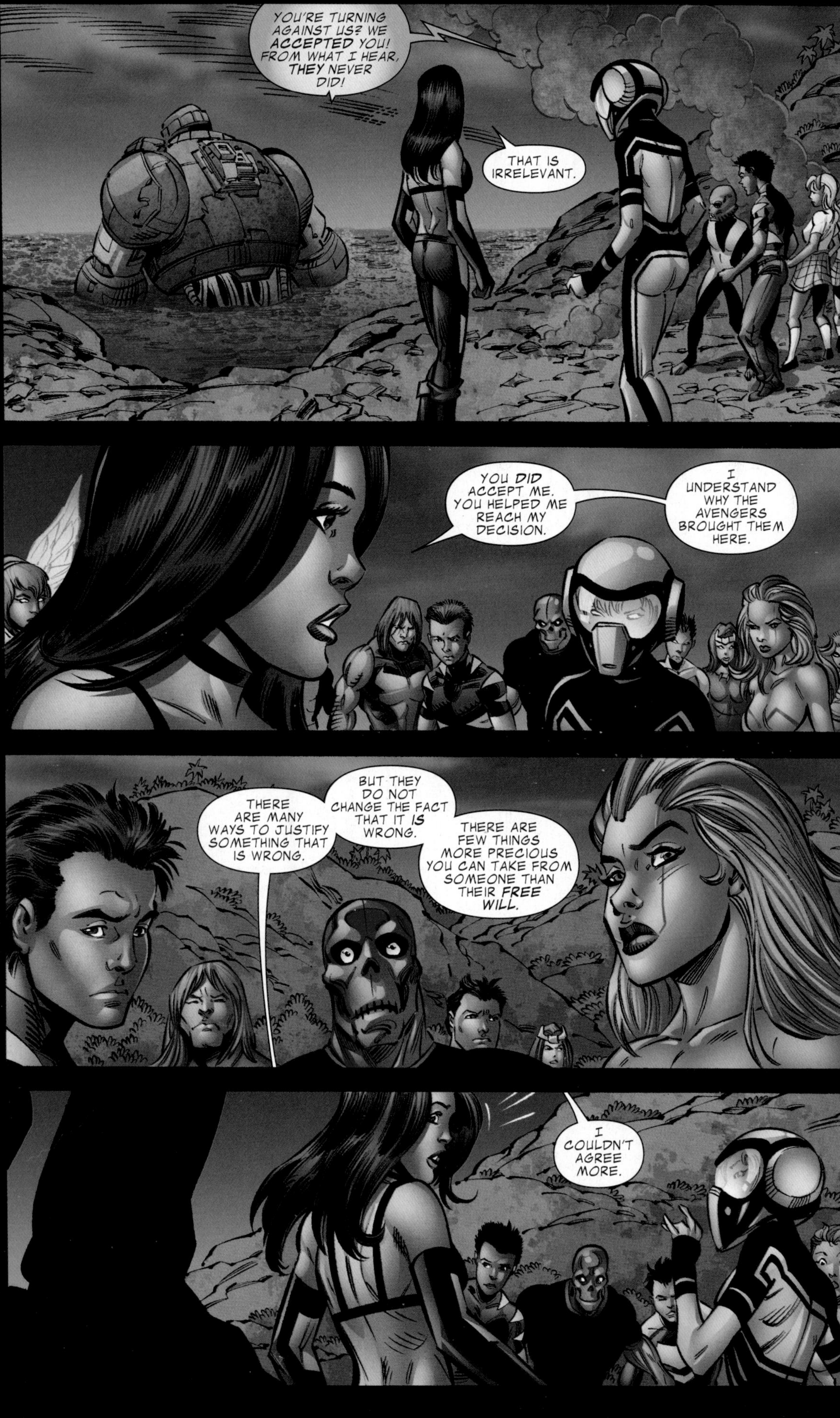
YOU'RE TURNING AGAINST US? WE ACCEPTED YOU! FROM WHAT I HEAR, THEY NEVER DID!
THAT IS IRRELEVANT.
YOU DID ACCEPT ME. YOU HELPED ME REACH MY DECISION.
I UNDERSTAND WHY THE AVENGERS BROUGHT THEM HERE.
THERE ARE MANY WAYS TO JUSTIFY SOMETHING THAT IS WRONG.
BUT THEY DO NOT CHANGE THE FACT THAT IT IS WRONG.
THERE ARE FEW THINGS MORE PRECIOUS YOU CAN TAKE FROM SOMEONE THAN THEIR FREE WILL.
I COULDN'T AGREE MORE.

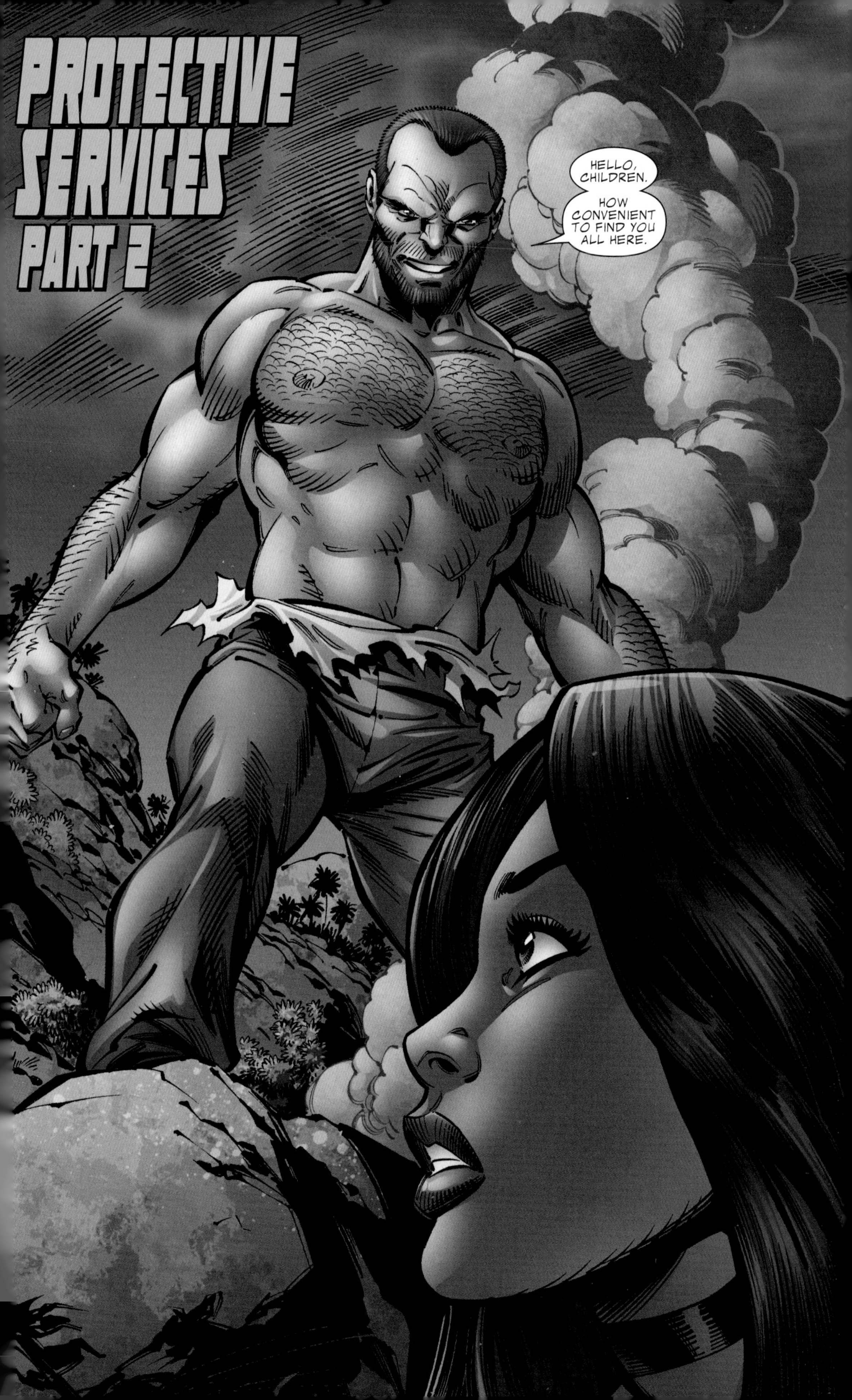
PROTECTIVE SERVICES PART 2
HELLO, CHILDREN.
HOW CONVENIENT TO FIND YOU ALL HERE.

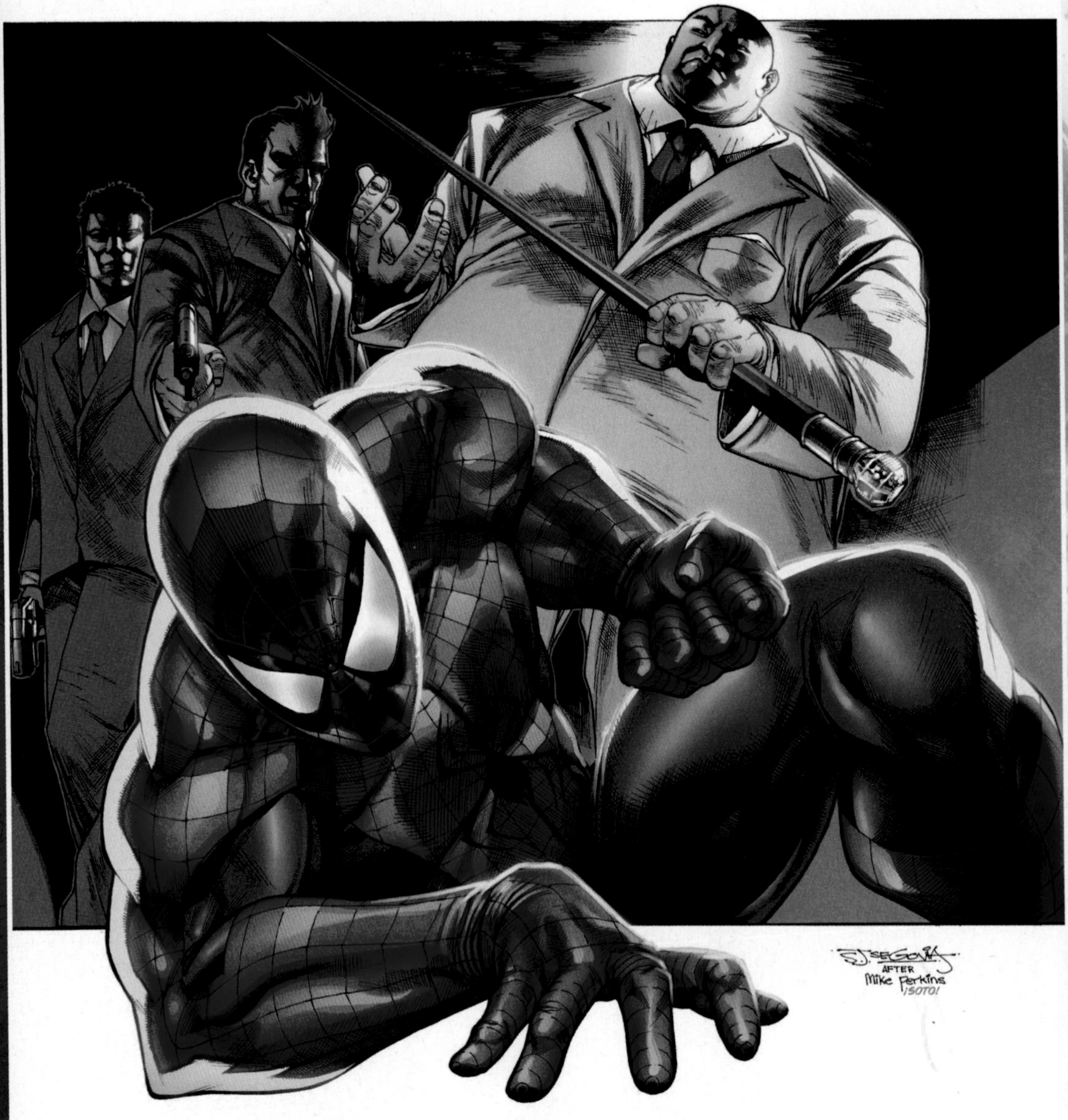
S.J. SEGOVIA
AFTER
Mike Perkins
¡SOTO!

#31 ASM IN MOTION VARIANT

BY **STEPHEN SEGOVIA & CHRIS SOTOMAYOR**

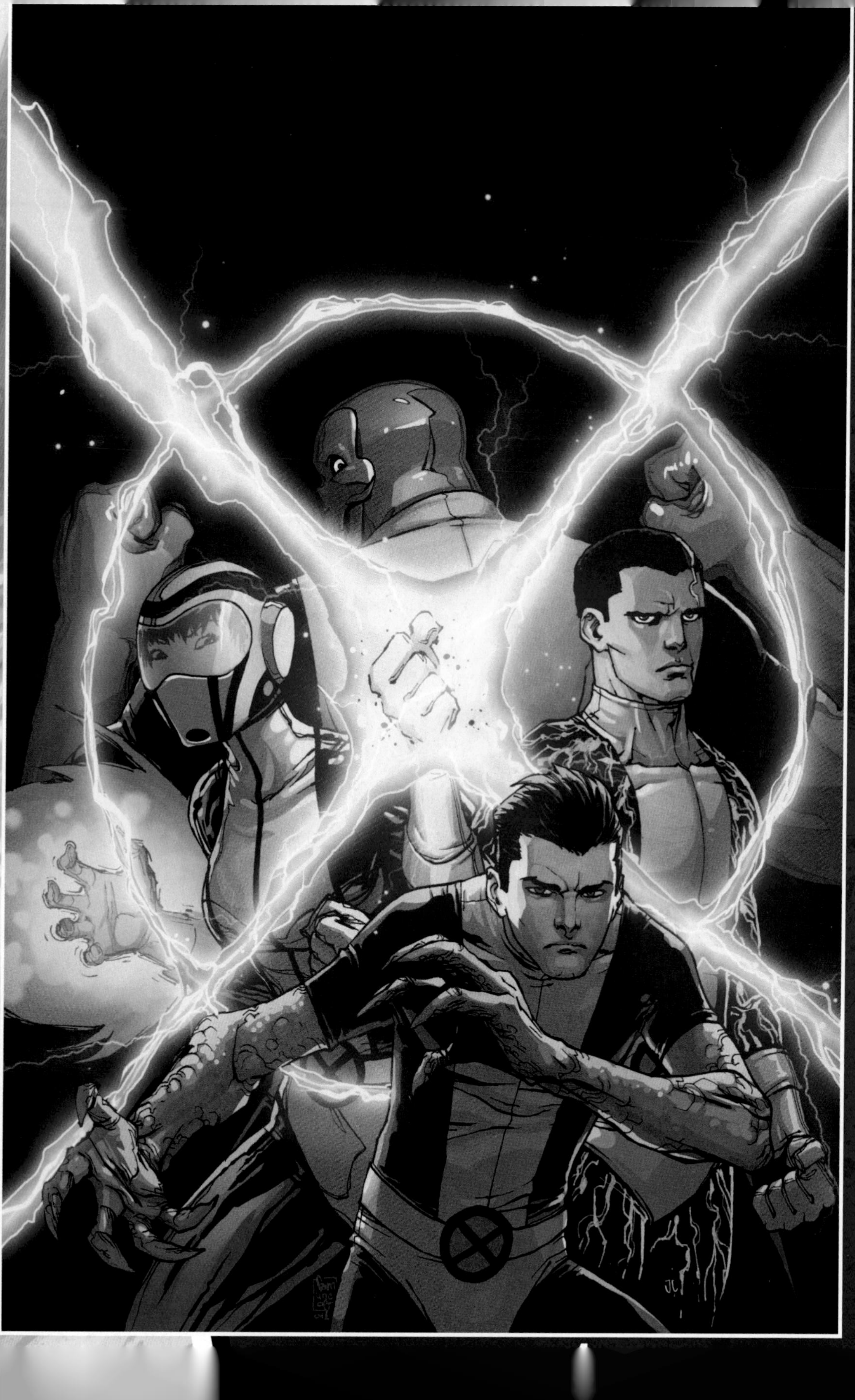

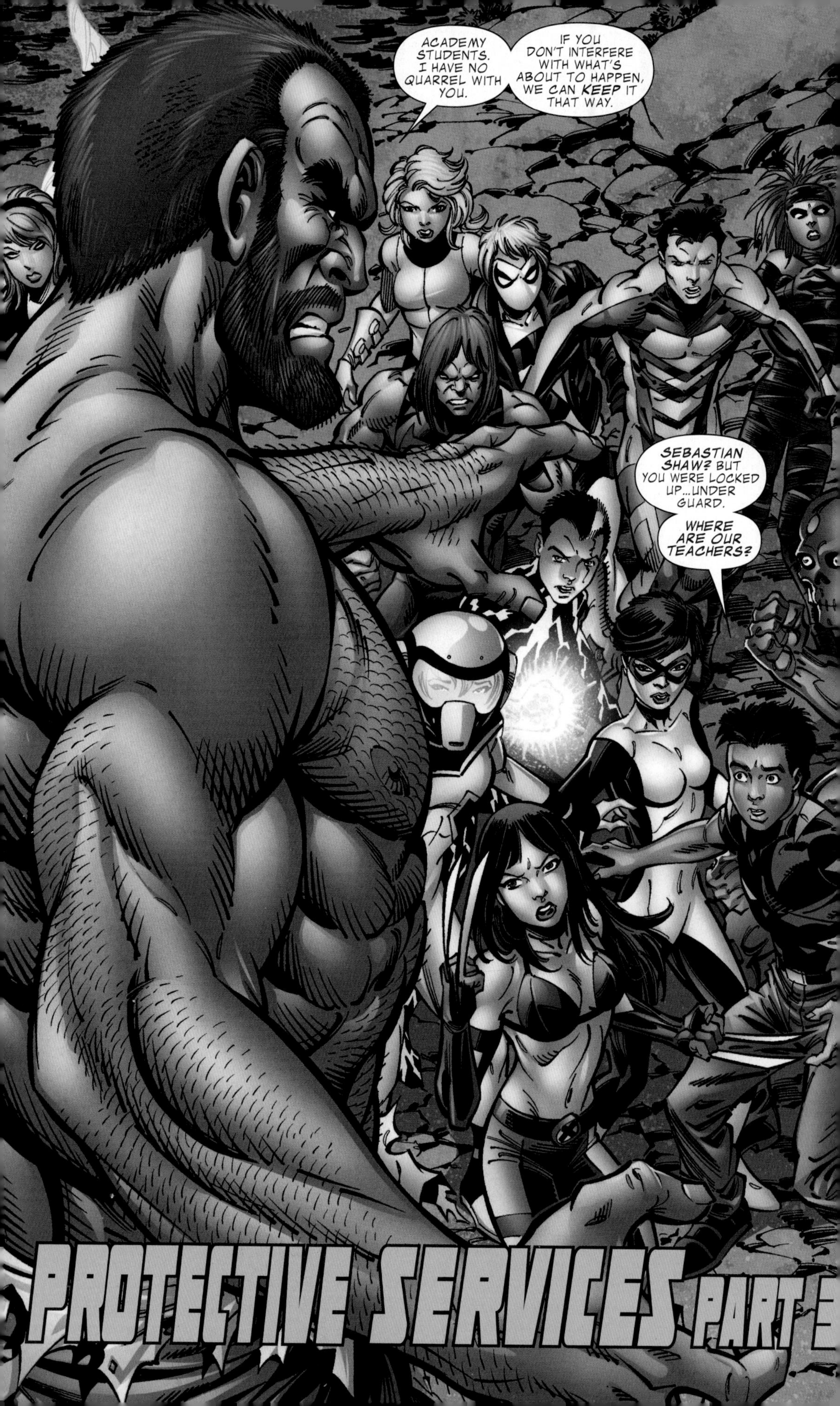
ACADEMY STUDENTS. I HAVE NO QUARREL WITH YOU.
IF YOU DON'T INTERFERE WITH WHAT'S ABOUT TO HAPPEN, WE CAN KEEP IT THAT WAY.
SEBASTIAN SHAW? BUT YOU WERE LOCKED UP...UNDER GUARD.
WHERE ARE OUR TEACHERS?
PROTECTIVE SERVICES PART 3

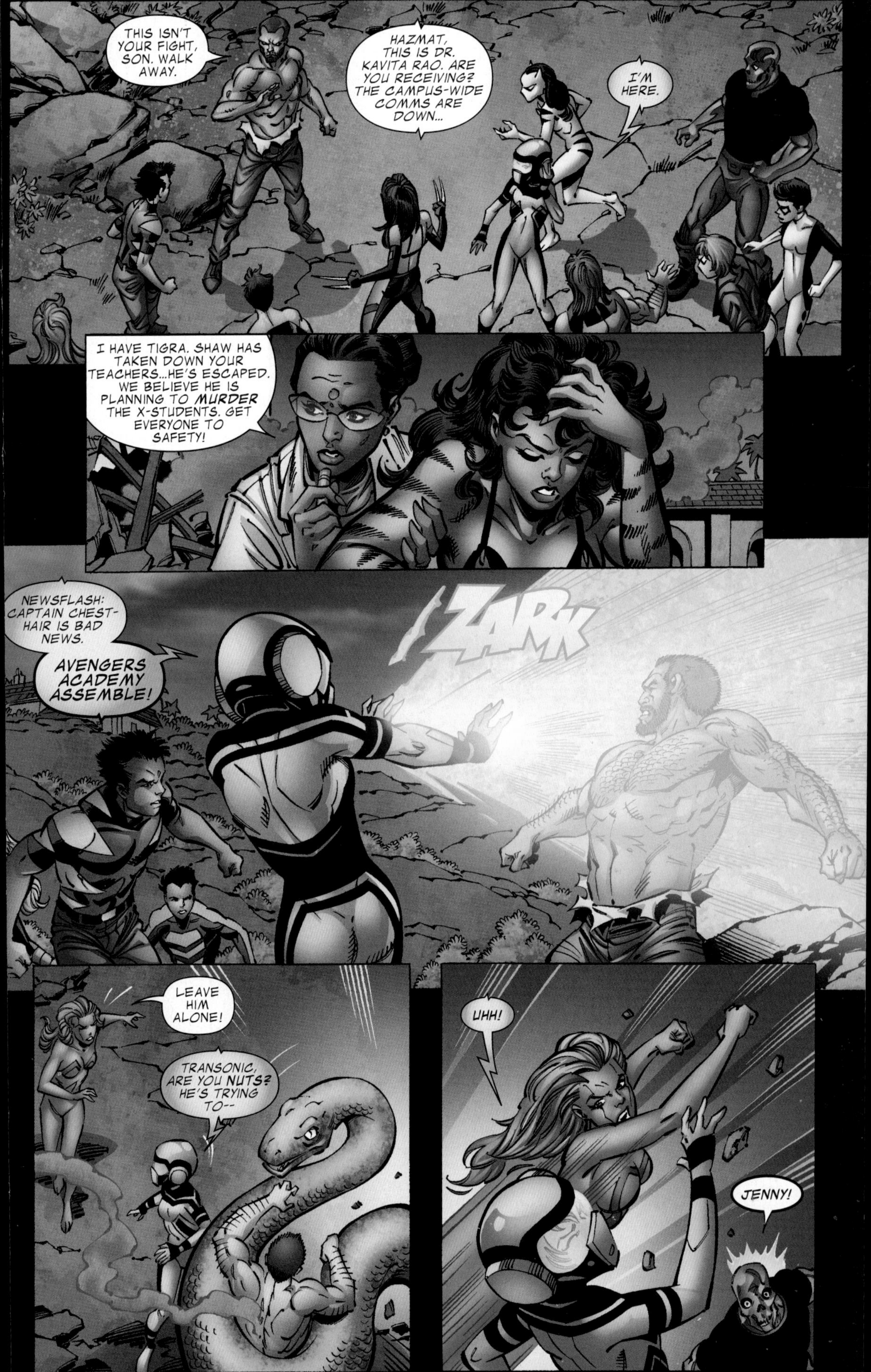
THIS ISN'T YOUR FIGHT, SON. WALK AWAY.
HAZMAT, THIS IS DR. KAVITA RAO. ARE YOU RECEIVING? THE CAMPUS-WIDE COMMS ARE DOWN...
I'M HERE.
I HAVE TIGRA. SHAW HAS TAKEN DOWN YOUR TEACHERS...HE'S ESCAPED. WE BELIEVE HE IS PLANNING TO MURDER THE X-STUDENTS. GET EVERYONE TO SAFETY!
NEWSFLASH: CAPTAIN CHEST-HAIR IS BAD NEWS.
AVENGERS ACADEMY ASSEMBLE!
ZARK
LEAVE HIM ALONE!
TRANSONIC, ARE YOU NUTS? HE'S TRYING TO--
UHH!
JENNY!

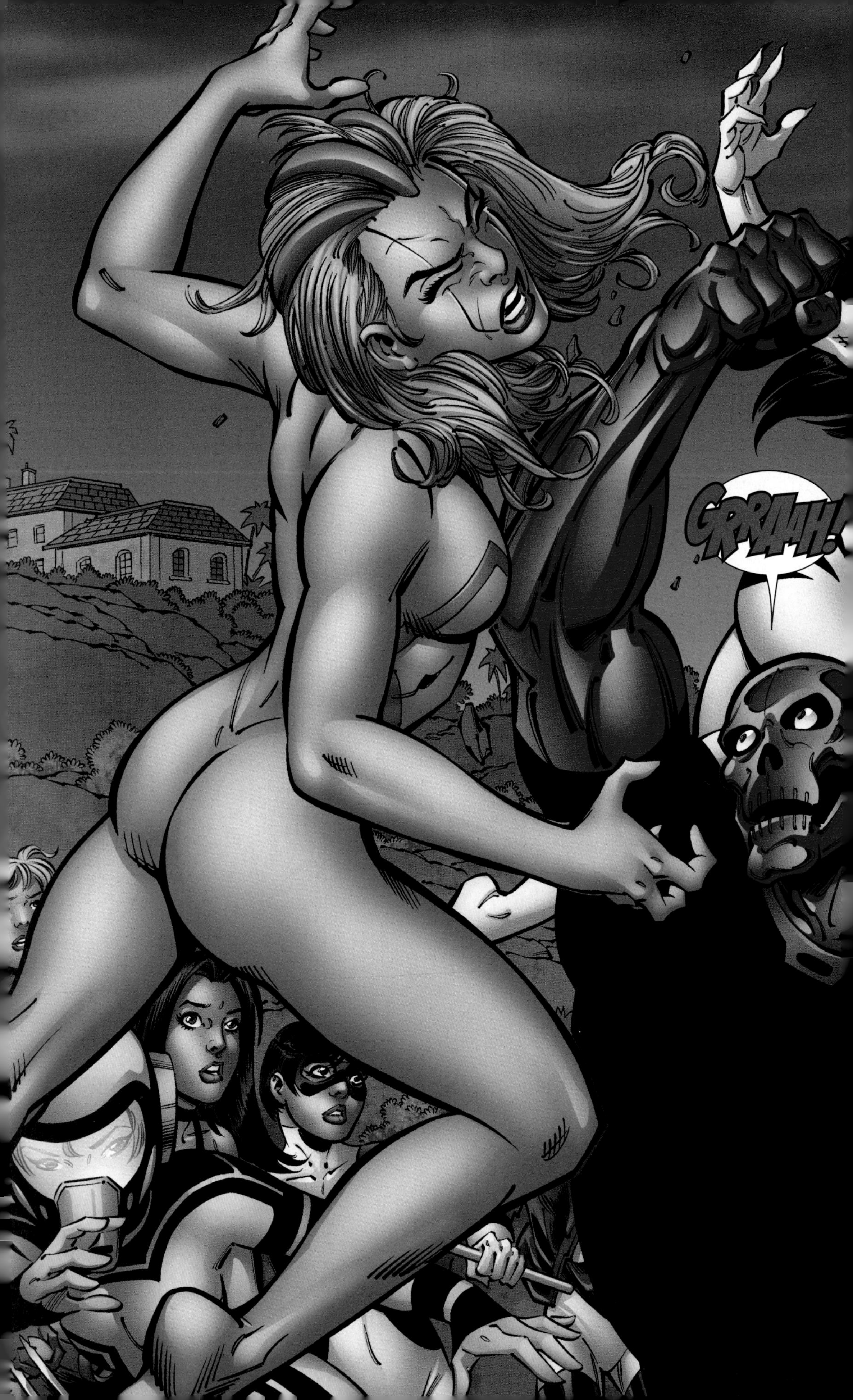
GRRAAH!

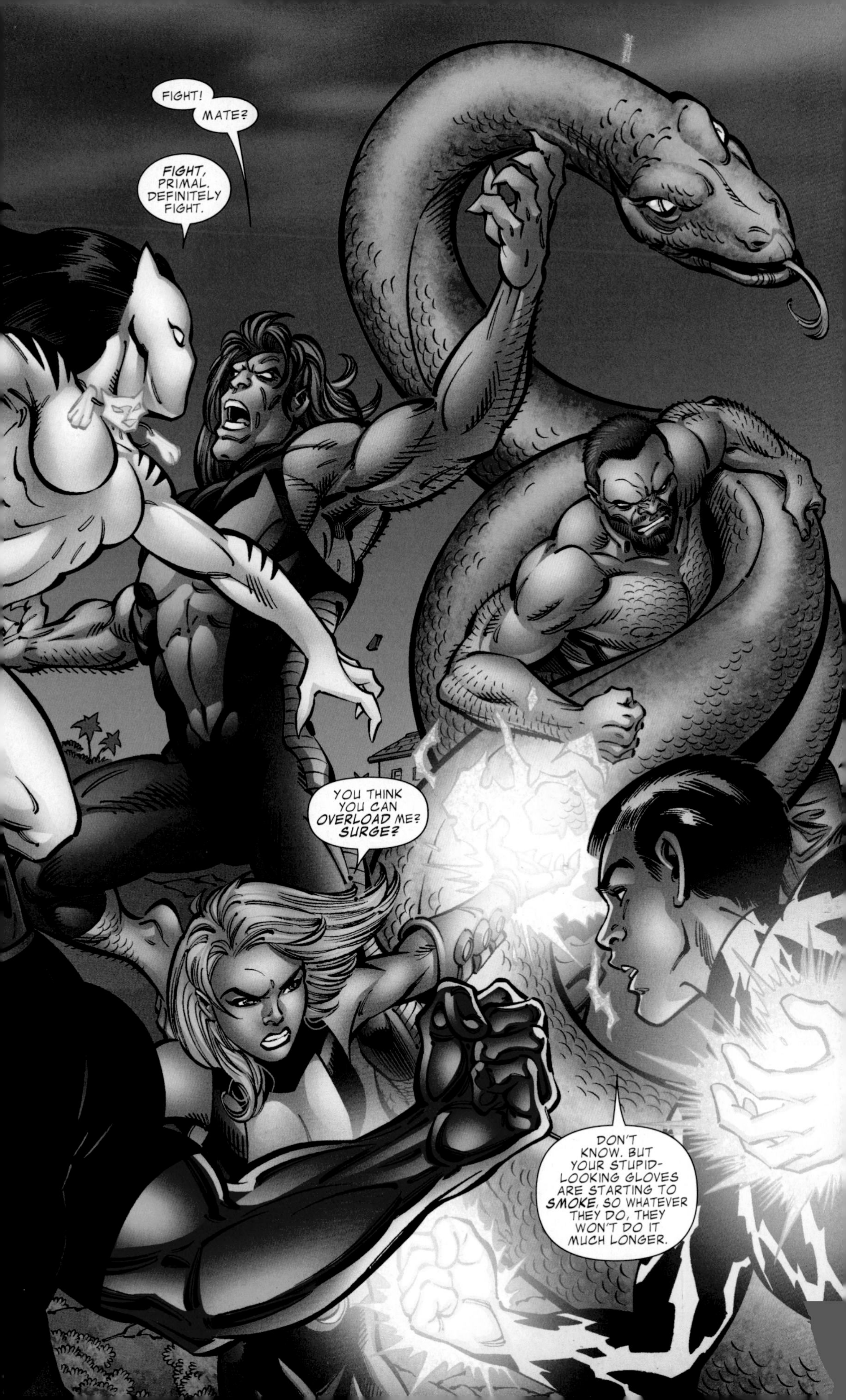
FIGHT!
MATE?
FIGHT, PRIMAL. DEFINITELY FIGHT.
YOU THINK YOU CAN OVERLOAD ME? SURGE?
DON'T KNOW. BUT YOUR STUPID-LOOKING GLOVES ARE STARTING TO SMOKE, SO WHATEVER THEY DO, THEY WON'T DO IT MUCH LONGER.

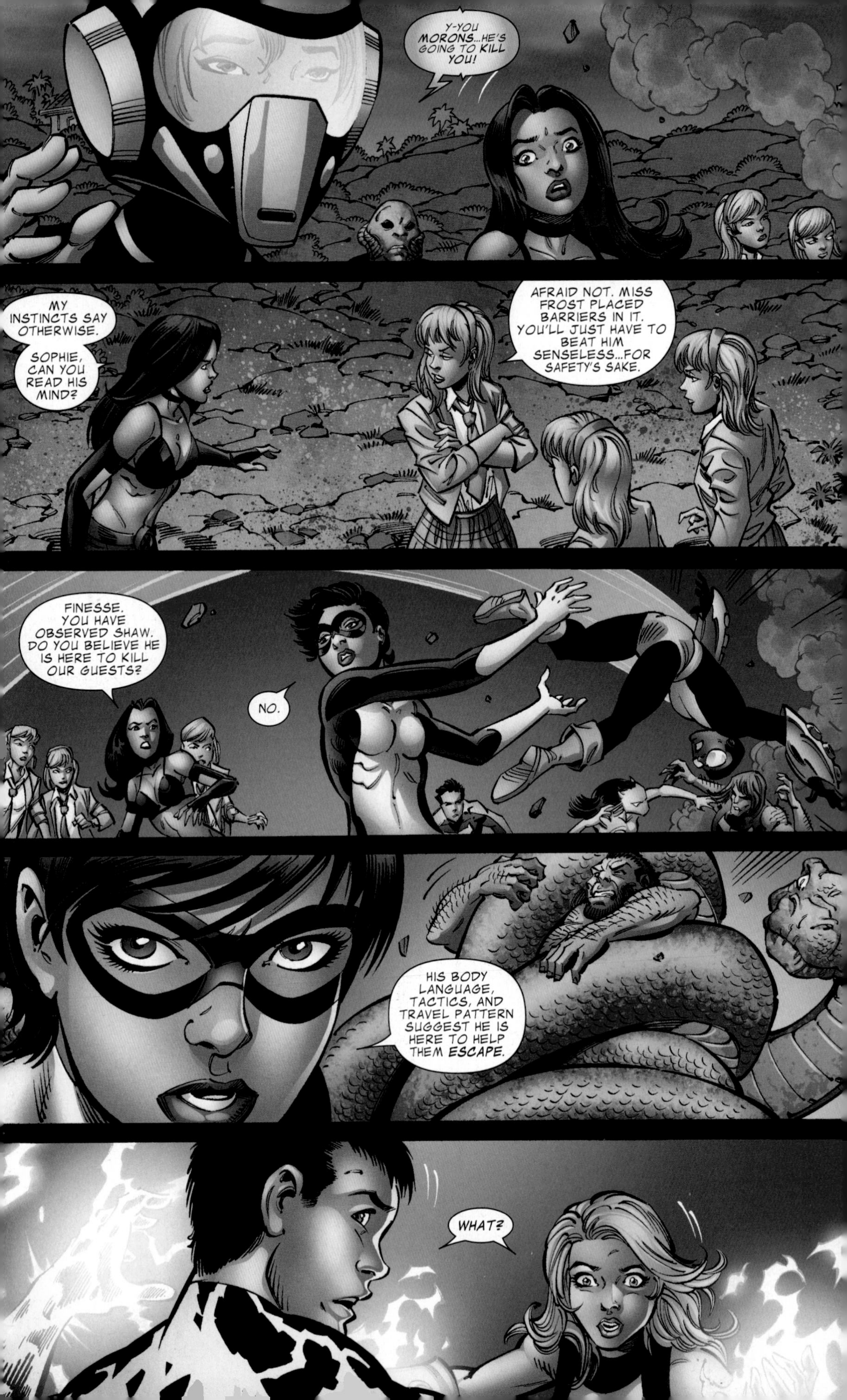

Y-YOU MORONS...HE'S GOING TO KILL YOU!
MY INSTINCTS SAY OTHERWISE.
SOPHIE, CAN YOU READ HIS MIND?
AFRAID NOT. MISS FROST PLACED BARRIERS IN IT. YOU'LL JUST HAVE TO BEAT HIM SENSELESS...FOR SAFETY'S SAKE.
FINESSE. YOU HAVE OBSERVED SHAW. DO YOU BELIEVE HE IS HERE TO KILL OUR GUESTS?
NO.
HIS BODY LANGUAGE, TACTICS, AND TRAVEL PATTERN SUGGEST HE IS HERE TO HELP THEM ESCAPE.
WHAT?

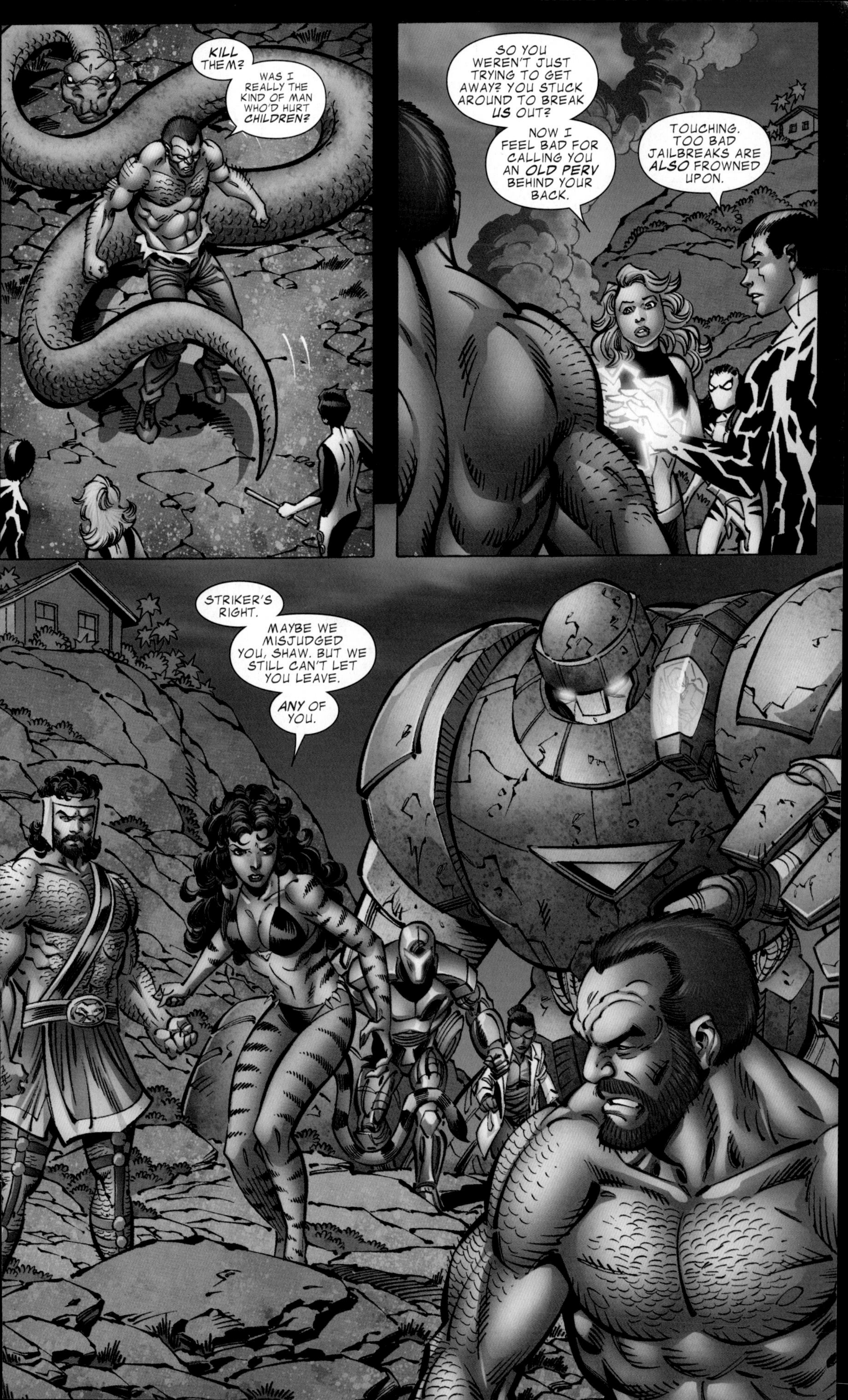
KILL THEM?
WAS I REALLY THE KIND OF MAN WHO'D HURT CHILDREN?
SO YOU WEREN'T JUST TRYING TO GET AWAY? YOU STUCK AROUND TO BREAK US OUT?
NOW I FEEL BAD FOR CALLING YOU AN OLD PERV BEHIND YOUR BACK.
TOUCHING. TOO BAD JAILBREAKS ARE ALSO FROWNED UPON.
STRIKER'S RIGHT.
MAYBE WE MISJUDGED YOU, SHAW. BUT WE STILL CAN'T LET YOU LEAVE.
ANY OF YOU.

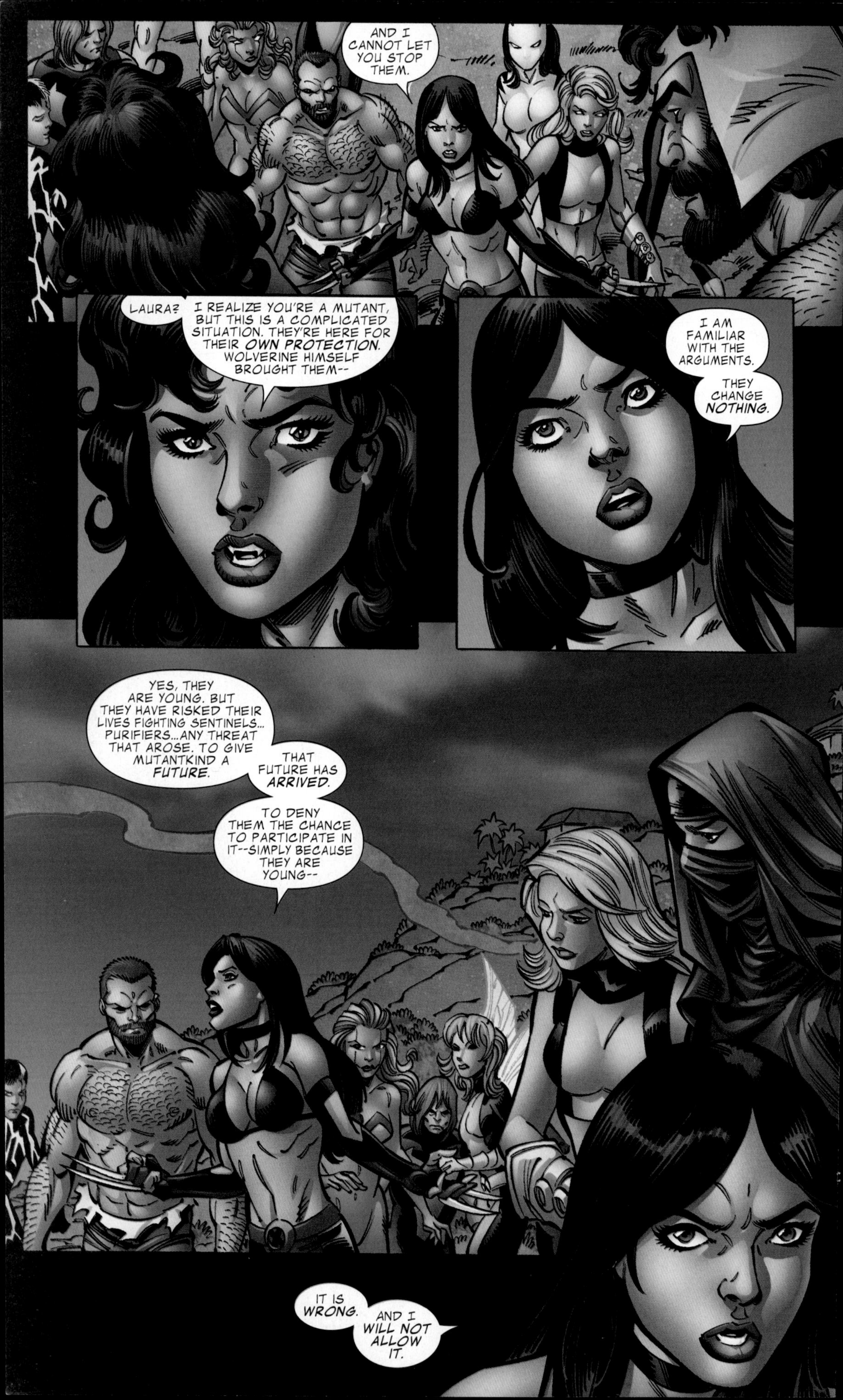
AND I CANNOT LET YOU STOP THEM.
LAURA?
I REALIZE YOU'RE A MUTANT, BUT THIS IS A COMPLICATED SITUATION. THEY'RE HERE FOR THEIR OWN PROTECTION. WOLVERINE HIMSELF BROUGHT THEM--
I AM FAMILIAR WITH THE ARGUMENTS.
THEY CHANGE NOTHING.
YES, THEY ARE YOUNG. BUT THEY HAVE RISKED THEIR LIVES FIGHTING SENTINELS... PURIFIERS...ANY THREAT THAT AROSE. TO GIVE MUTANTKIND A FUTURE.
THAT FUTURE HAS ARRIVED.
TO DENY THEM THE CHANCE TO PARTICIPATE IN IT--SIMPLY BECAUSE THEY ARE YOUNG--
IT IS WRONG.
AND I WILL NOT ALLOW IT.

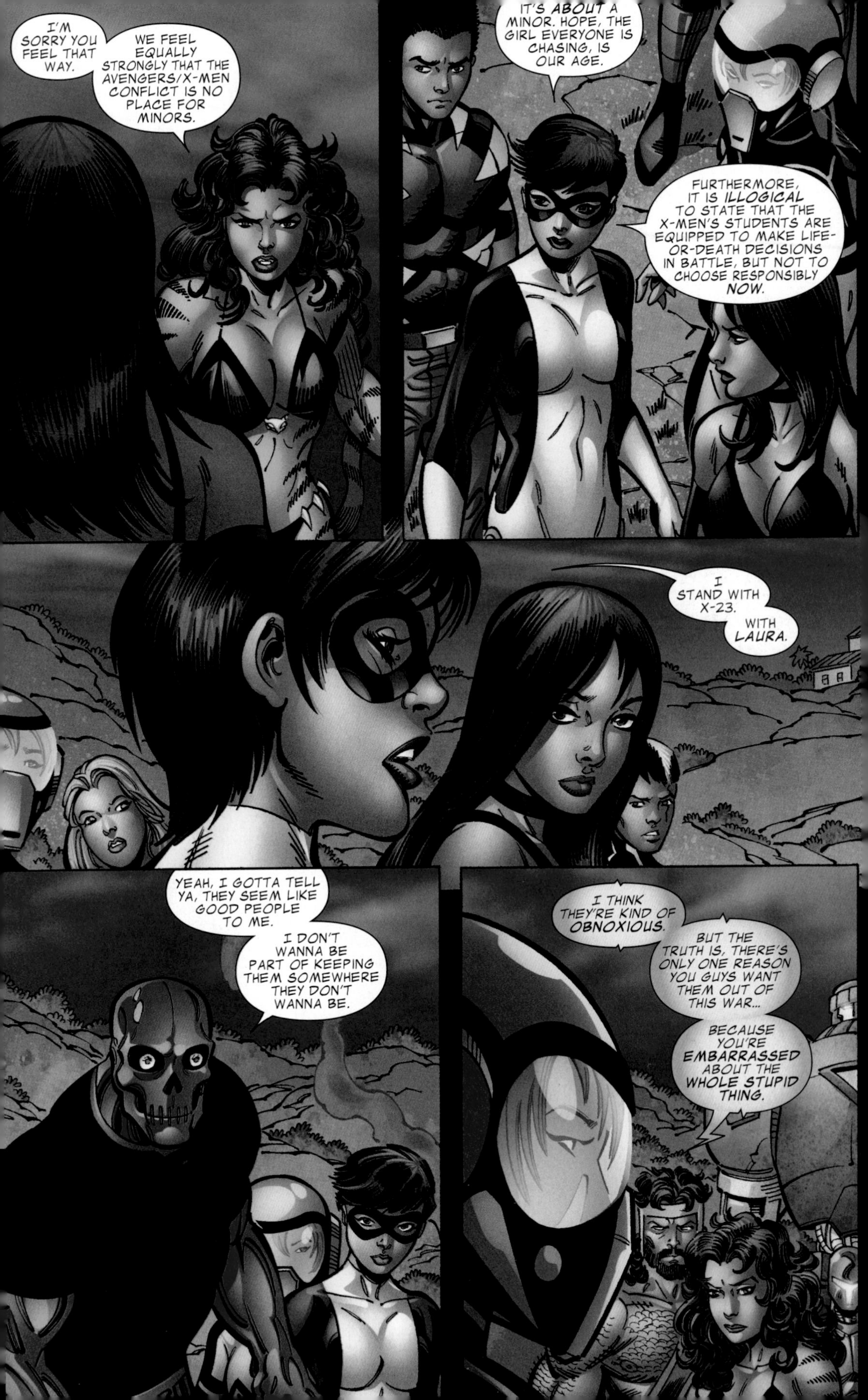
I'M SORRY YOU FEEL THAT WAY.
WE FEEL EQUALLY STRONGLY THAT THE AVENGERS/X-MEN CONFLICT IS NO PLACE FOR MINORS.
IT'S ABOUT A MINOR. HOPE, THE GIRL EVERYONE IS CHASING, IS OUR AGE.
FURTHERMORE, IT IS ILLOGICAL TO STATE THAT THE X-MEN'S STUDENTS ARE EQUIPPED TO MAKE LIFE-OR-DEATH DECISIONS IN BATTLE, BUT NOT TO CHOOSE RESPONSIBLY NOW.
I STAND WITH X-23.
WITH LAURA.
YEAH, I GOTTA TELL YA, THEY SEEM LIKE GOOD PEOPLE TO ME.
I DON'T WANNA BE PART OF KEEPING THEM SOMEWHERE THEY DON'T WANNA BE.
I THINK THEY'RE KIND OF OBNOXIOUS.
BUT THE TRUTH IS, THERE'S ONLY ONE REASON YOU GUYS WANT THEM OUT OF THIS WAR...
BECAUSE YOU'RE EMBARRASSED ABOUT THE WHOLE STUPID THING.

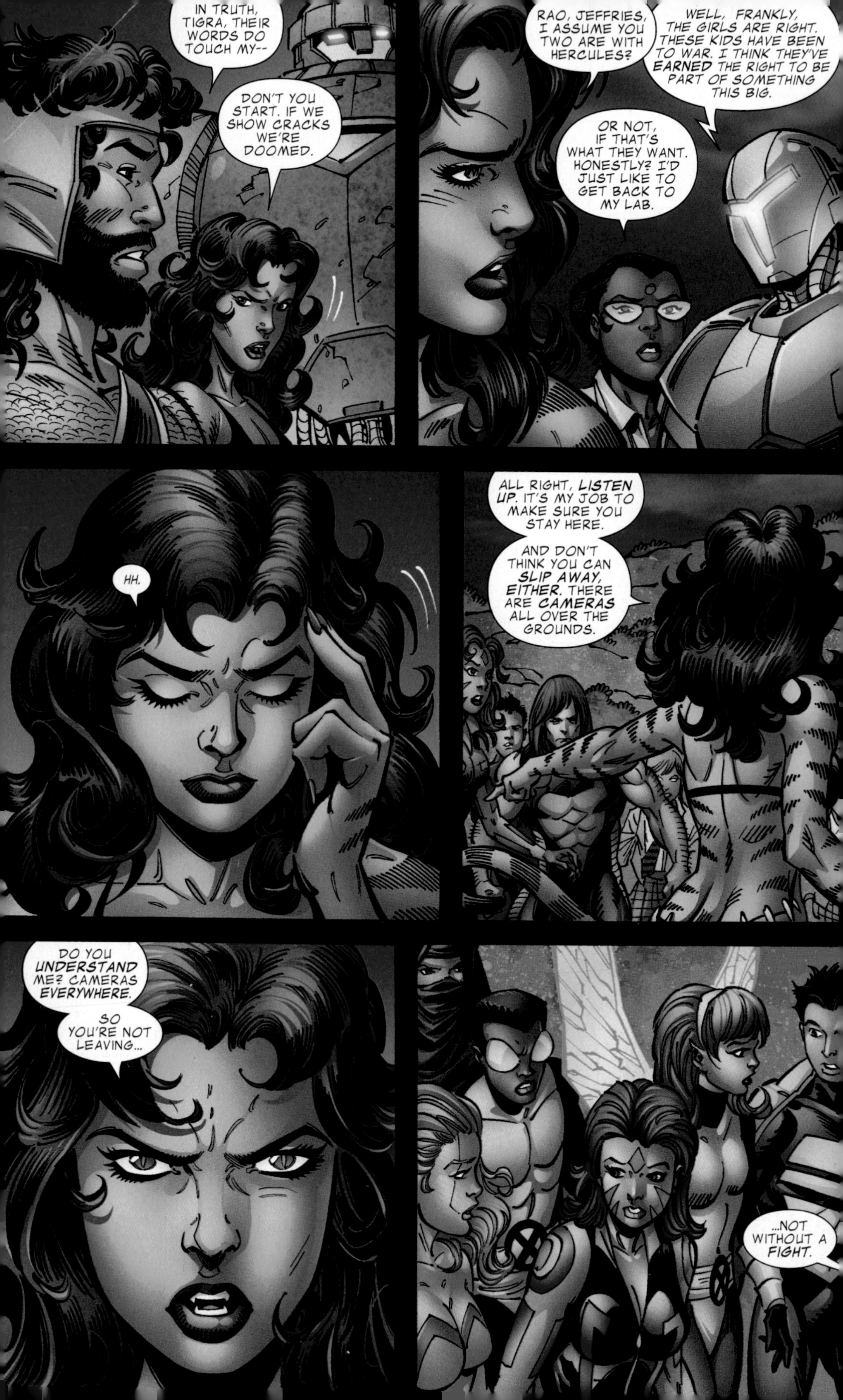
IN TRUTH, TIGRA, THEIR WORDS DO TOUCH MY--
DON'T YOU START. IF WE SHOW CRACKS WE'RE DOOMED.
RAO, JEFFRIES, I ASSUME YOU TWO ARE WITH HERCULES?
WELL, FRANKLY, THE GIRLS ARE RIGHT. THESE KIDS HAVE BEEN TO WAR. I THINK THEY'VE EARNED THE RIGHT TO BE PART OF SOMETHING THIS BIG.
OR NOT, IF THAT'S WHAT THEY WANT. HONESTLY? I'D JUST LIKE TO GET BACK TO MY LAB.
HH.
ALL RIGHT, LISTEN UP. IT'S MY JOB TO MAKE SURE YOU STAY HERE.
AND DON'T THINK YOU CAN SLIP AWAY, EITHER. THERE ARE CAMERAS ALL OVER THE GROUNDS.
DO YOU UNDERSTAND ME? CAMERAS EVERYWHERE.
SO YOU'RE NOT LEAVING...
...NOT WITHOUT A FIGHT.

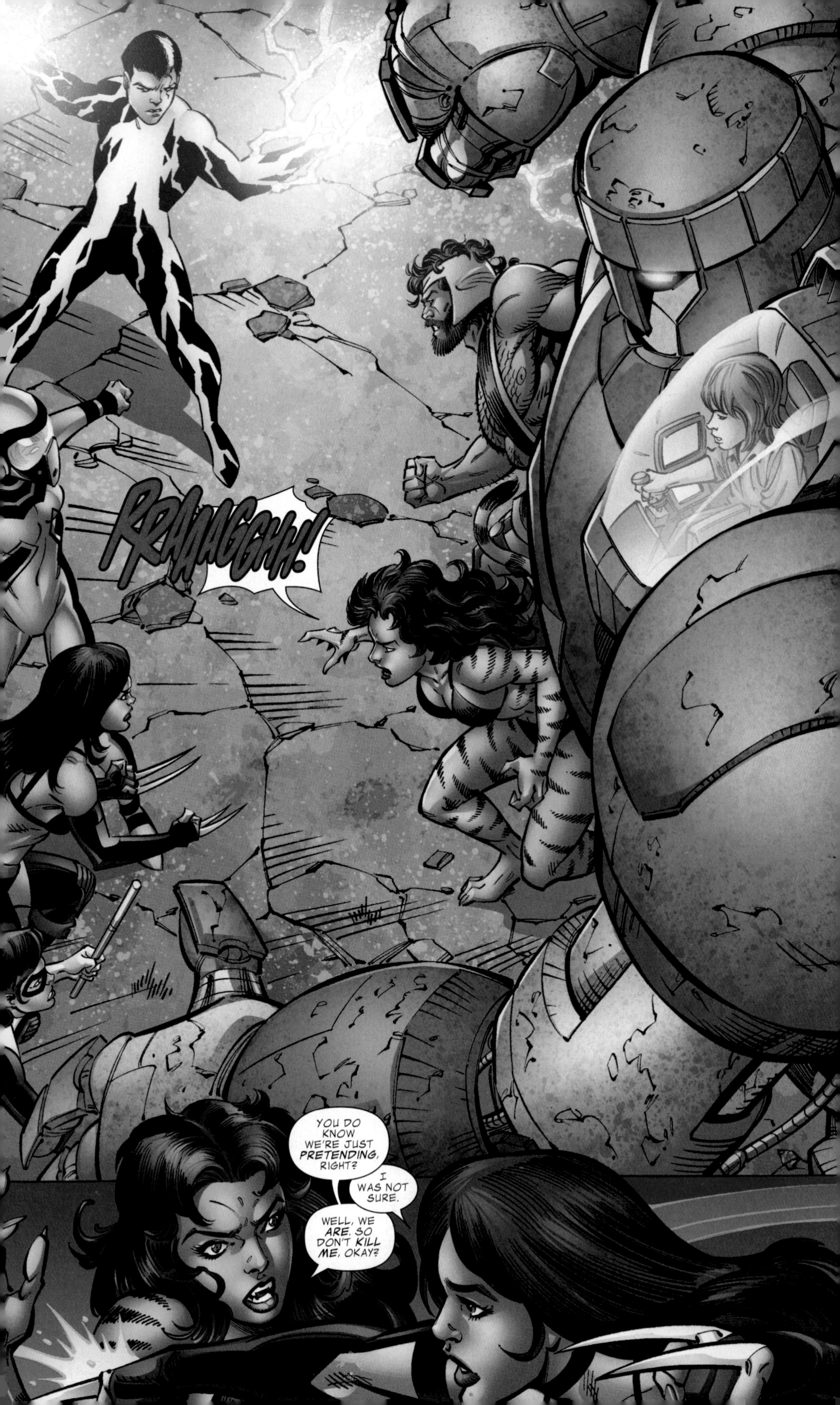

RRAAAGGHH!
YOU DO KNOW WE'RE JUST PRETENDING, RIGHT?
I WAS NOT SURE.
WELL, WE ARE. SO DON'T KILL ME, OKAY?

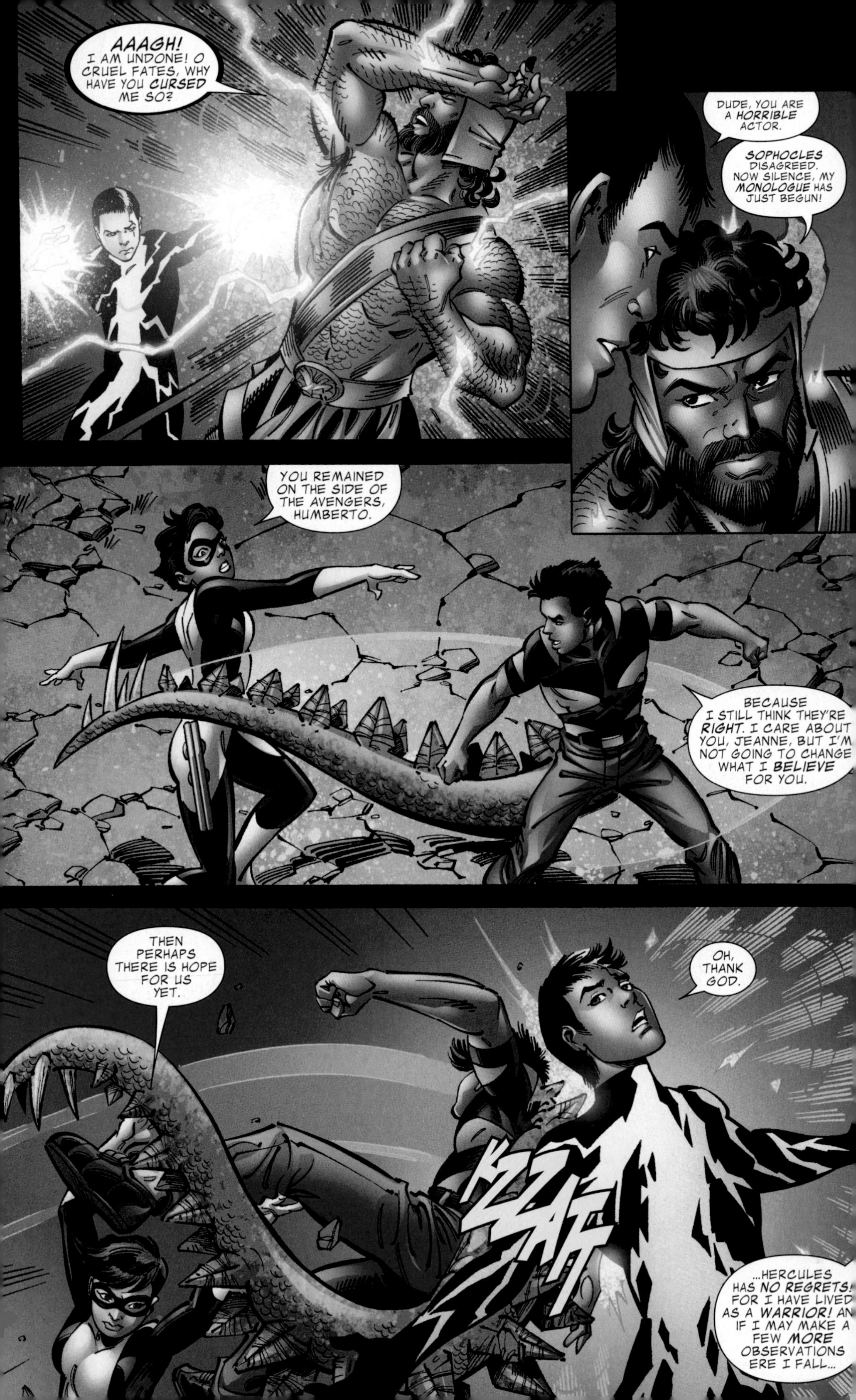
AAAGH! I AM UNDONE! O CRUEL FATES, WHY HAVE YOU CURSED ME SO?
DUDE, YOU ARE A HORRIBLE ACTOR.
SOPHOCLES DISAGREED. NOW SILENCE, MY MONOLOGUE HAS JUST BEGUN!
YOU REMAINED ON THE SIDE OF THE AVENGERS, HUMBERTO.
BECAUSE I STILL THINK THEY'RE RIGHT. I CARE ABOUT YOU, JEANNE, BUT I'M NOT GOING TO CHANGE WHAT I BELIEVE FOR YOU.
THEN PERHAPS THERE IS HOPE FOR US YET.
OH, THANK GOD.
KZZAT
...HERCULES HAS NO REGRETS! FOR I HAVE LIVED AS A WARRIOR! AN IF I MAY MAKE A FEW MORE OBSERVATIONS ERE I FALL...

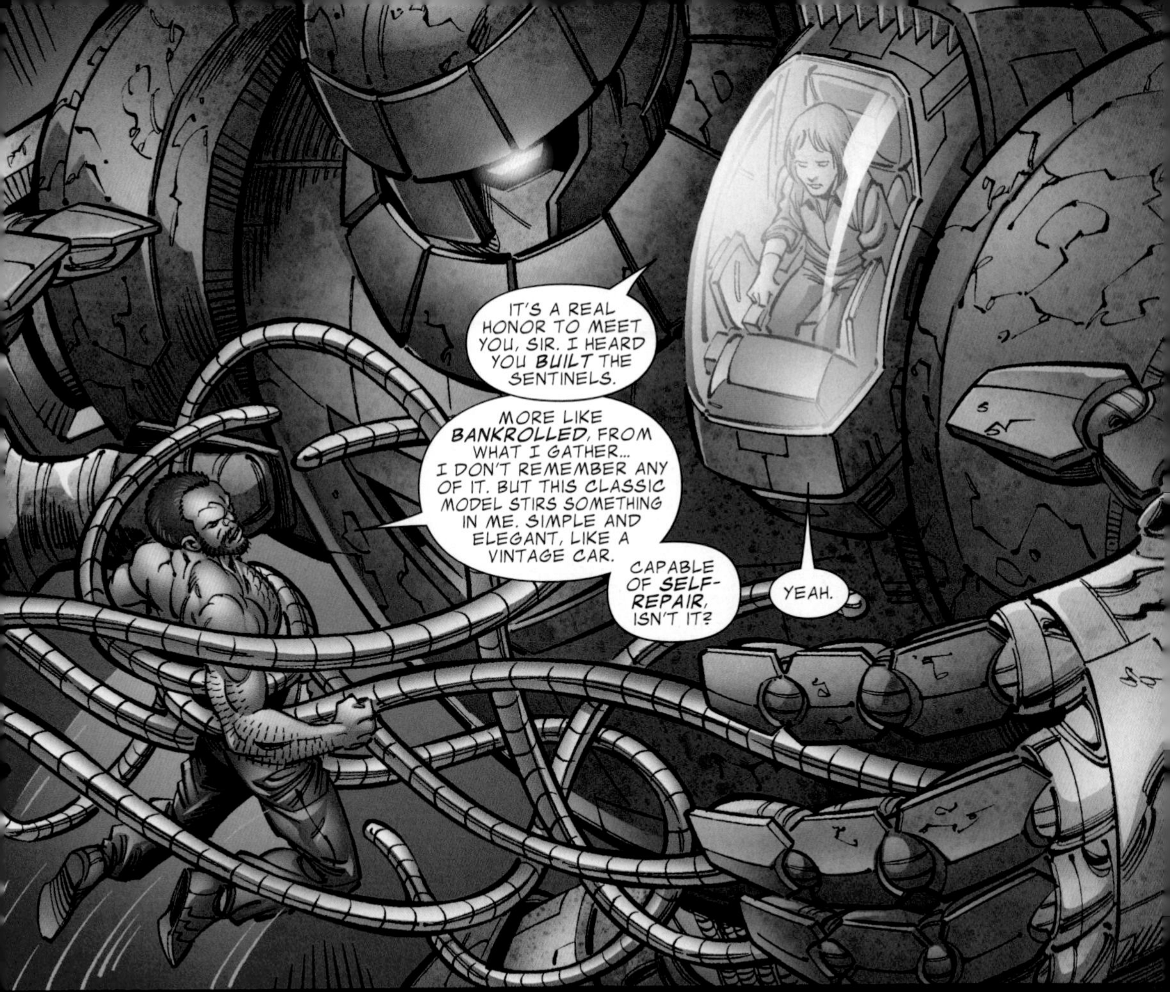
IT'S A REAL HONOR TO MEET YOU, SIR. I HEARD YOU BUILT THE SENTINELS.
MORE LIKE BANKROLLED, FROM WHAT I GATHER... I DON'T REMEMBER ANY OF IT. BUT THIS CLASSIC MODEL STIRS SOMETHING IN ME. SIMPLE AND ELEGANT, LIKE A VINTAGE CAR.
CAPABLE OF SELF-REPAIR, ISN'T IT?
YEAH.
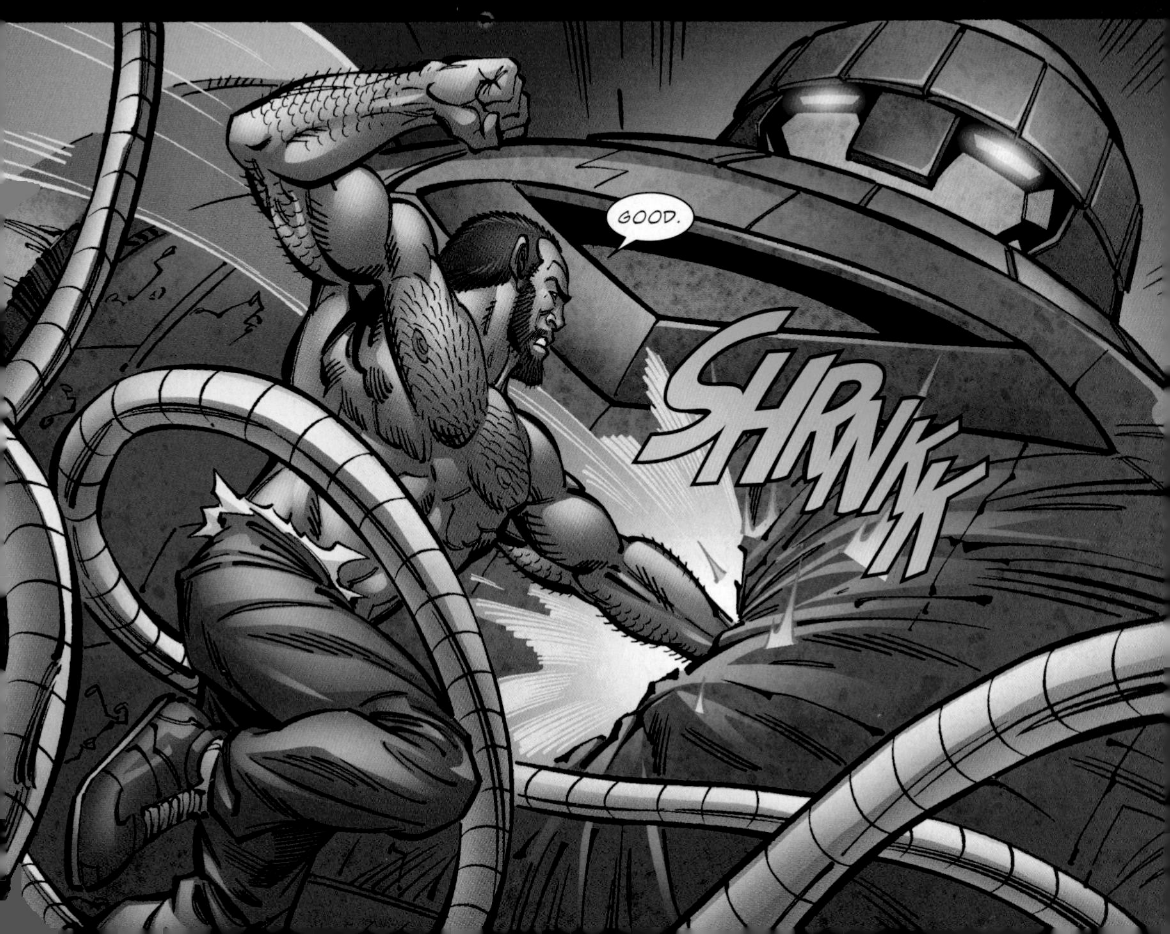
GOOD.
SHRNKK

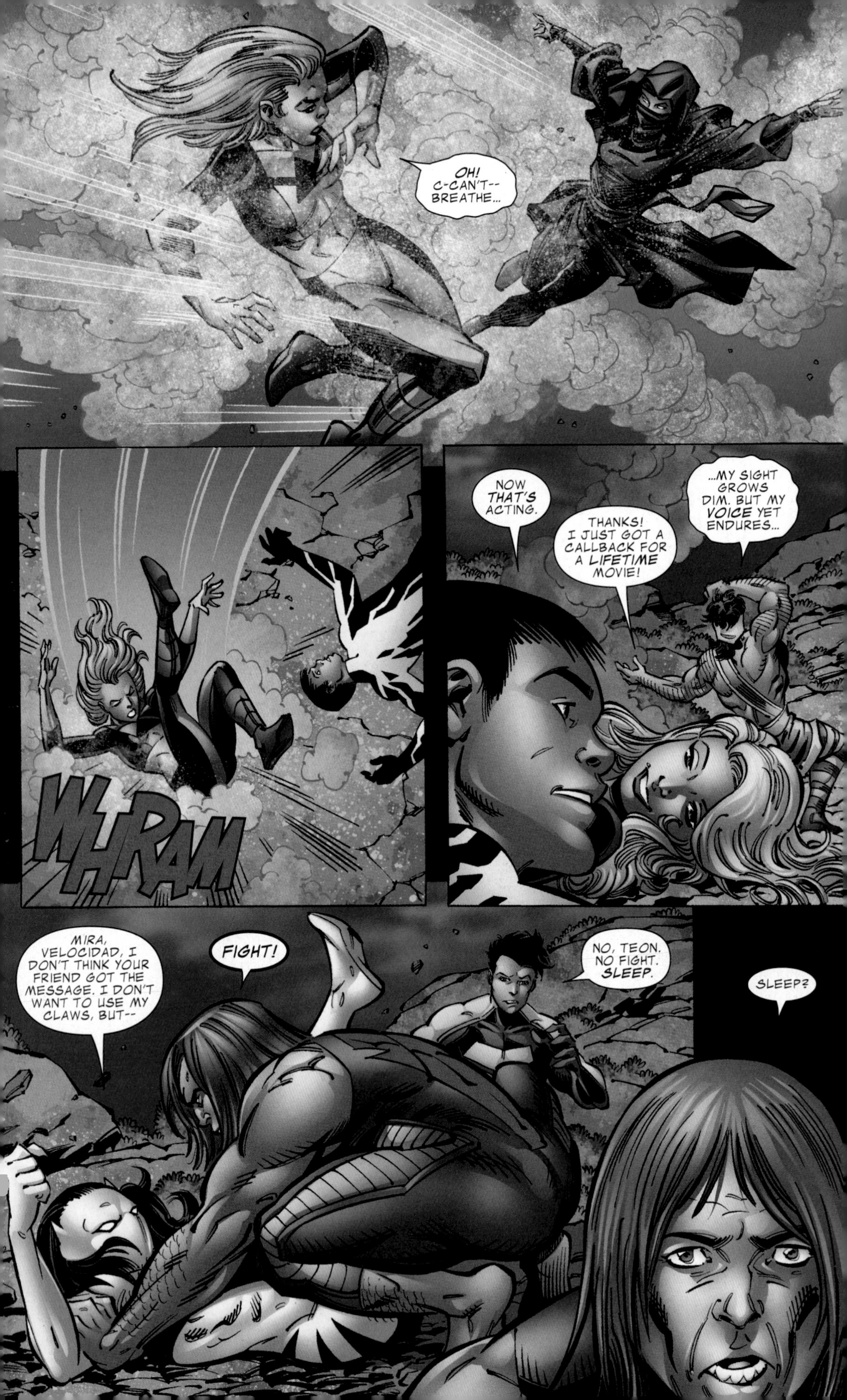
OH! C-CAN'T-- BREATHE...
WHRAM
NOW THAT'S ACTING.
THANKS! I JUST GOT A CALLBACK FOR A LIFETIME MOVIE!
...MY SIGHT GROWS DIM. BUT MY VOICE YET ENDURES...
MIRA, VELOCIDAD, I DON'T THINK YOUR FRIEND GOT THE MESSAGE. I DON'T WANT TO USE MY CLAWS, BUT--
FIGHT!
NO, TEON. NO FIGHT. SLEEP.
SLEEP?

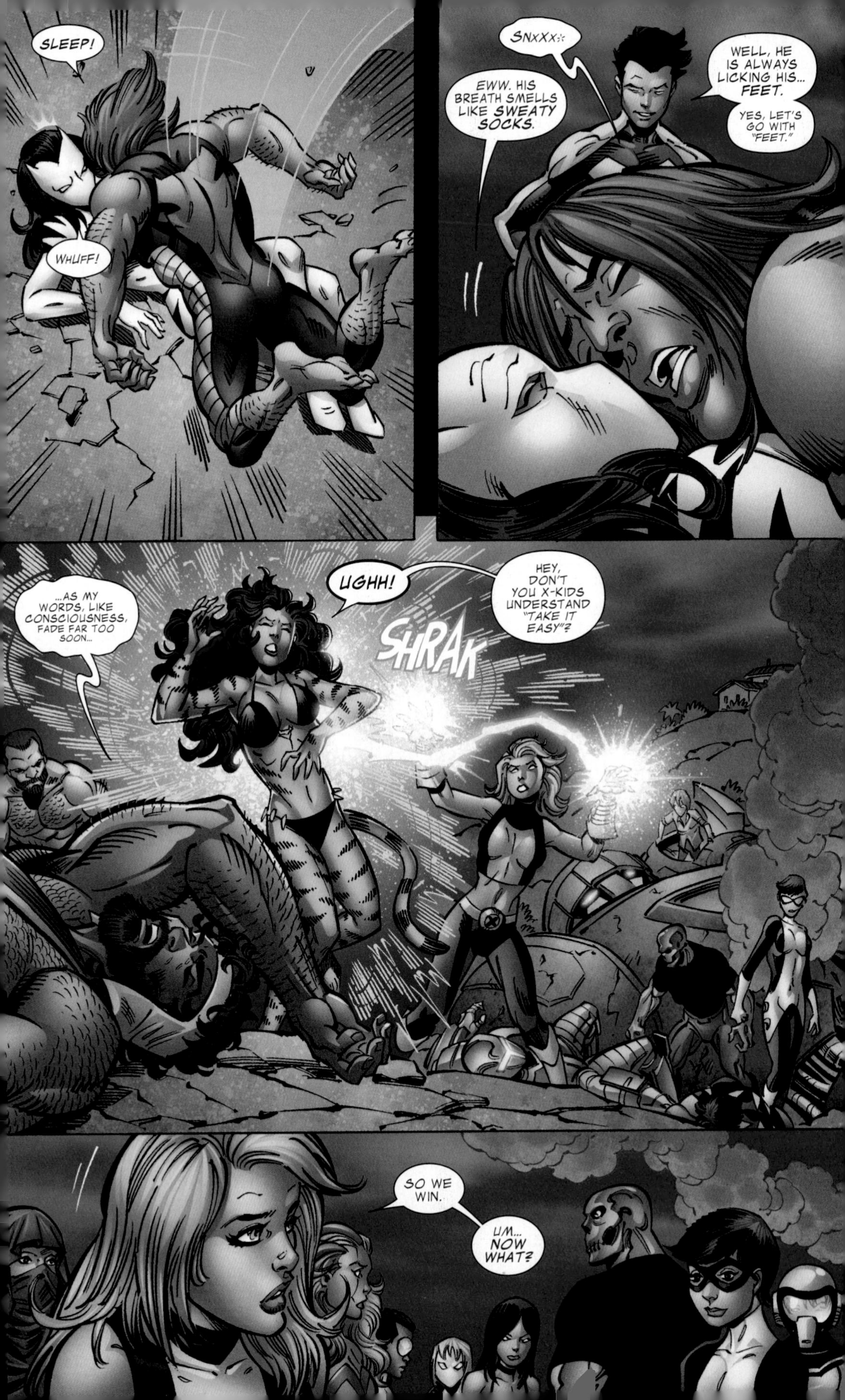
SLEEP!
WHUFF!
SNXXX
EWW. HIS BREATH SMELLS LIKE SWEATY SOCKS.
WELL, HE IS ALWAYS LICKING HIS... FEET.
YES, LET'S GO WITH "FEET."
...AS MY WORDS, LIKE CONSCIOUSNESS, FADE FAR TOO SOON...
UGHH!
SHRAK
HEY, DON'T YOU X-KIDS UNDERSTAND "TAKE IT EASY"?
SO WE WIN.
UM... NOW WHAT?

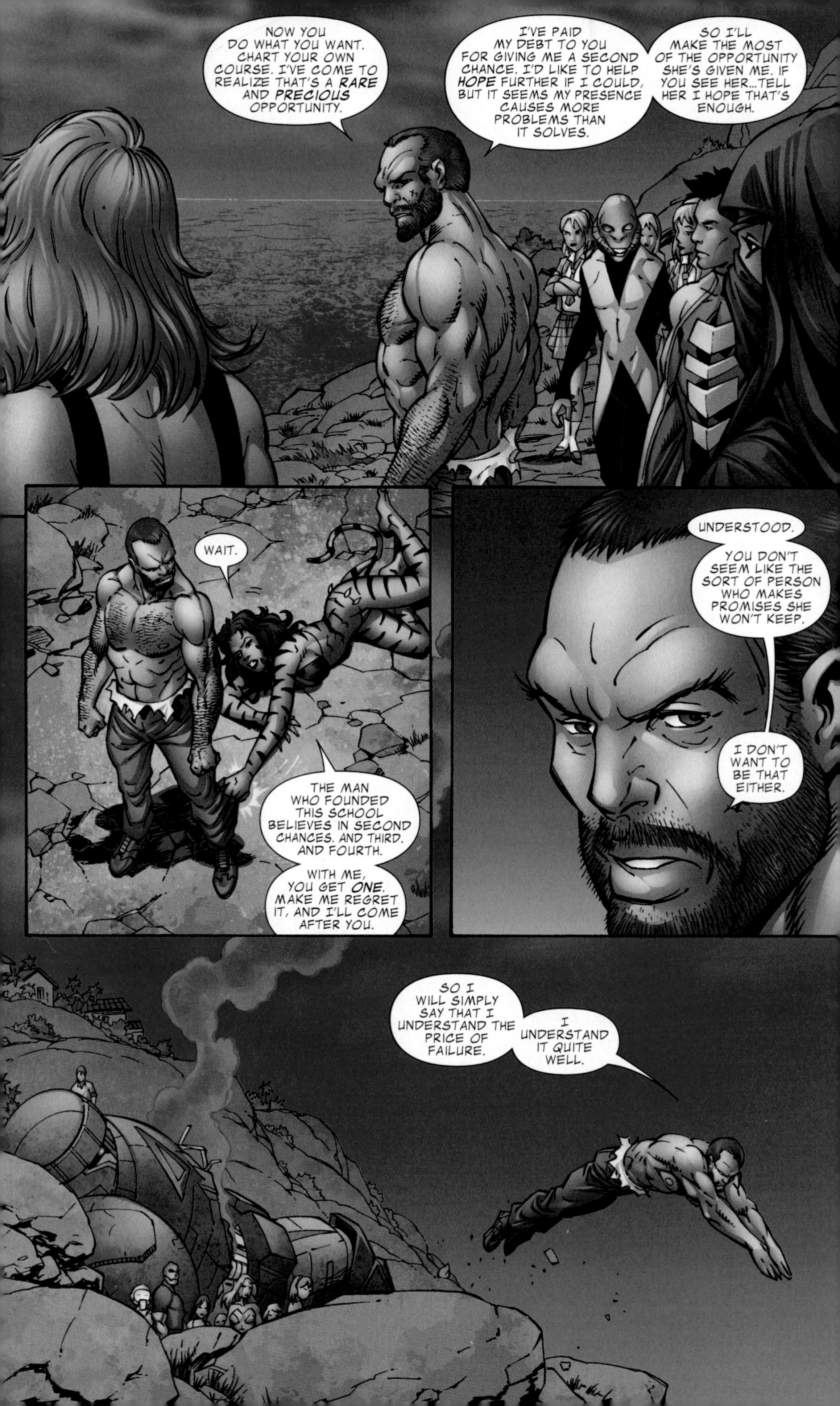

NOW YOU DO WHAT YOU WANT. CHART YOUR OWN COURSE. I'VE COME TO REALIZE THAT'S A RARE AND PRECIOUS OPPORTUNITY.
I'VE PAID MY DEBT TO YOU FOR GIVING ME A SECOND CHANCE. I'D LIKE TO HELP HOPE FURTHER IF I COULD, BUT IT SEEMS MY PRESENCE CAUSES MORE PROBLEMS THAN IT SOLVES.
SO I'LL MAKE THE MOST OF THE OPPORTUNITY SHE'S GIVEN ME. IF YOU SEE HER...TELL HER I HOPE THAT'S ENOUGH.
WAIT.
THE MAN WHO FOUNDED THIS SCHOOL BELIEVES IN SECOND CHANCES. AND THIRD. AND FOURTH.
WITH ME, YOU GET ONE. MAKE ME REGRET IT, AND I'LL COME AFTER YOU.
UNDERSTOOD.
YOU DON'T SEEM LIKE THE SORT OF PERSON WHO MAKES PROMISES SHE WON'T KEEP.
I DON'T WANT TO BE THAT EITHER.
SO I WILL SIMPLY SAY THAT I UNDERSTAND THE PRICE OF FAILURE.
I UNDERSTAND IT QUITE WELL.

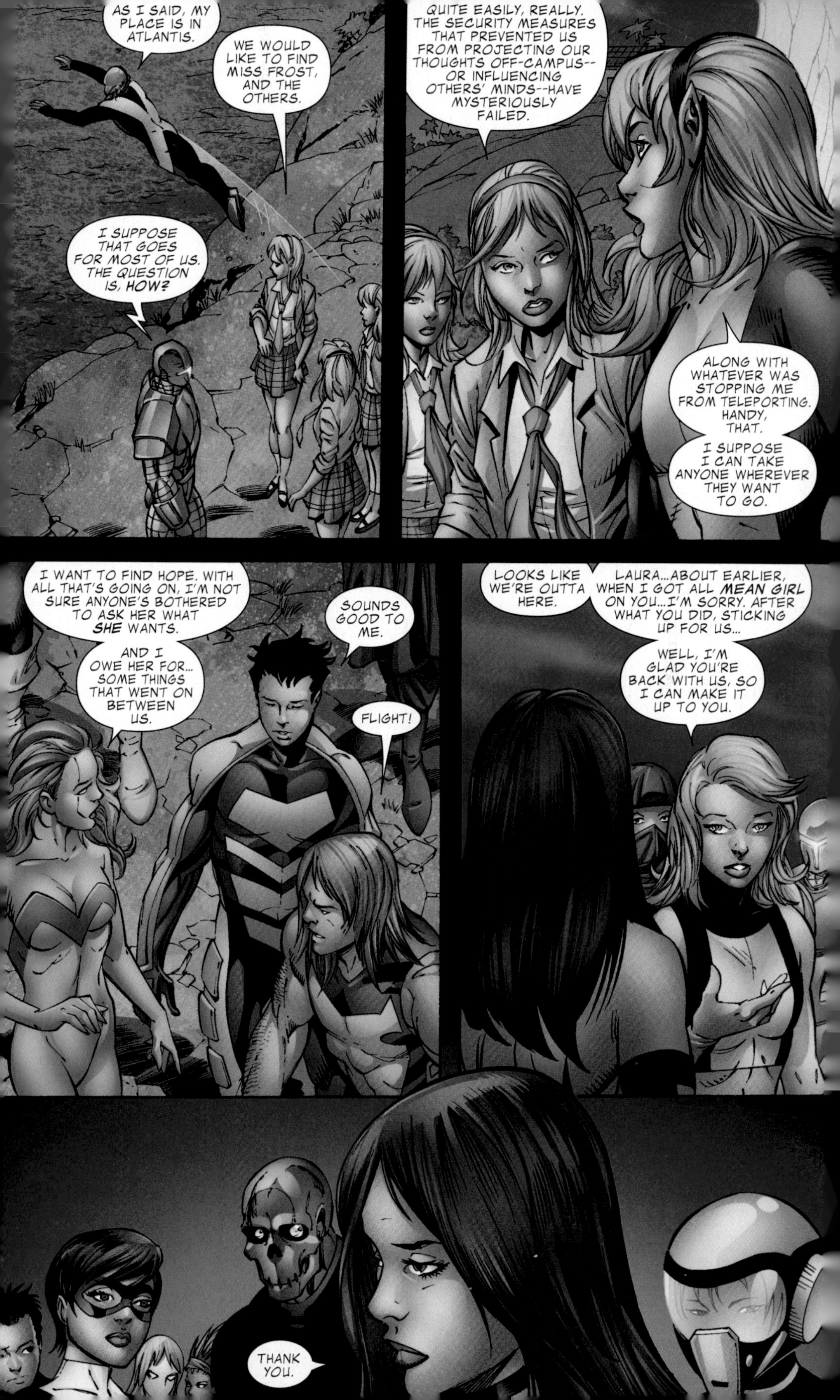

AS I SAID, MY PLACE IS IN ATLANTIS.
WE WOULD LIKE TO FIND MISS FROST, AND THE OTHERS.
I SUPPOSE THAT GOES FOR MOST OF US. THE QUESTION IS, HOW?
QUITE EASILY, REALLY. THE SECURITY MEASURES THAT PREVENTED US FROM PROJECTING OUR THOUGHTS OFF-CAMPUS--OR INFLUENCING OTHERS' MINDS--HAVE MYSTERIOUSLY FAILED.
ALONG WITH WHATEVER WAS STOPPING ME FROM TELEPORTING. HANDY, THAT.
I SUPPOSE I CAN TAKE ANYONE WHEREVER THEY WANT TO GO.
I WANT TO FIND HOPE. WITH ALL THAT'S GOING ON, I'M NOT SURE ANYONE'S BOTHERED TO ASK HER WHAT SHE WANTS.
AND I OWE HER FOR... SOME THINGS THAT WENT ON BETWEEN US.
SOUNDS GOOD TO ME.
FLIGHT!
LOOKS LIKE WE'RE OUTTA HERE.
LAURA...ABOUT EARLIER, WHEN I GOT ALL MEAN GIRL ON YOU...I'M SORRY. AFTER WHAT YOU DID, STICKING UP FOR US...
WELL, I'M GLAD YOU'RE BACK WITH US, SO I CAN MAKE IT UP TO YOU.
THANK YOU.

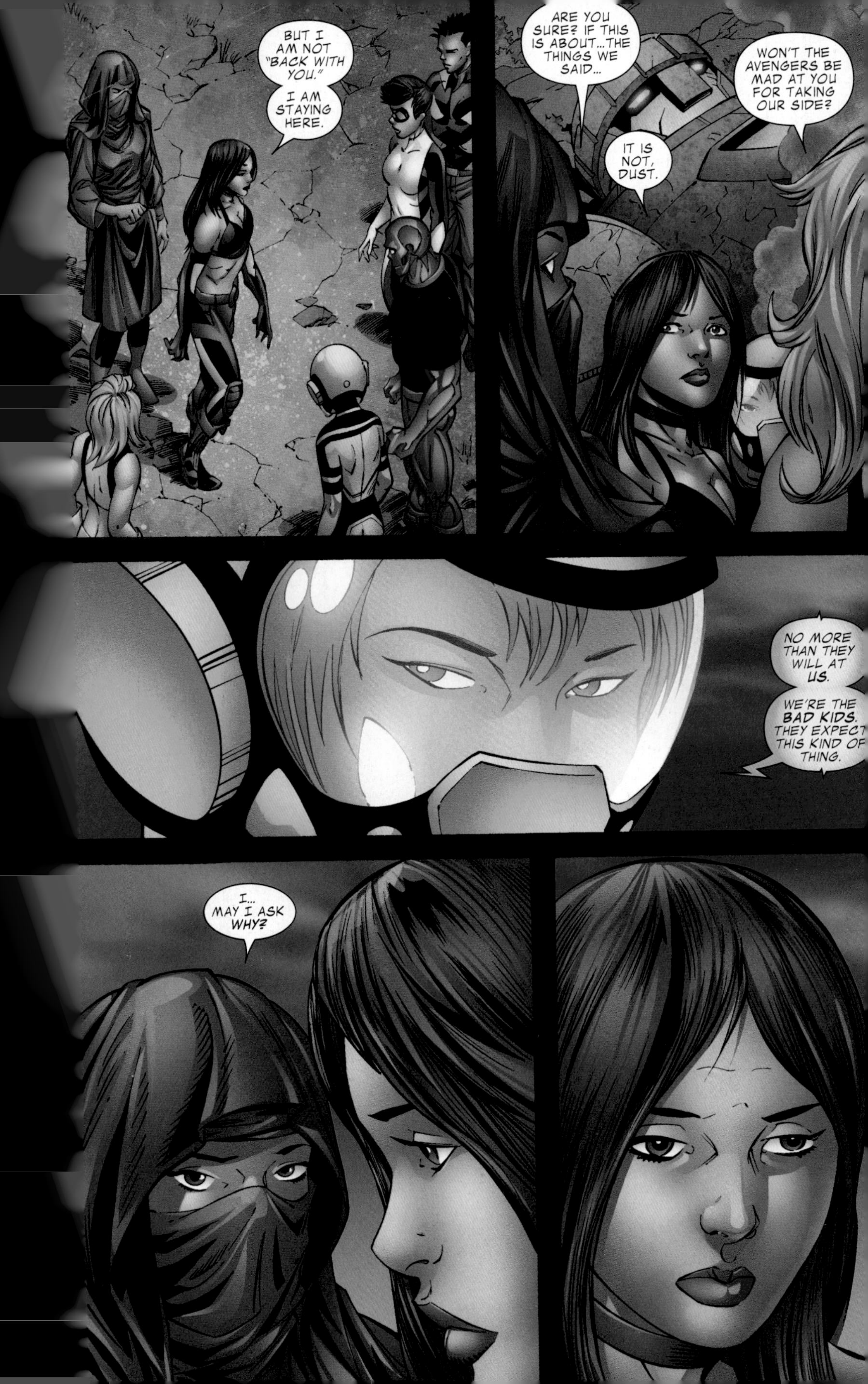
BUT I AM NOT "BACK WITH YOU."
I AM STAYING HERE.
ARE YOU SURE? IF THIS IS ABOUT...THE THINGS WE SAID...
IT IS NOT, DUST.
WON'T THE AVENGERS BE MAD AT YOU FOR TAKING OUR SIDE?
NO MORE THAN THEY WILL AT US.
WE'RE THE BAD KIDS. THEY EXPECT THIS KIND OF THING.
I... MAY I ASK WHY?

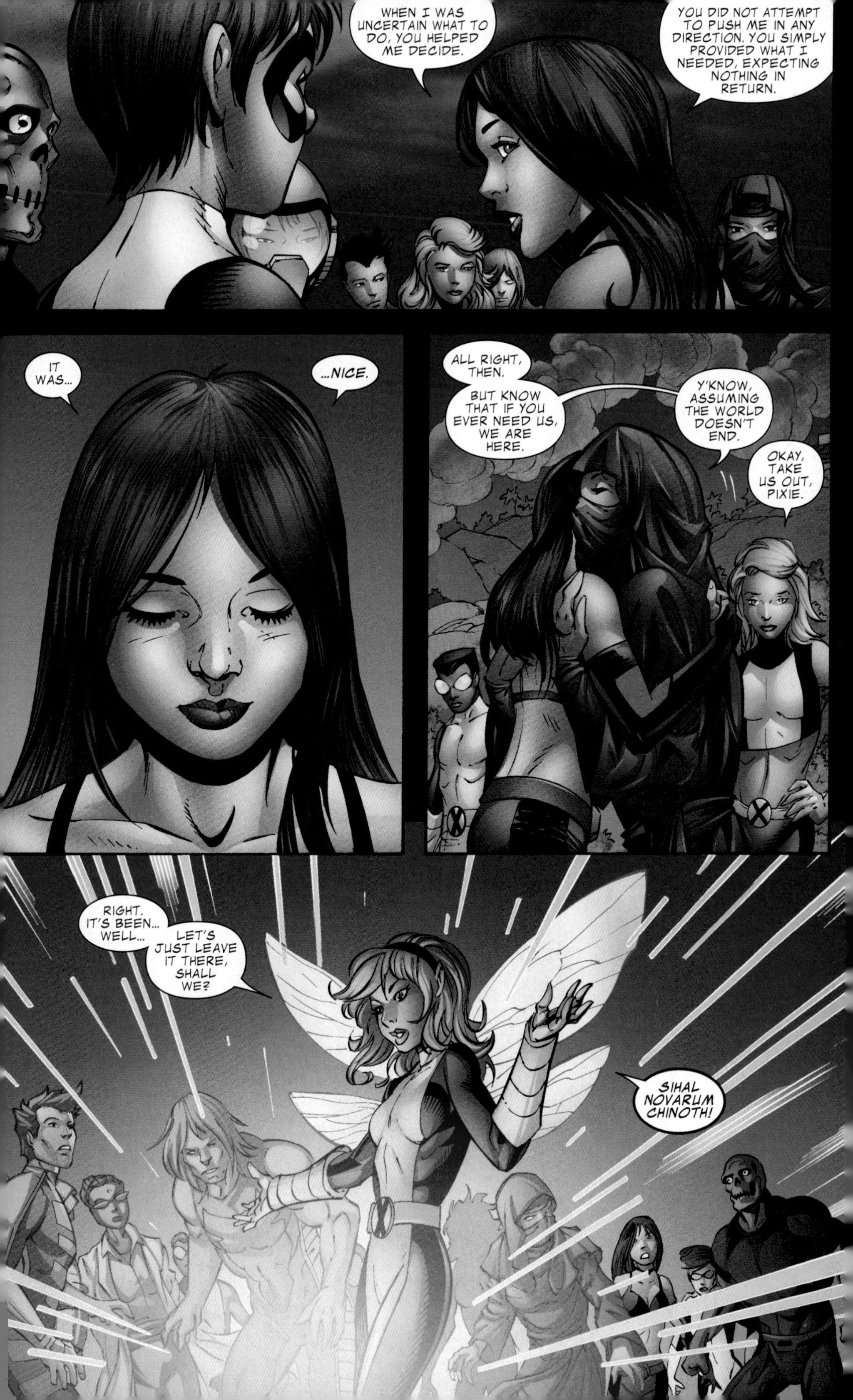

WHEN I WAS UNCERTAIN WHAT TO DO, YOU HELPED ME DECIDE.
YOU DID NOT ATTEMPT TO PUSH ME IN ANY DIRECTION. YOU SIMPLY PROVIDED WHAT I NEEDED, EXPECTING NOTHING IN RETURN.
IT WAS...
...NICE.
ALL RIGHT, THEN.
BUT KNOW THAT IF YOU EVER NEED US, WE ARE HERE.
Y'KNOW, ASSUMING THE WORLD DOESN'T END.
OKAY, TAKE US OUT, PIXIE.
RIGHT. IT'S BEEN... WELL...
LET'S JUST LEAVE IT THERE, SHALL WE?
SIHAL NOVARUM CHINOTH!

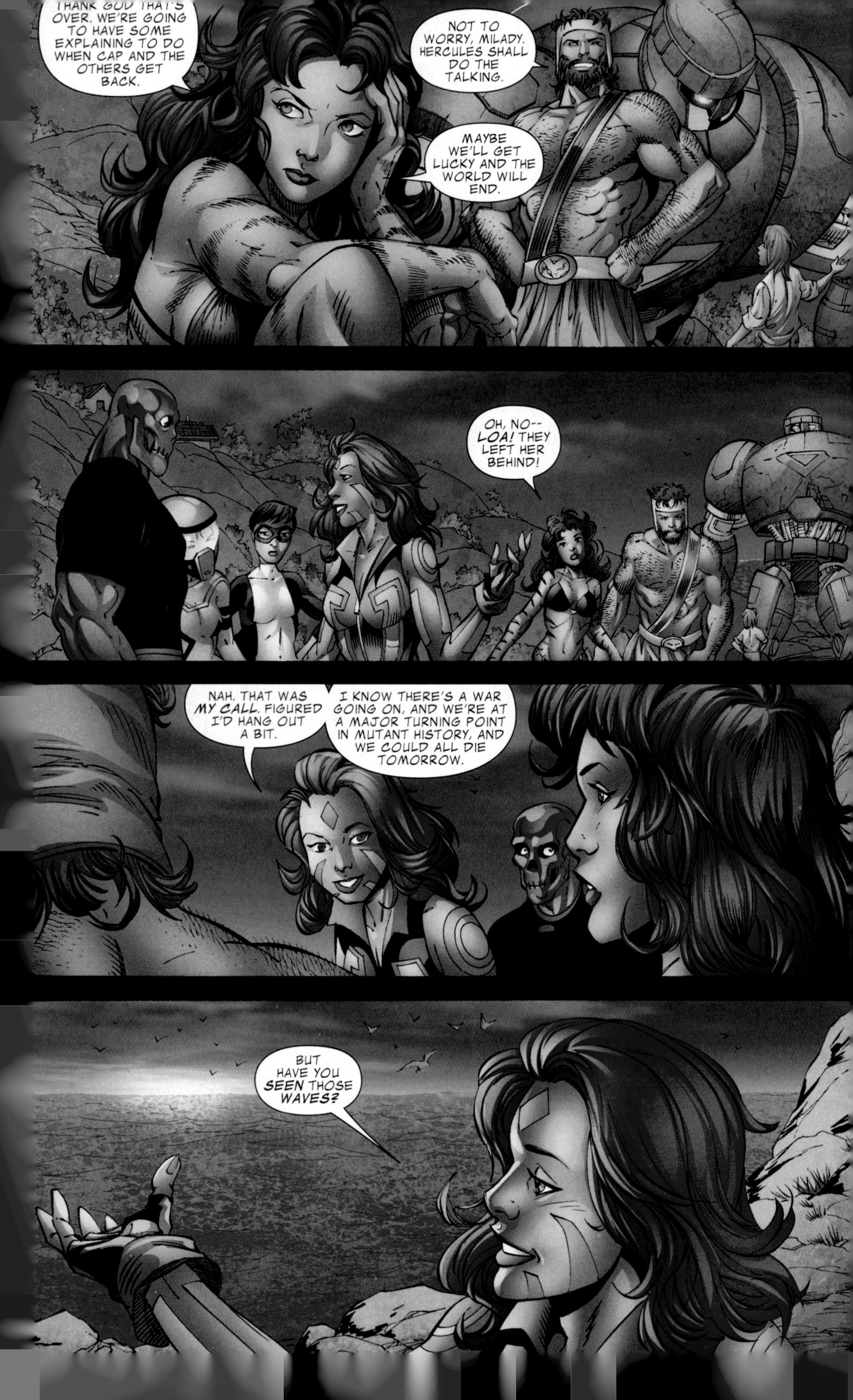
THANK GOD THAT'S OVER. WE'RE GOING TO HAVE SOME EXPLAINING TO DO WHEN CAP AND THE OTHERS GET BACK.
NOT TO WORRY, MILADY. HERCULES SHALL DO THE TALKING.
MAYBE WE'LL GET LUCKY AND THE WORLD WILL END.
OH, NO-- LOA! THEY LEFT HER BEHIND!
NAH. THAT WAS MY CALL. FIGURED I'D HANG OUT A BIT.
I KNOW THERE'S A WAR GOING ON, AND WE'RE AT A MAJOR TURNING POINT IN MUTANT HISTORY, AND WE COULD ALL DIE TOMORROW.
BUT HAVE YOU SEEN THOSE WAVES?

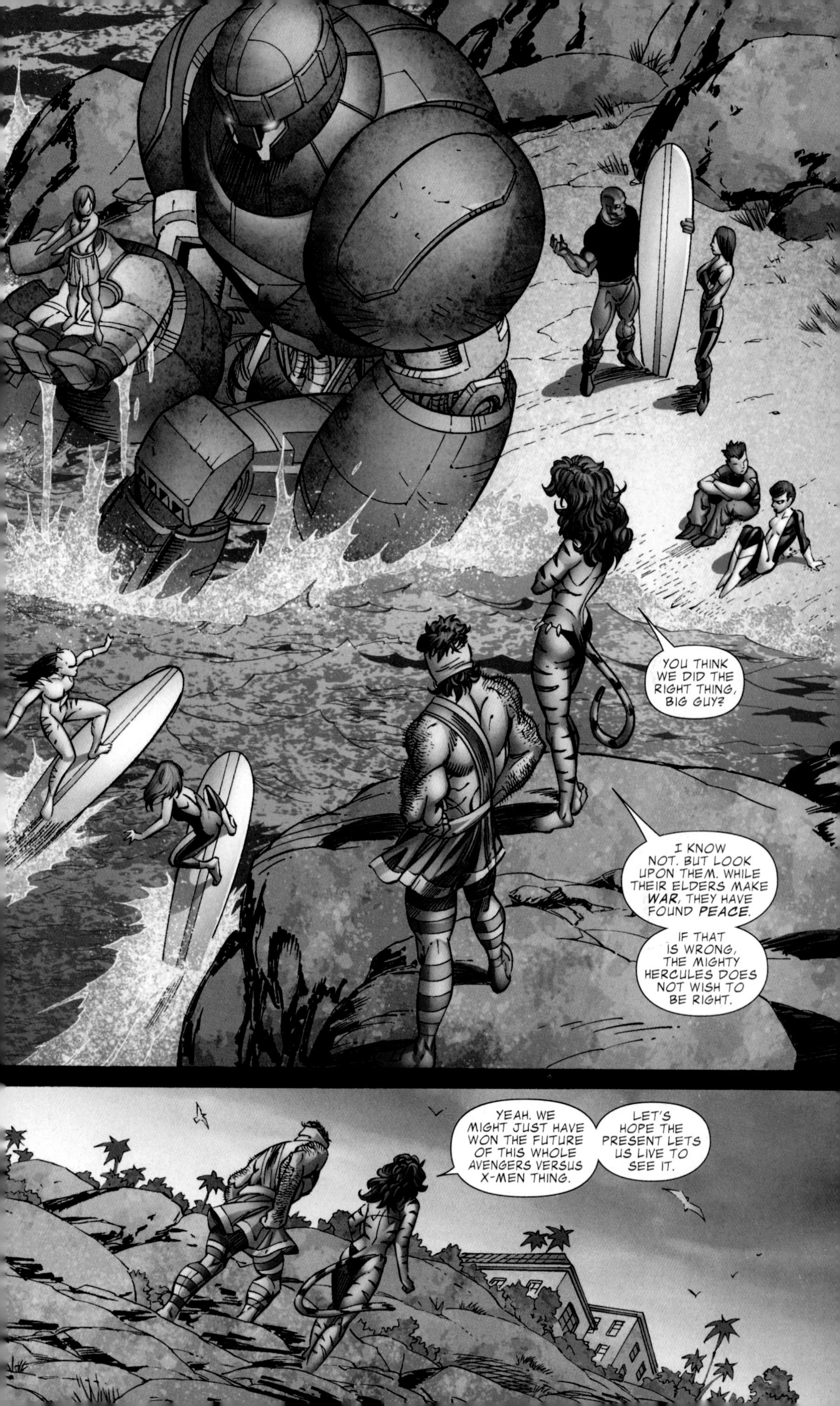
YOU THINK WE DID THE RIGHT THING, BIG GUY?
I KNOW NOT. BUT LOOK UPON THEM. WHILE THEIR ELDERS MAKE WAR, THEY HAVE FOUND PEACE.
IF THAT IS WRONG, THE MIGHTY HERCULES DOES NOT WISH TO BE RIGHT.
YEAH. WE MIGHT JUST HAVE WON THE FUTURE OF THIS WHOLE AVENGERS VERSUS X-MEN THING.
LET'S HOPE THE PRESENT LETS US LIVE TO SEE IT.

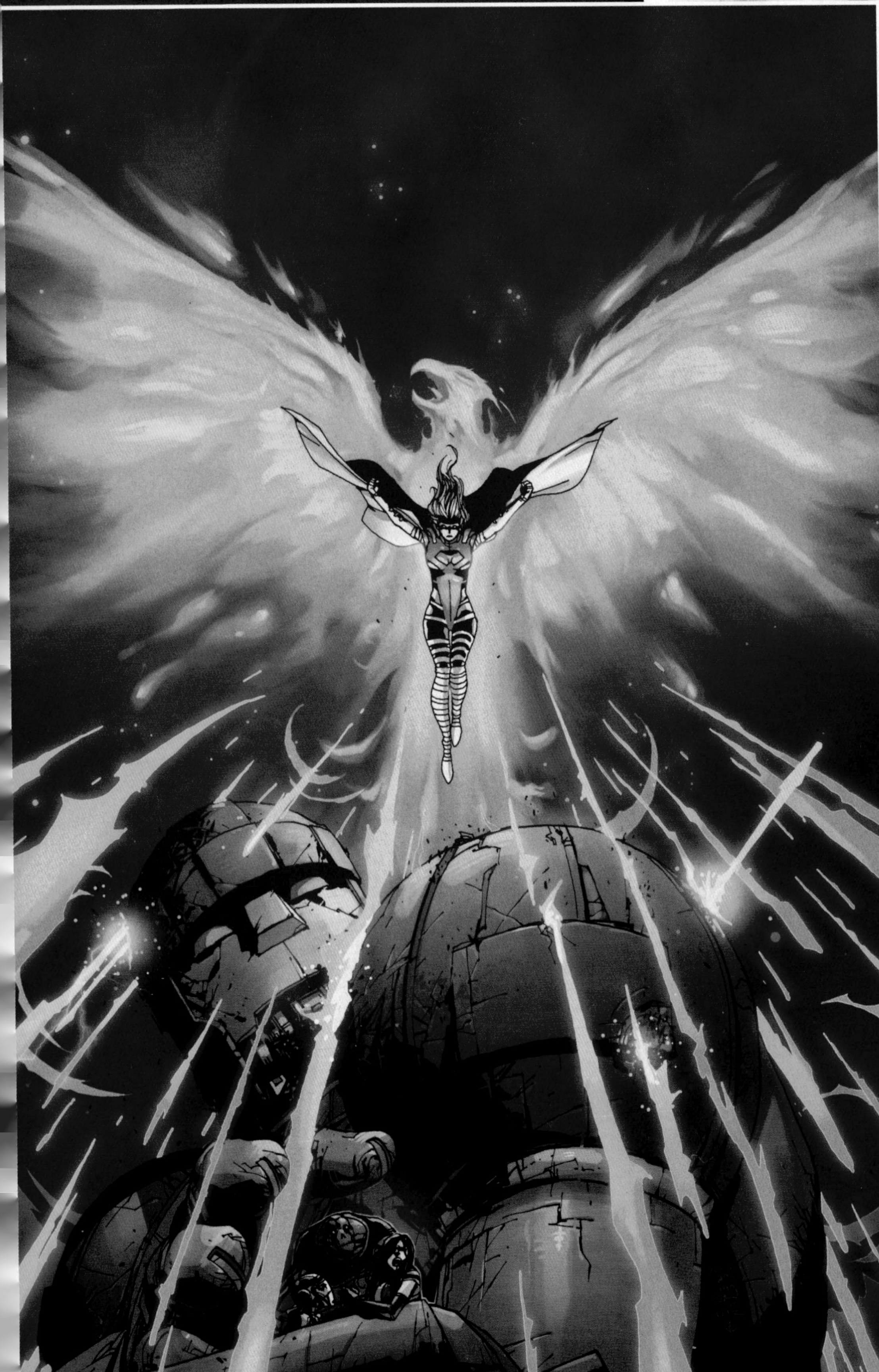

ISSUE #32

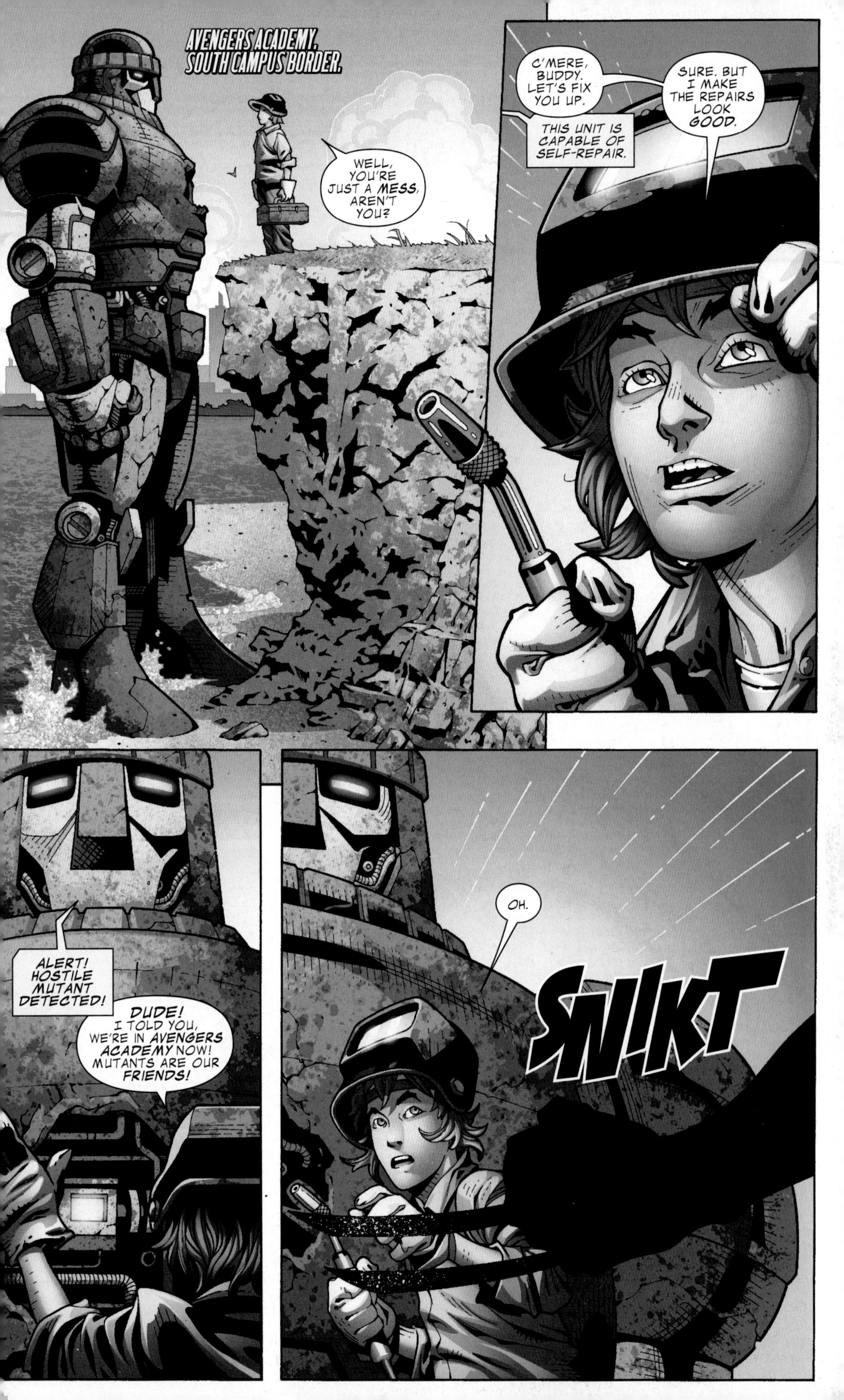
AVENGERS ACADEMY. SOUTH CAMPUS BORDER.
WELL, YOU'RE JUST A MESS, AREN'T YOU?
C'MERE, BUDDY. LET'S FIX YOU UP.
THIS UNIT IS CAPABLE OF SELF-REPAIR.
SURE. BUT I MAKE THE REPAIRS LOOK GOOD.
ALERT! HOSTILE MUTANT DETECTED!
DUDE! I TOLD YOU, WE'RE IN AVENGERS ACADEMY NOW! MUTANTS ARE OUR FRIENDS!
OH.
SNIKT

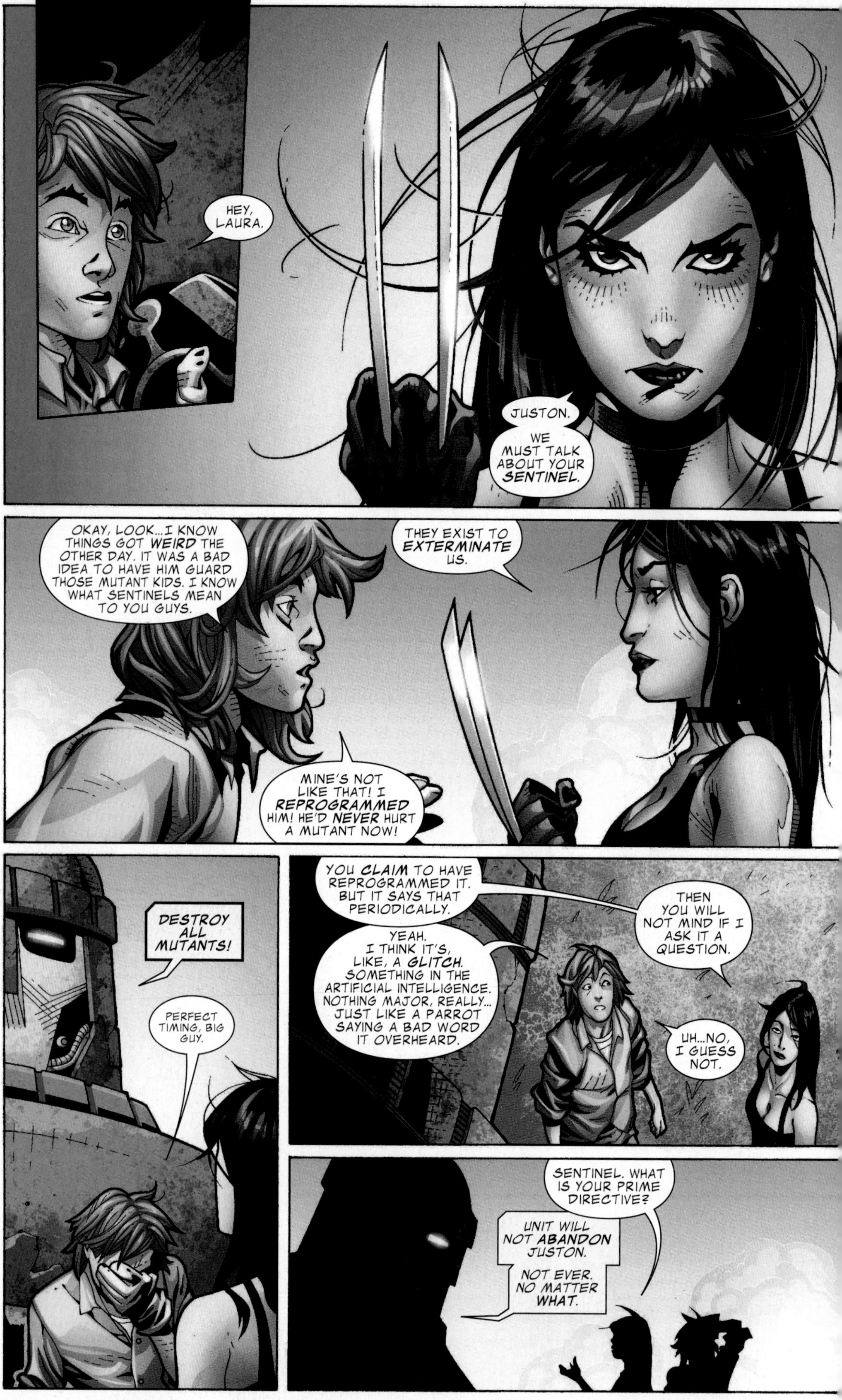
HEY, LAURA.
JUSTON.
WE MUST TALK ABOUT YOUR SENTINEL.
OKAY, LOOK...I KNOW THINGS GOT WEIRD THE OTHER DAY. IT WAS A BAD IDEA TO HAVE HIM GUARD THOSE MUTANT KIDS. I KNOW WHAT SENTINELS MEAN TO YOU GUYS.
THEY EXIST TO EXTERMINATE US.
MINE'S NOT LIKE THAT! I REPROGRAMMED HIM! HE'D NEVER HURT A MUTANT NOW!
DESTROY ALL MUTANTS!
PERFECT TIMING, BIG GUY.
YOU CLAIM TO HAVE REPROGRAMMED IT. BUT IT SAYS THAT PERIODICALLY.
YEAH. I THINK IT'S, LIKE, A GLITCH. SOMETHING IN THE ARTIFICIAL INTELLIGENCE. NOTHING MAJOR, REALLY... JUST LIKE A PARROT SAYING A BAD WORD IT OVERHEARD.
THEN YOU WILL NOT MIND IF I ASK IT A QUESTION.
UH...NO, I GUESS NOT.
SENTINEL. WHAT IS YOUR PRIME DIRECTIVE?
UNIT WILL NOT ABANDON JUSTON.
NOT EVER. NO MATTER WHAT.

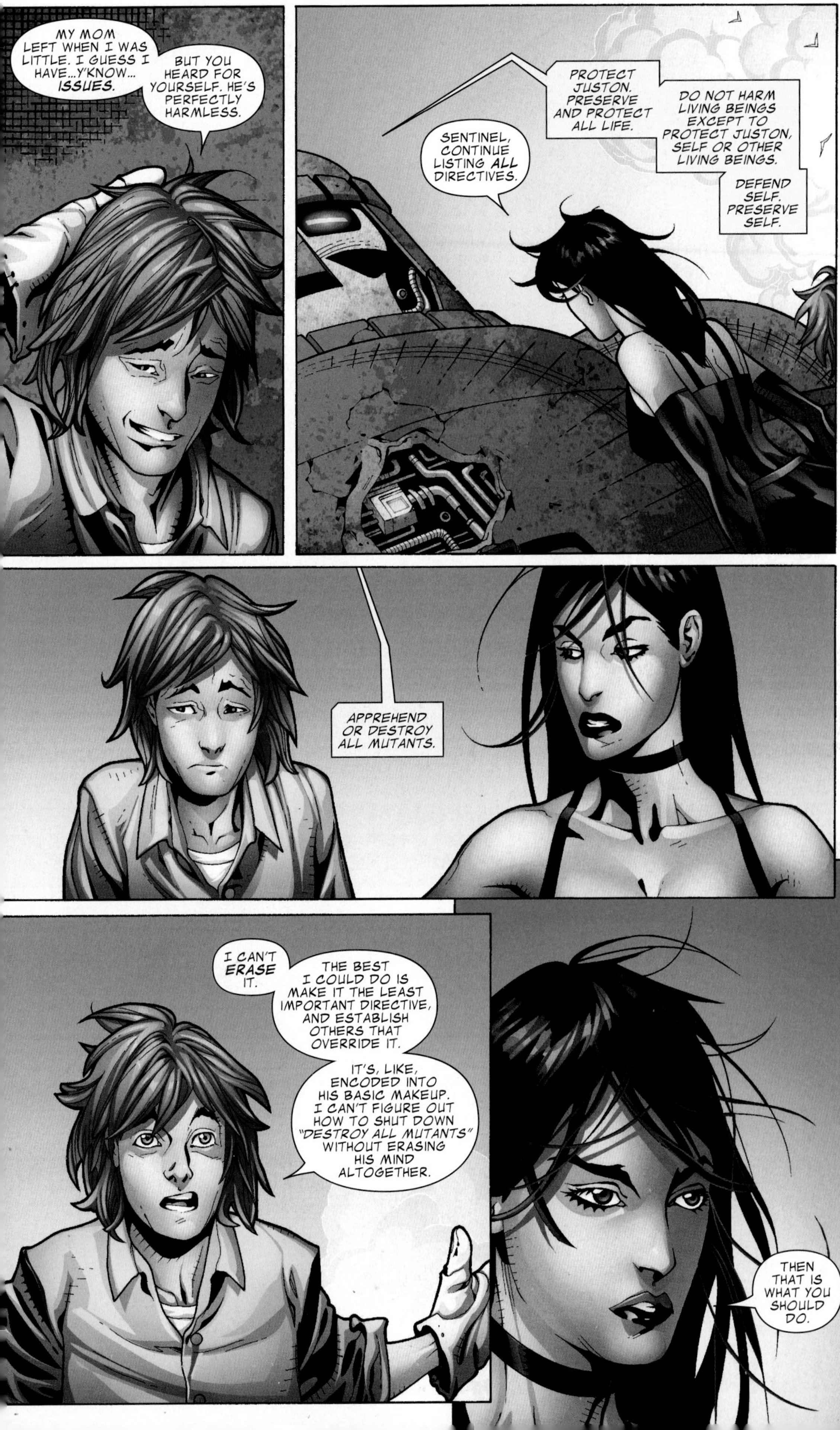

MY MOM LEFT WHEN I WAS LITTLE. I GUESS I HAVE...Y'KNOW... ISSUES.
BUT YOU HEARD FOR YOURSELF. HE'S PERFECTLY HARMLESS.
SENTINEL, CONTINUE LISTING ALL DIRECTIVES.
PROTECT JUSTON. PRESERVE AND PROTECT ALL LIFE.
DO NOT HARM LIVING BEINGS EXCEPT TO PROTECT JUSTON, SELF OR OTHER LIVING BEINGS.
DEFEND SELF. PRESERVE SELF.
APPREHEND OR DESTROY ALL MUTANTS.
I CAN'T ERASE IT.
THE BEST I COULD DO IS MAKE IT THE LEAST IMPORTANT DIRECTIVE, AND ESTABLISH OTHERS THAT OVERRIDE IT.
IT'S, LIKE, ENCODED INTO HIS BASIC MAKEUP. I CAN'T FIGURE OUT HOW TO SHUT DOWN "DESTROY ALL MUTANTS" WITHOUT ERASING HIS MIND ALTOGETHER.
THEN THAT IS WHAT YOU SHOULD DO.

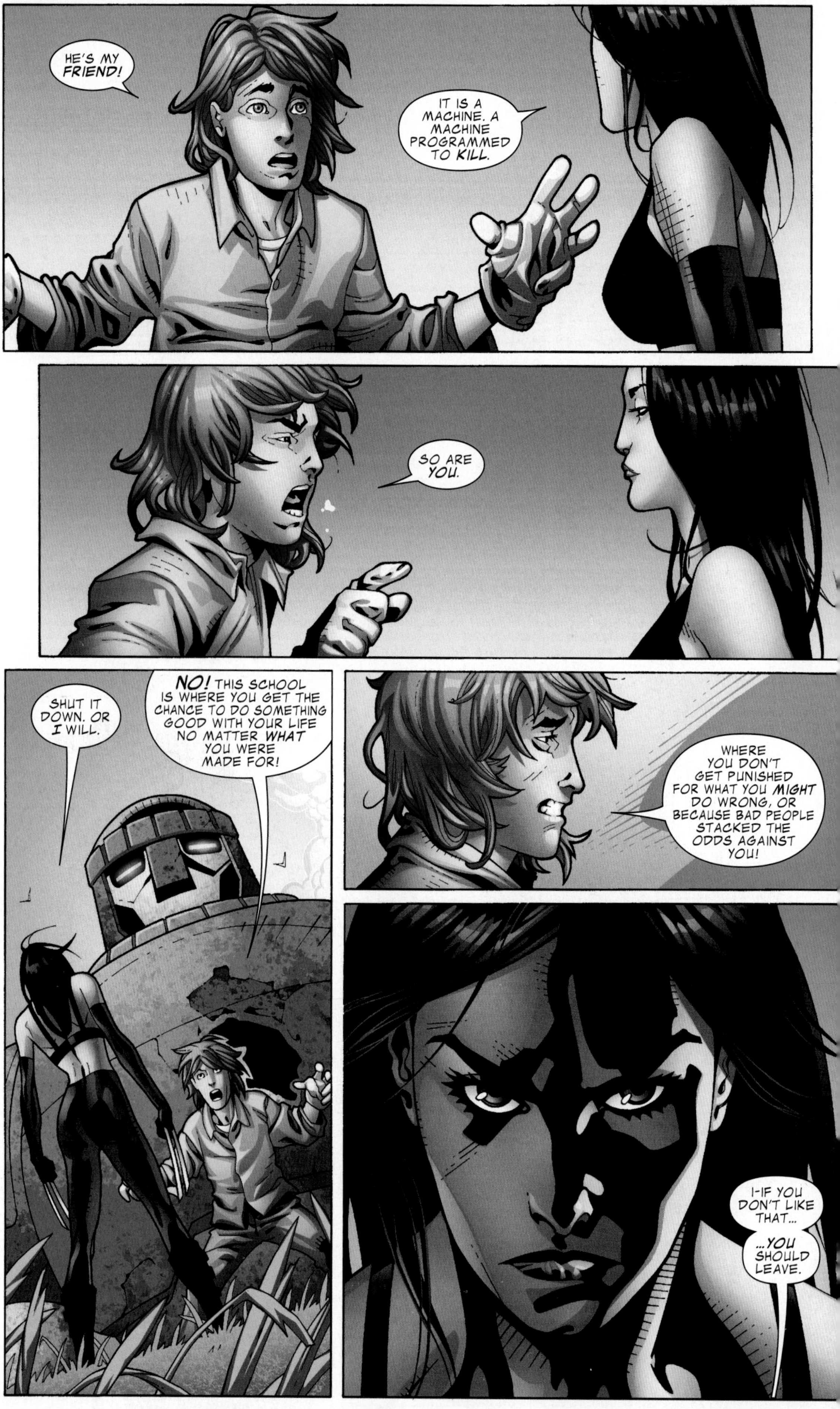
HE'S MY FRIEND!
IT IS A MACHINE. A MACHINE PROGRAMMED TO KILL.
SO ARE YOU.
SHUT IT DOWN. OR I WILL.
NO! THIS SCHOOL IS WHERE YOU GET THE CHANCE TO DO SOMETHING GOOD WITH YOUR LIFE NO MATTER WHAT YOU WERE MADE FOR!
WHERE YOU DON'T GET PUNISHED FOR WHAT YOU MIGHT DO WRONG, OR BECAUSE BAD PEOPLE STACKED THE ODDS AGAINST YOU!
I-IF YOU DON'T LIKE THAT...
...YOU SHOULD LEAVE.

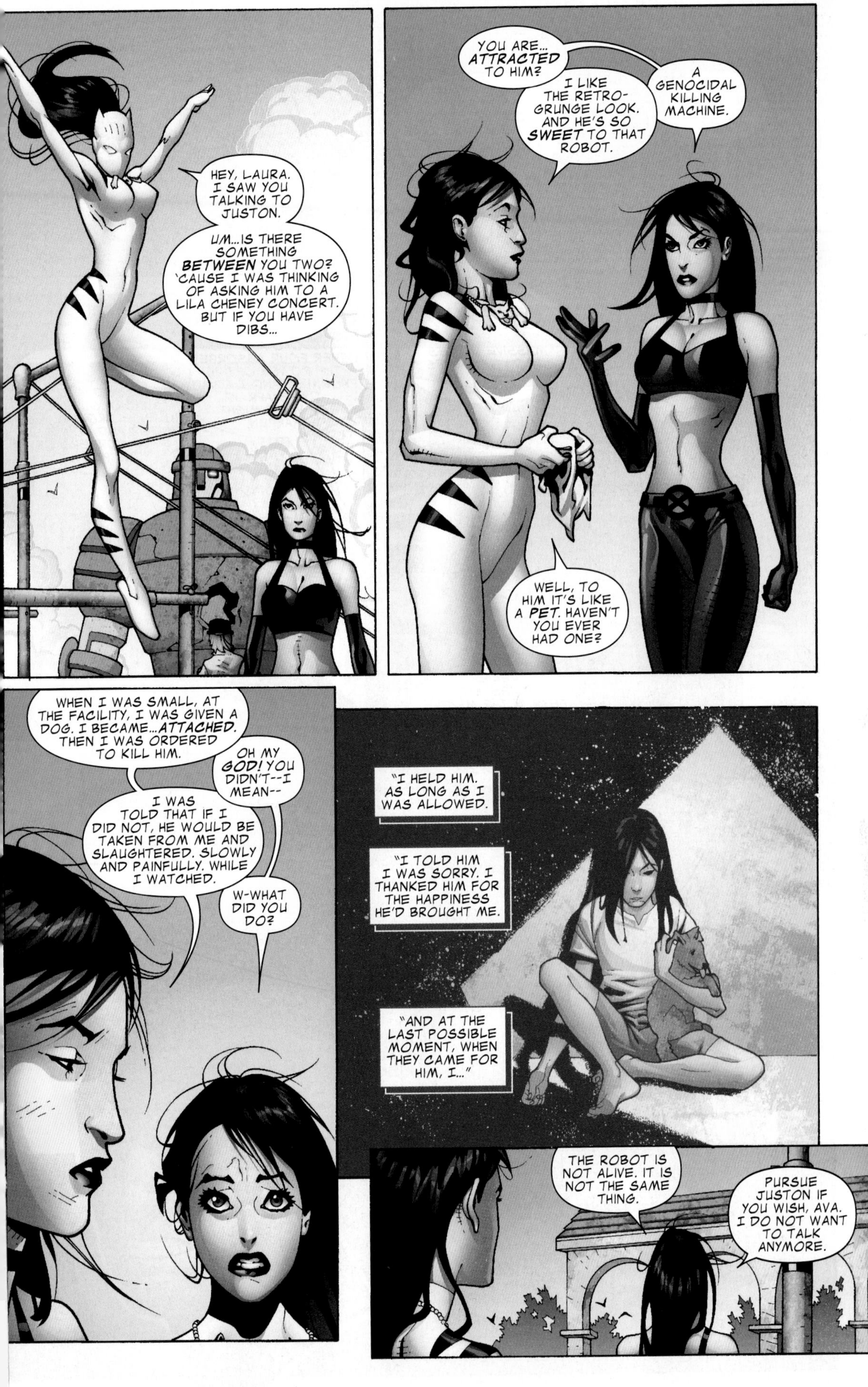
HEY, LAURA. I SAW YOU TALKING TO JUSTON.
UM...IS THERE SOMETHING BETWEEN YOU TWO? 'CAUSE I WAS THINKING OF ASKING HIM TO A LILA CHENEY CONCERT. BUT IF YOU HAVE DIBS...
YOU ARE... ATTRACTED TO HIM?
A GENOCIDAL KILLING MACHINE.
I LIKE THE RETRO-GRUNGE LOOK. AND HE'S SO SWEET TO THAT ROBOT.
WELL, TO HIM IT'S LIKE A PET. HAVEN'T YOU EVER HAD ONE?
WHEN I WAS SMALL, AT THE FACILITY, I WAS GIVEN A DOG. I BECAME...ATTACHED. THEN I WAS ORDERED TO KILL HIM.
OH MY GOD! YOU DIDN'T--I MEAN--
I WAS TOLD THAT IF I DID NOT, HE WOULD BE TAKEN FROM ME AND SLAUGHTERED. SLOWLY AND PAINFULLY. WHILE I WATCHED.
W-WHAT DID YOU DO?
"I HELD HIM. AS LONG AS I WAS ALLOWED.
"I TOLD HIM I WAS SORRY. I THANKED HIM FOR THE HAPPINESS HE'D BROUGHT ME.
"AND AT THE LAST POSSIBLE MOMENT, WHEN THEY CAME FOR HIM, I..."
THE ROBOT IS NOT ALIVE. IT IS NOT THE SAME THING.
PURSUE JUSTON IF YOU WISH, AVA. I DO NOT WANT TO TALK ANYMORE.

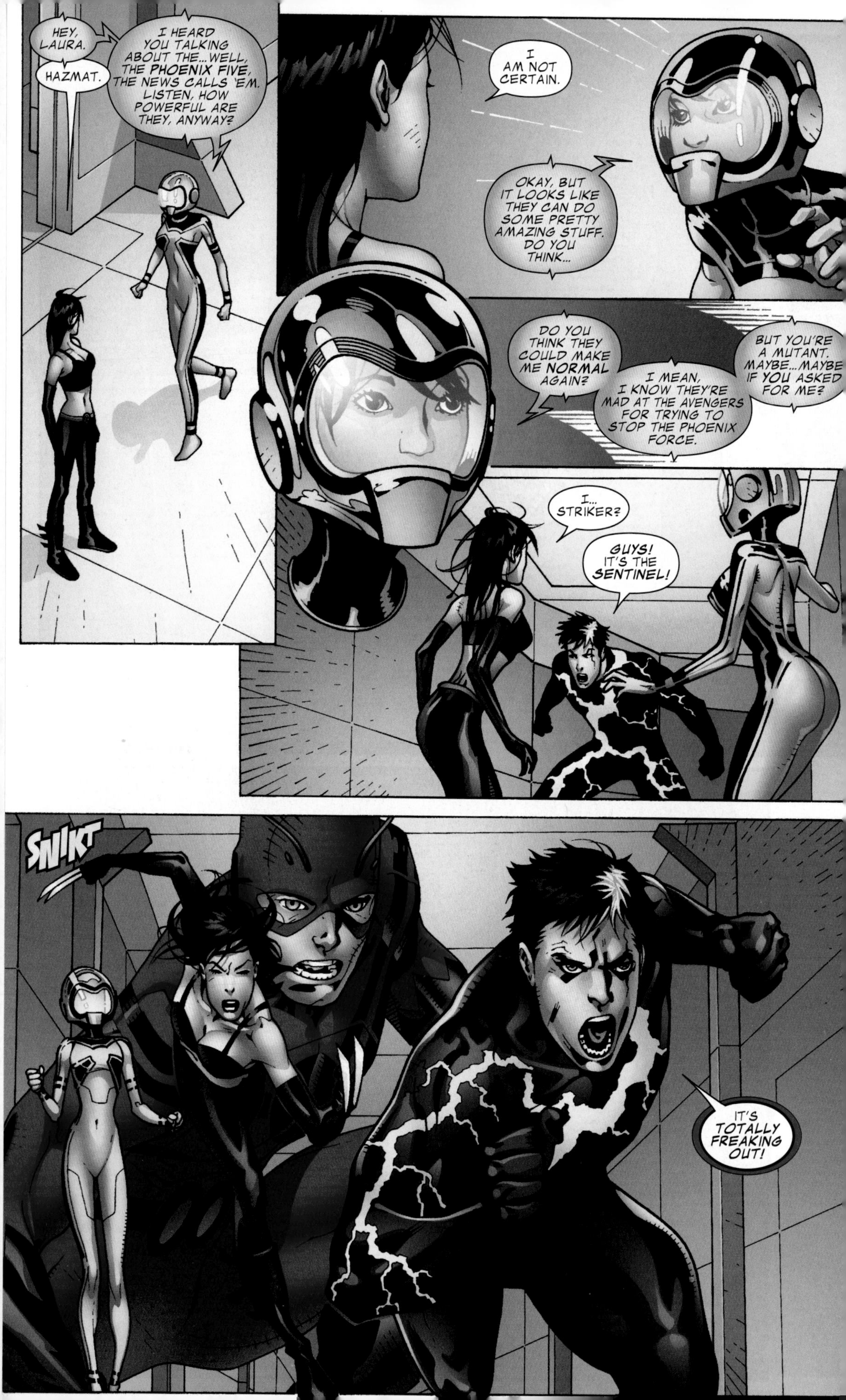
HEY, LAURA.
HAZMAT.
I HEARD YOU TALKING ABOUT THE...WELL, THE PHOENIX FIVE, THE NEWS CALLS 'EM. LISTEN, HOW POWERFUL ARE THEY, ANYWAY?
I AM NOT CERTAIN.
OKAY, BUT IT LOOKS LIKE THEY CAN DO SOME PRETTY AMAZING STUFF. DO YOU THINK...
DO YOU THINK THEY COULD MAKE ME NORMAL AGAIN?
I MEAN, I KNOW THEY'RE MAD AT THE AVENGERS FOR TRYING TO STOP THE PHOENIX FORCE.
BUT YOU'RE A MUTANT. MAYBE...MAYBE IF YOU ASKED FOR ME?
I... STRIKER?
GUYS! IT'S THE SENTINEL!
SNIKT
IT'S TOTALLY FREAKING OUT!

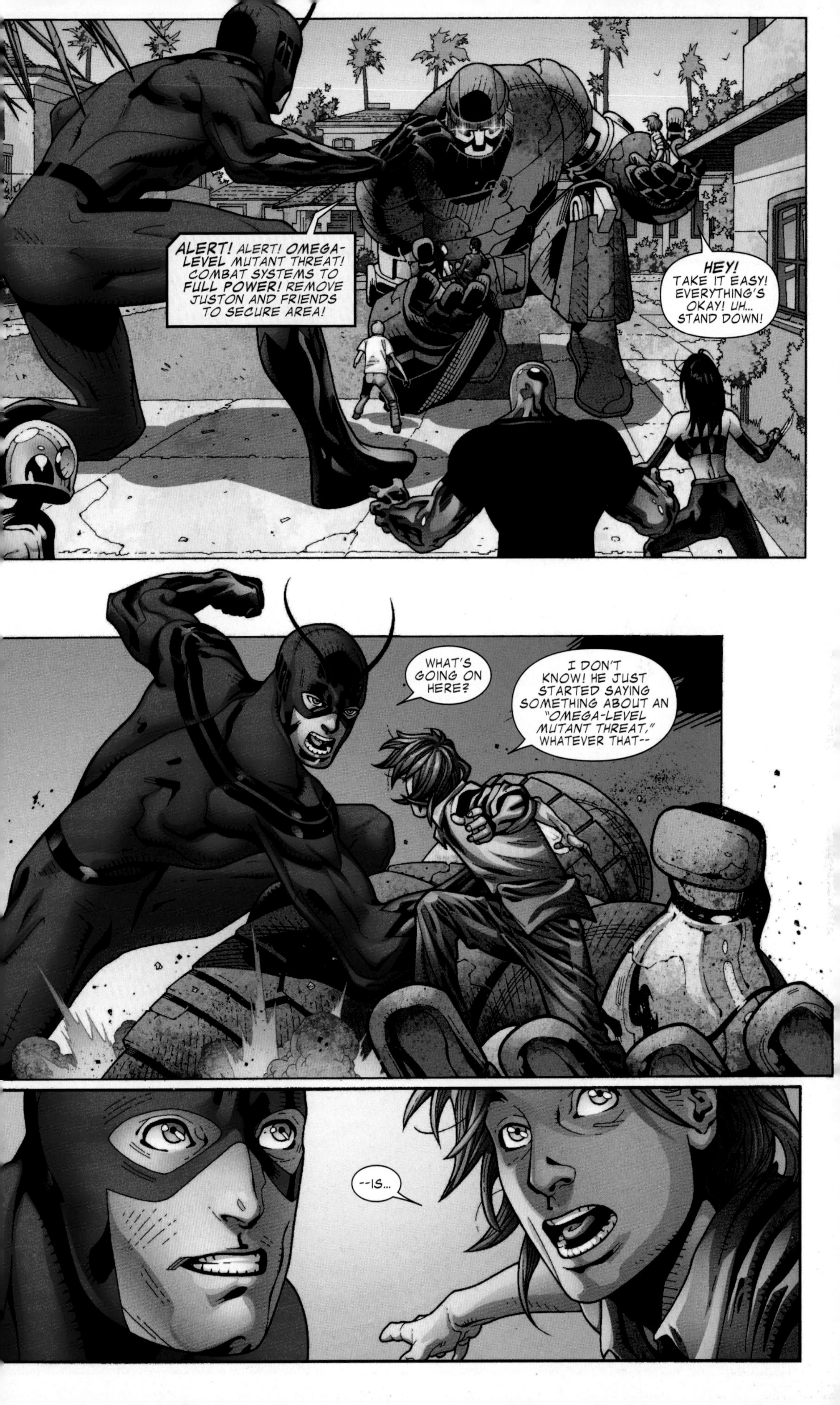

ALERT! ALERT! OMEGA-LEVEL MUTANT THREAT! COMBAT SYSTEMS TO FULL POWER! REMOVE JUSTON AND FRIENDS TO SECURE AREA!
HEY! TAKE IT EASY! EVERYTHING'S OKAY! UH... STAND DOWN!
WHAT'S GOING ON HERE?
I DON'T KNOW! HE JUST STARTED SAYING SOMETHING ABOUT AN "OMEGA-LEVEL MUTANT THREAT," WHATEVER THAT--
--IS...

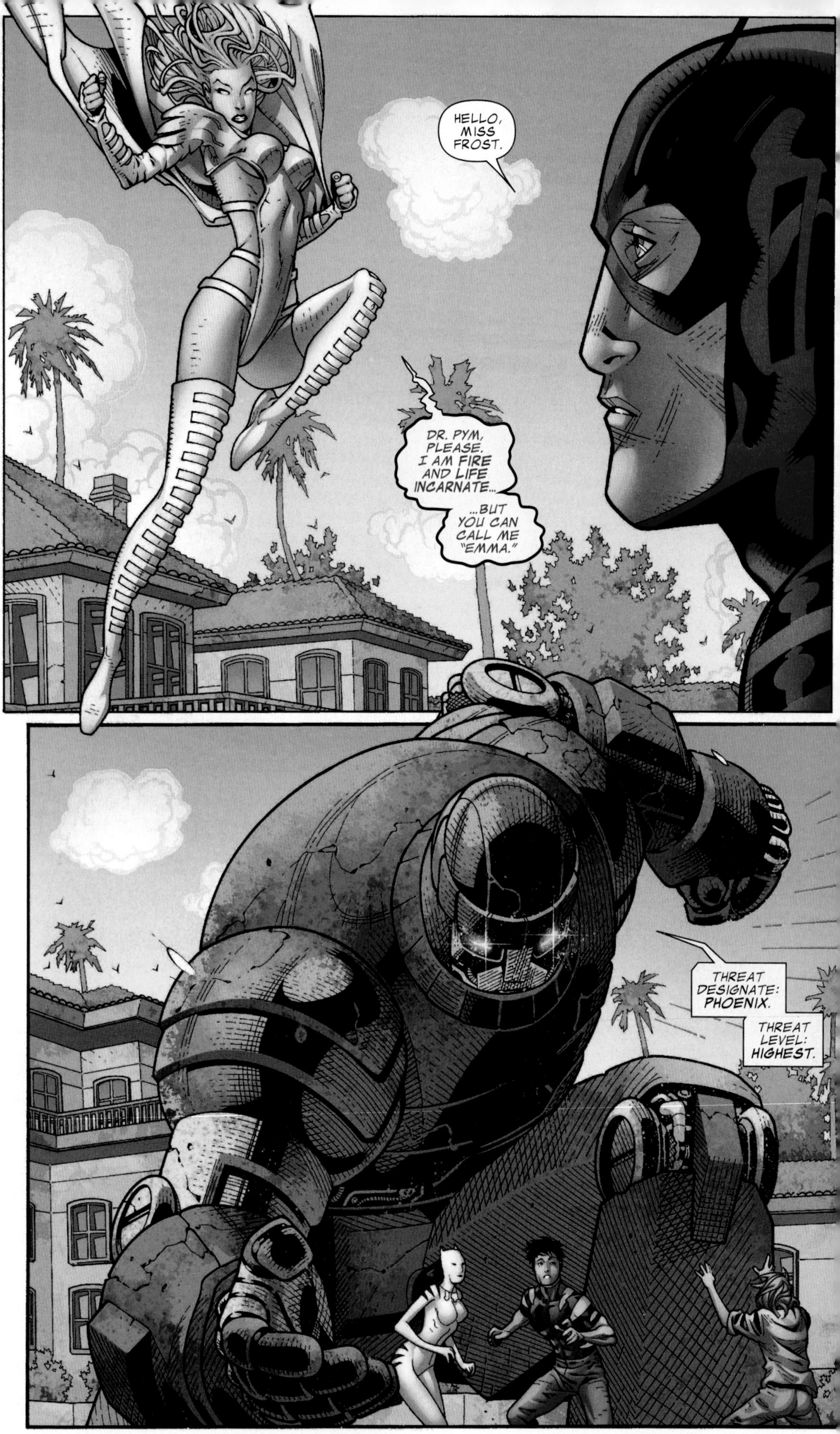

HELLO, MISS FROST.
DR. PYM, PLEASE. I AM FIRE AND LIFE INCARNATE...
...BUT YOU CAN CALL ME "EMMA."
THREAT DESIGNATE: PHOENIX.
THREAT LEVEL: HIGHEST.

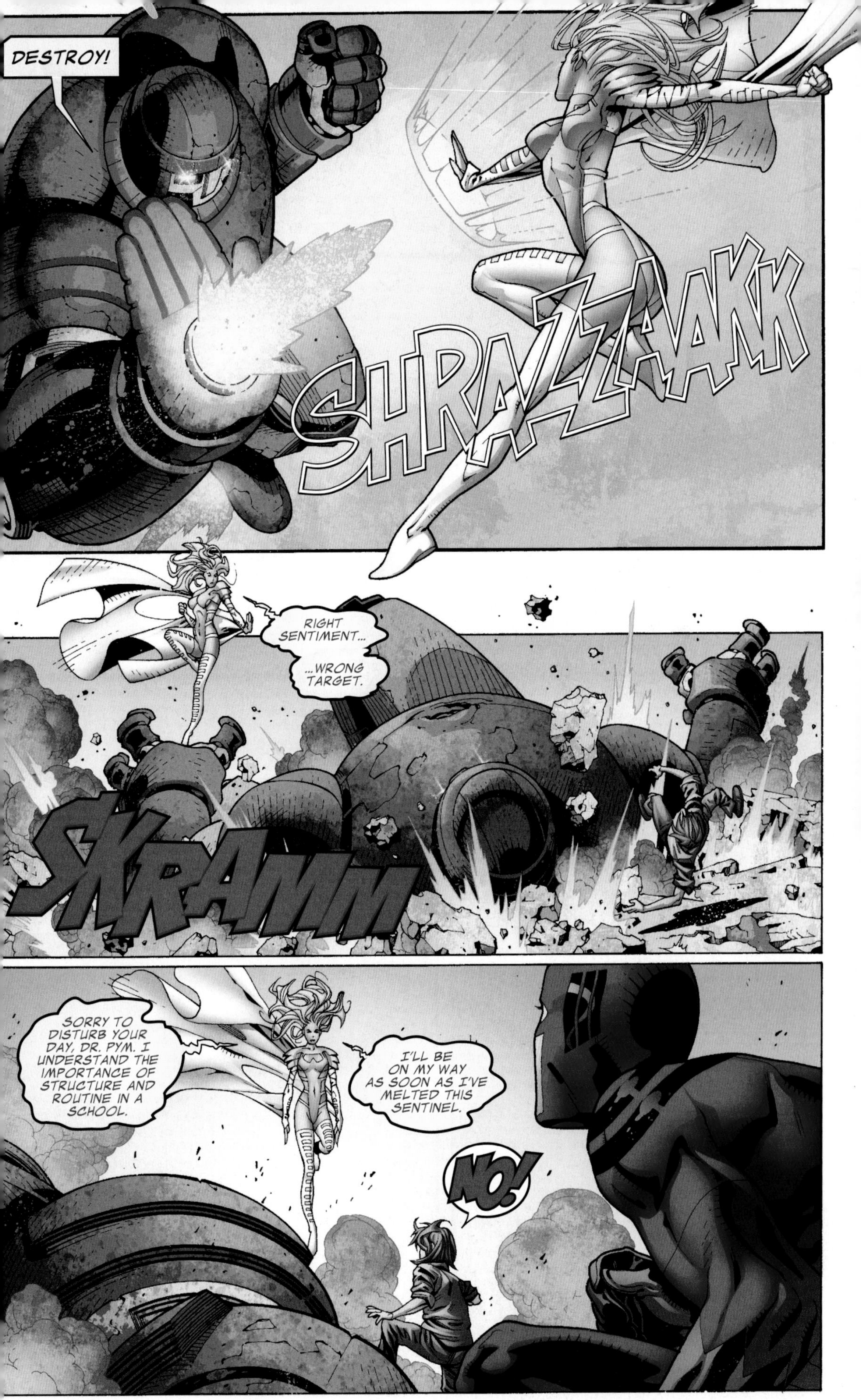
DESTROY!
SHRAZZAAKK
RIGHT SENTIMENT...
...WRONG TARGET.
SKRAMM
SORRY TO DISTURB YOUR DAY, DR. PYM. I UNDERSTAND THE IMPORTANCE OF STRUCTURE AND ROUTINE IN A SCHOOL.
I'LL BE ON MY WAY AS SOON AS I'VE MELTED THIS SENTINEL.
NO!

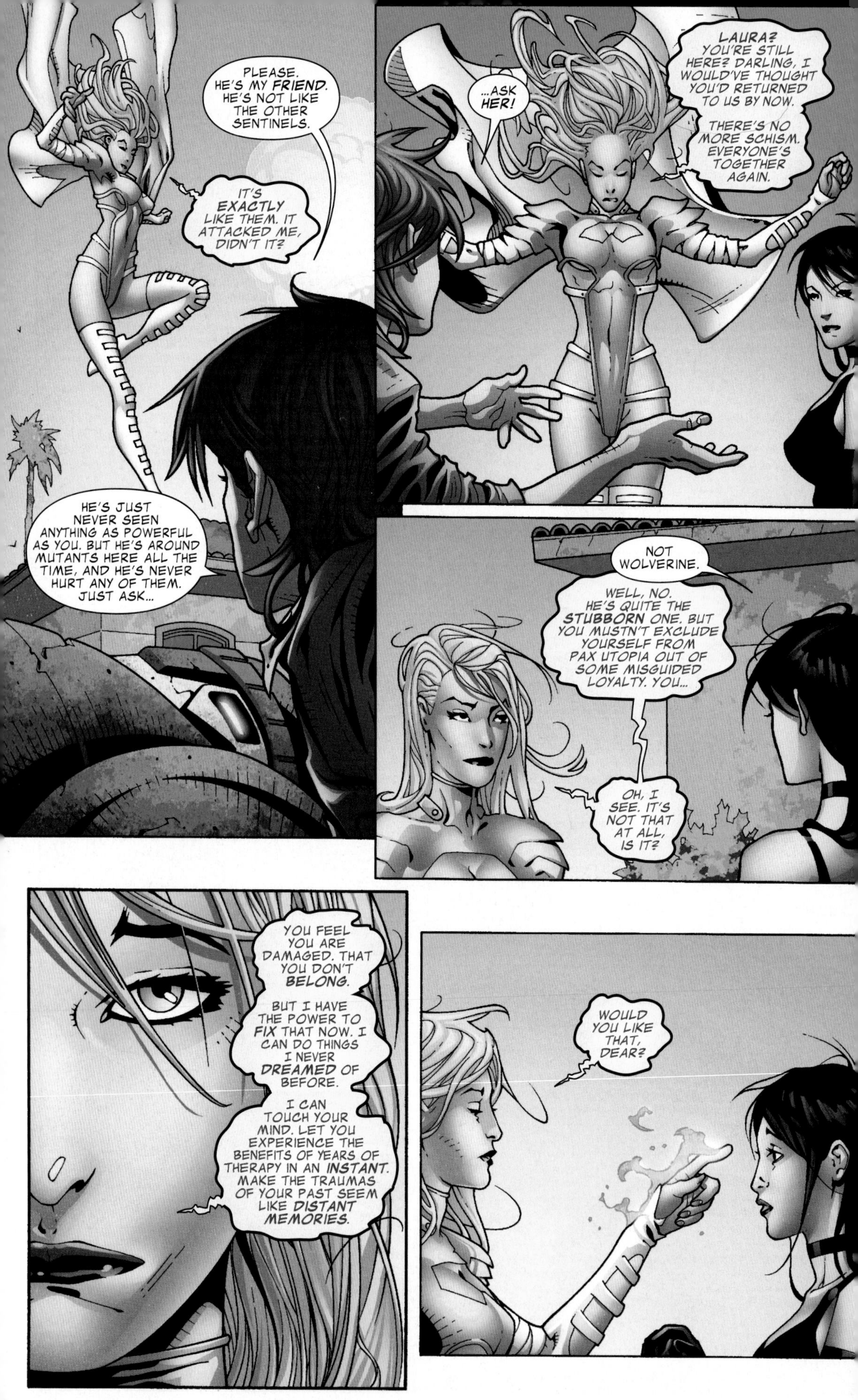
PLEASE. HE'S MY FRIEND. HE'S NOT LIKE THE OTHER SENTINELS.
IT'S EXACTLY LIKE THEM. IT ATTACKED ME, DIDN'T IT?
HE'S JUST NEVER SEEN ANYTHING AS POWERFUL AS YOU. BUT HE'S AROUND MUTANTS HERE ALL THE TIME, AND HE'S NEVER HURT ANY OF THEM. JUST ASK...
...ASK HER!
LAURA? YOU'RE STILL HERE? DARLING, I WOULD'VE THOUGHT YOU'D RETURNED TO US BY NOW.
THERE'S NO MORE SCHISM. EVERYONE'S TOGETHER AGAIN.
NOT WOLVERINE.
WELL, NO. HE'S QUITE THE STUBBORN ONE. BUT YOU MUSTN'T EXCLUDE YOURSELF FROM PAX UTOPIA OUT OF SOME MISGUIDED LOYALTY. YOU...
OH, I SEE. IT'S NOT THAT AT ALL, IS IT?
YOU FEEL YOU ARE DAMAGED. THAT YOU DON'T BELONG.
BUT I HAVE THE POWER TO FIX THAT NOW. I CAN DO THINGS I NEVER DREAMED OF BEFORE.
I CAN TOUCH YOUR MIND. LET YOU EXPERIENCE THE BENEFITS OF YEARS OF THERAPY IN AN INSTANT. MAKE THE TRAUMAS OF YOUR PAST SEEM LIKE DISTANT MEMORIES.
WOULD YOU LIKE THAT, DEAR?

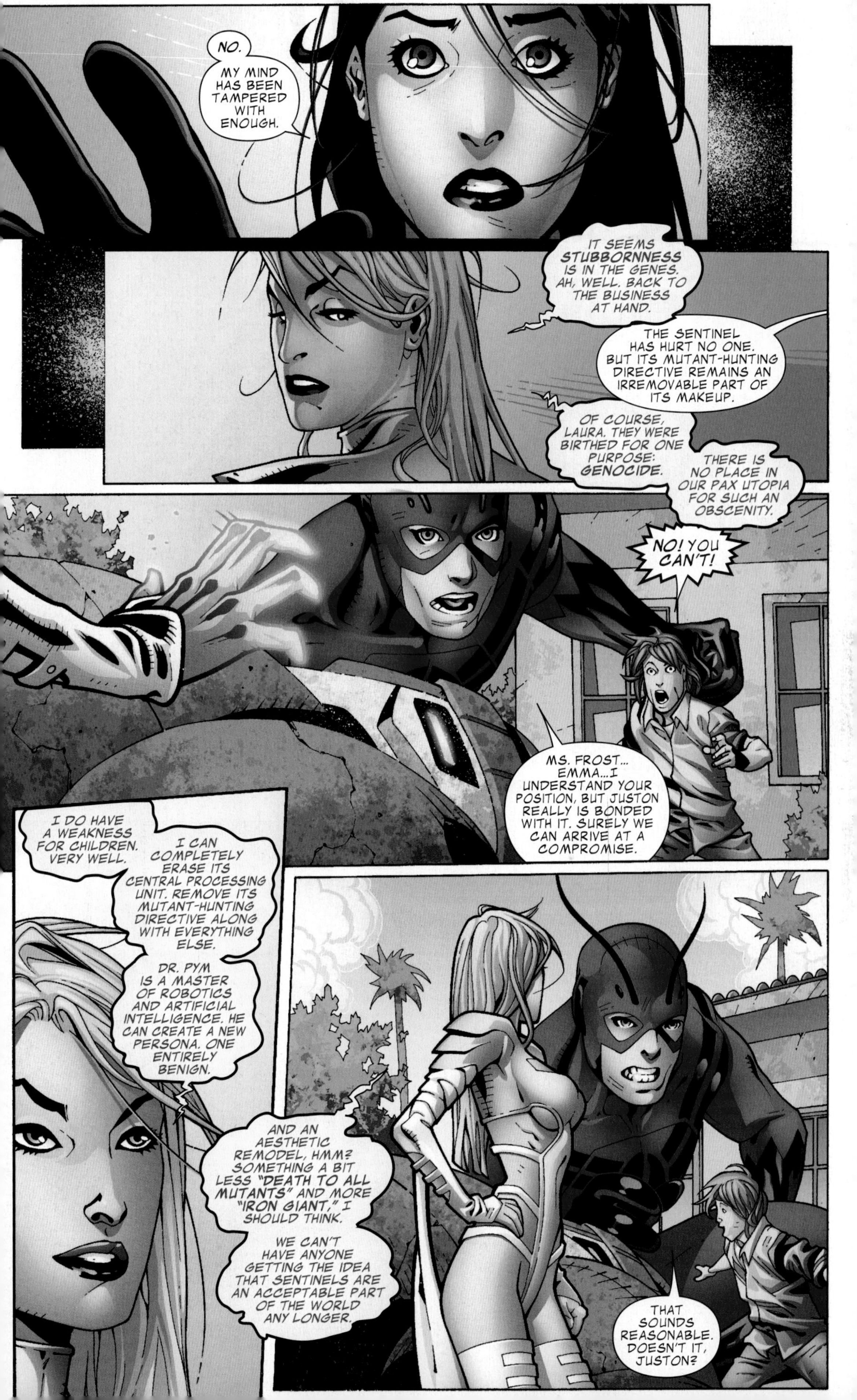
NO.
MY MIND HAS BEEN TAMPERED WITH ENOUGH.
IT SEEMS STUBBORNNESS IS IN THE GENES. AH, WELL. BACK TO THE BUSINESS AT HAND.
THE SENTINEL HAS HURT NO ONE. BUT ITS MUTANT-HUNTING DIRECTIVE REMAINS AN IRREMOVABLE PART OF ITS MAKEUP.
OF COURSE, LAURA. THEY WERE BIRTHED FOR ONE PURPOSE: GENOCIDE.
THERE IS NO PLACE IN OUR PAX UTOPIA FOR SUCH AN OBSCENITY.
NO! YOU CAN'T!
MS. FROST... EMMA...I UNDERSTAND YOUR POSITION, BUT JUSTON REALLY IS BONDED WITH IT. SURELY WE CAN ARRIVE AT A COMPROMISE.
I DO HAVE A WEAKNESS FOR CHILDREN. VERY WELL.
I CAN COMPLETELY ERASE ITS CENTRAL PROCESSING UNIT. REMOVE ITS MUTANT-HUNTING DIRECTIVE ALONG WITH EVERYTHING ELSE.
DR. PYM IS A MASTER OF ROBOTICS AND ARTIFICIAL INTELLIGENCE. HE CAN CREATE A NEW PERSONA. ONE ENTIRELY BENIGN.
AND AN AESTHETIC REMODEL, HMM? SOMETHING A BIT LESS "DEATH TO ALL MUTANTS" AND MORE "IRON GIANT," I SHOULD THINK.
WE CAN'T HAVE ANYONE GETTING THE IDEA THAT SENTINELS ARE AN ACCEPTABLE PART OF THE WORLD ANY LONGER.
THAT SOUNDS REASONABLE. DOESN'T IT, JUSTON?

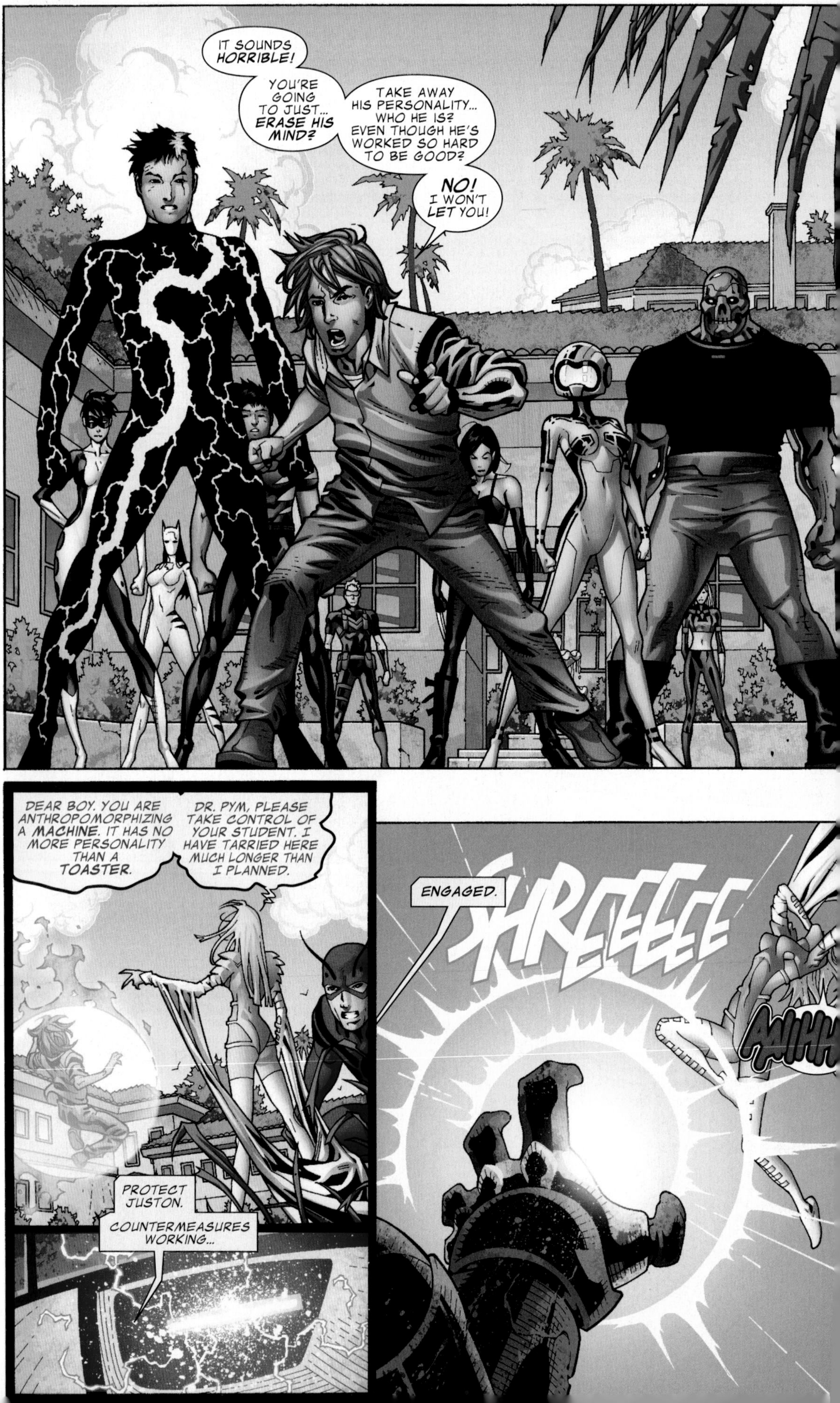
IT SOUNDS HORRIBLE!
YOU'RE GOING TO JUST... ERASE HIS MIND?
TAKE AWAY HIS PERSONALITY... WHO HE IS? EVEN THOUGH HE'S WORKED SO HARD TO BE GOOD?
NO! I WON'T LET YOU!
DEAR BOY. YOU ARE ANTHROPOMORPHIZING A MACHINE. IT HAS NO MORE PERSONALITY THAN A TOASTER.
DR. PYM, PLEASE TAKE CONTROL OF YOUR STUDENT. I HAVE TARRIED HERE MUCH LONGER THAN I PLANNED.
PROTECT JUSTON.
COUNTERMEASURES WORKING...
ENGAGED.
SHREEEEEE
AAIIHH

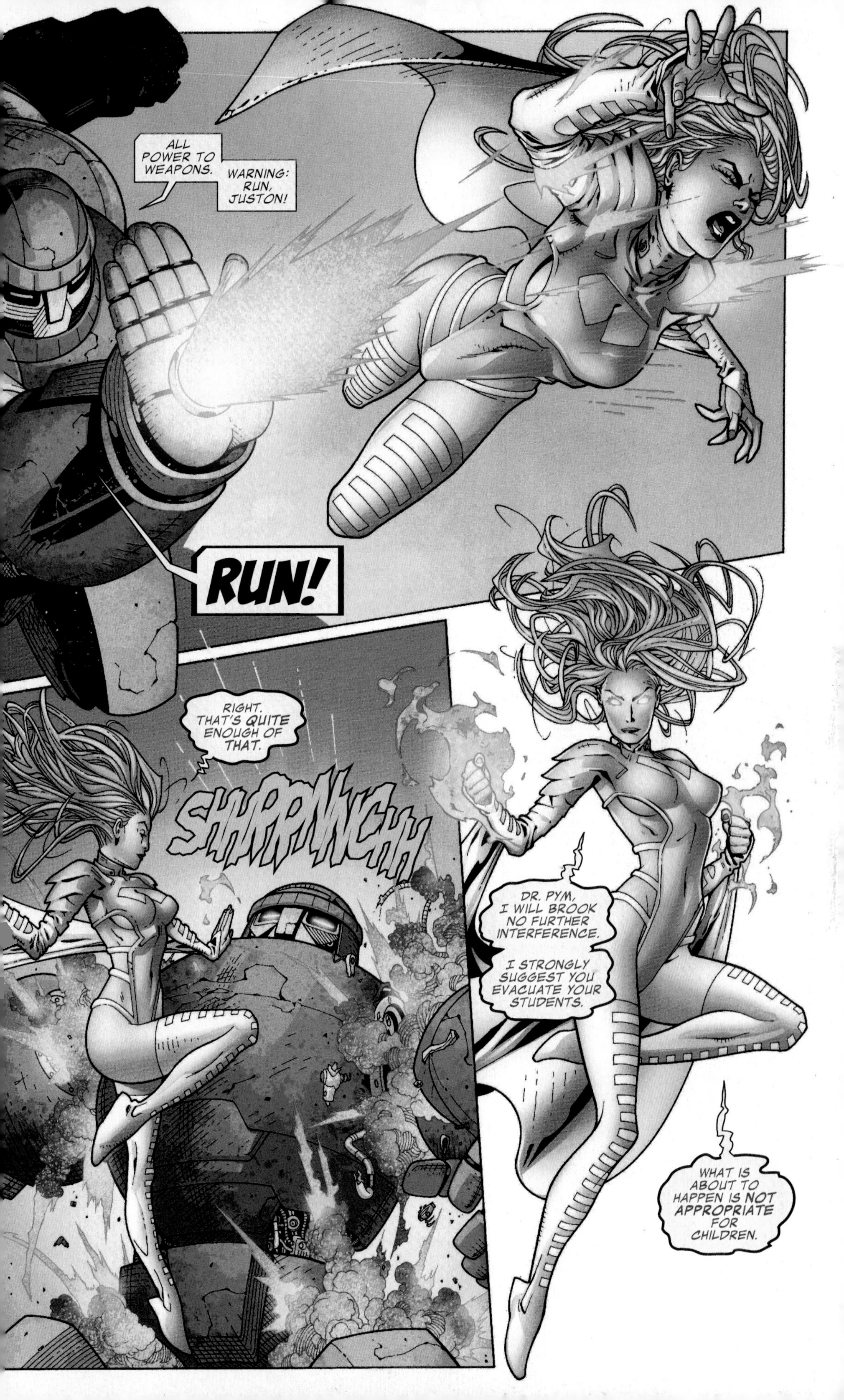
ALL POWER TO WEAPONS.
WARNING: RUN, JUSTON!
RUN!
RIGHT. THAT'S QUITE ENOUGH OF THAT.
SHRRNNCHH
DR. PYM, I WILL BROOK NO FURTHER INTERFERENCE.
I STRONGLY SUGGEST YOU EVACUATE YOUR STUDENTS.
WHAT IS ABOUT TO HAPPEN IS NOT APPROPRIATE FOR CHILDREN.

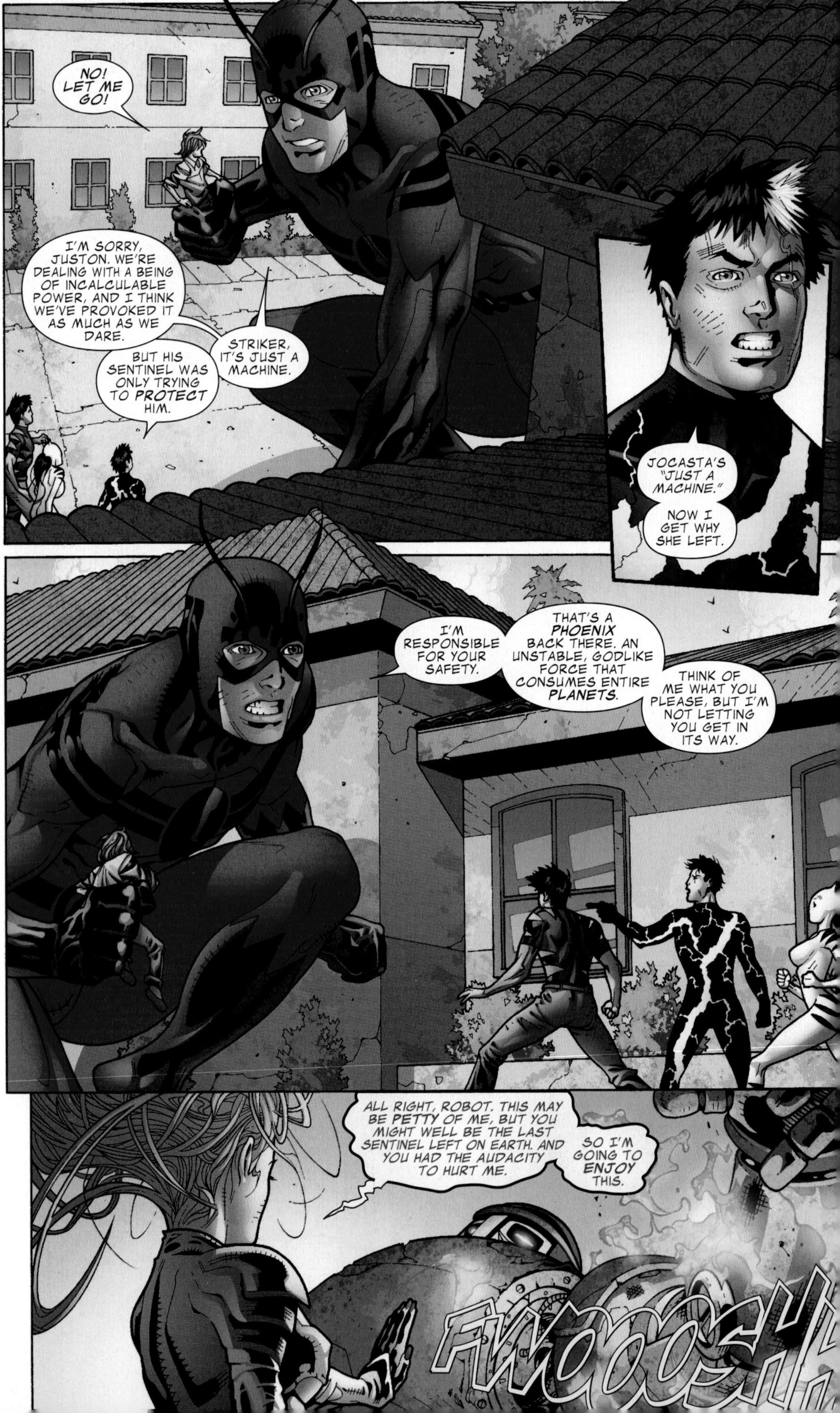
NO! LET ME GO!
I'M SORRY, JUSTON. WE'RE DEALING WITH A BEING OF INCALCULABLE POWER, AND I THINK WE'VE PROVOKED IT AS MUCH AS WE DARE.
BUT HIS SENTINEL WAS ONLY TRYING TO PROTECT HIM.
STRIKER, IT'S JUST A MACHINE.
JOCASTA'S "JUST A MACHINE."
NOW I GET WHY SHE LEFT.
I'M RESPONSIBLE FOR YOUR SAFETY.
THAT'S A PHOENIX BACK THERE. AN UNSTABLE, GODLIKE FORCE THAT CONSUMES ENTIRE PLANETS.
THINK OF ME WHAT YOU PLEASE, BUT I'M NOT LETTING YOU GET IN ITS WAY.
ALL RIGHT, ROBOT. THIS MAY BE PETTY OF ME, BUT YOU MIGHT WELL BE THE LAST SENTINEL LEFT ON EARTH. AND YOU HAD THE AUDACITY TO HURT ME.
SO I'M GOING TO ENJOY THIS.
FWOOOSH

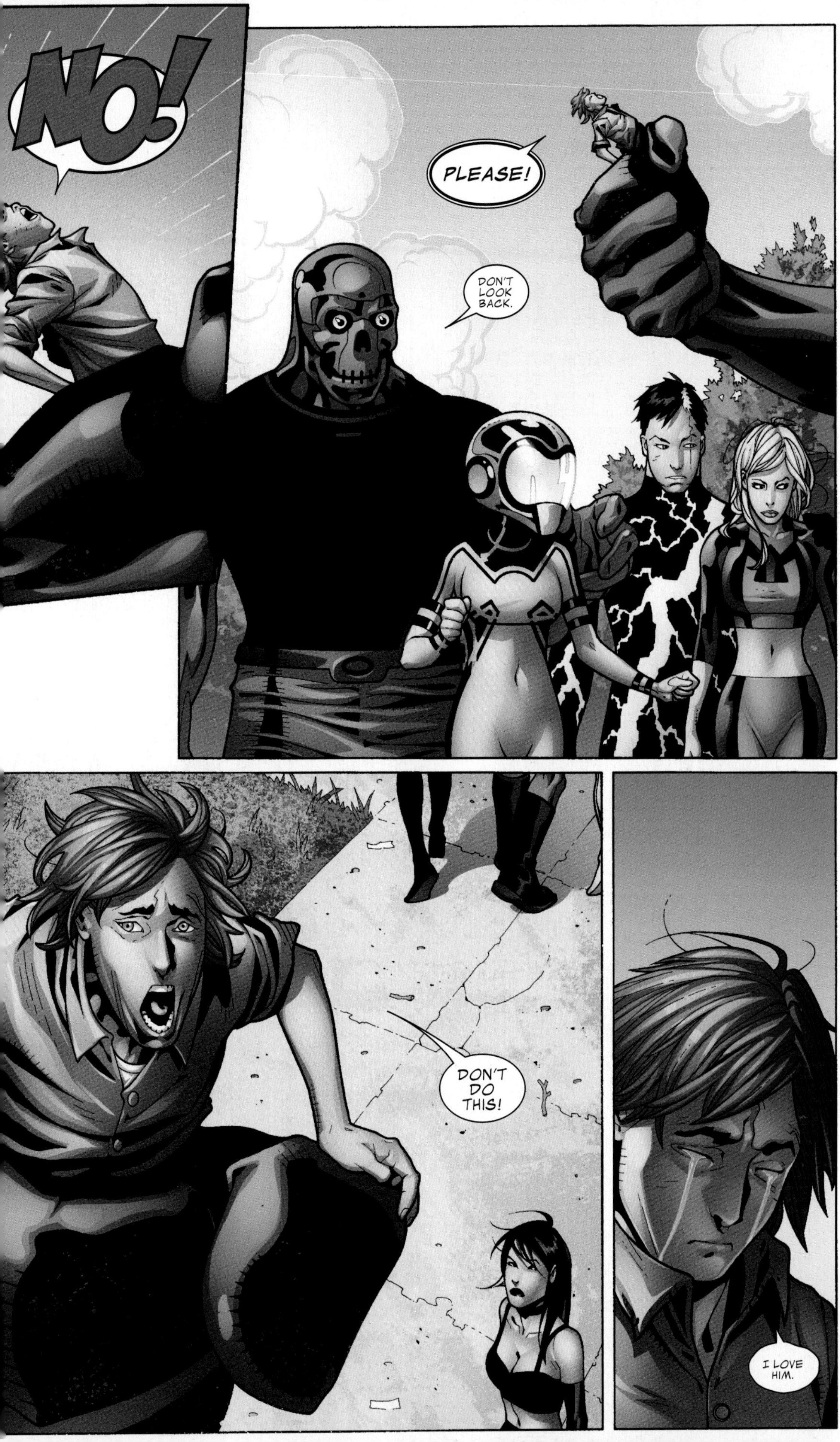
NO!
PLEASE!
DON'T LOOK BACK.
DON'T DO THIS!
I LOVE HIM.

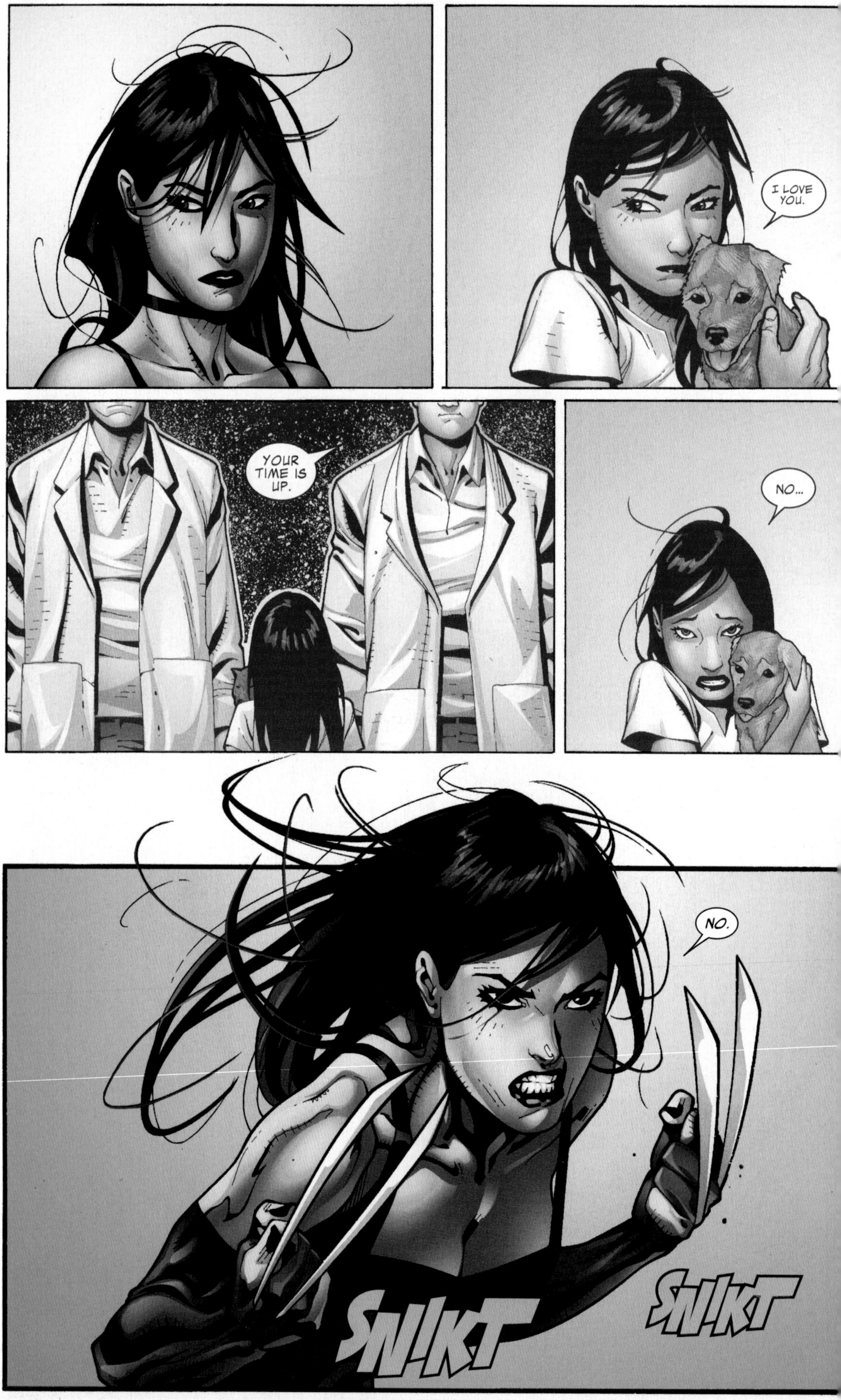
I LOVE YOU.
YOUR TIME IS UP.
NO...
NO.
SNIKT
SNIKT

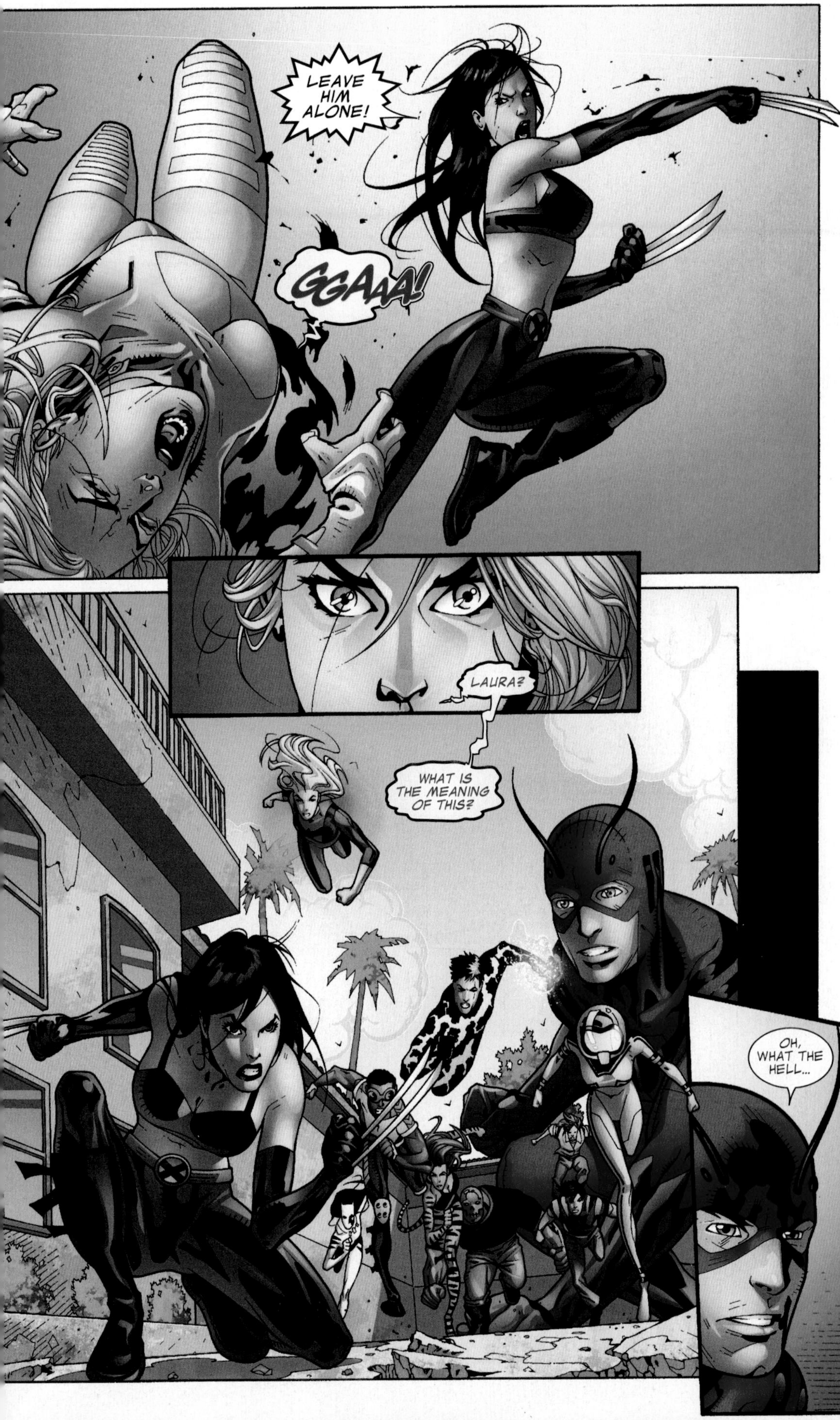
LEAVE HIM ALONE!
GGAAA!
LAURA?
WHAT IS THE MEANING OF THIS?
OH, WHAT THE HELL...

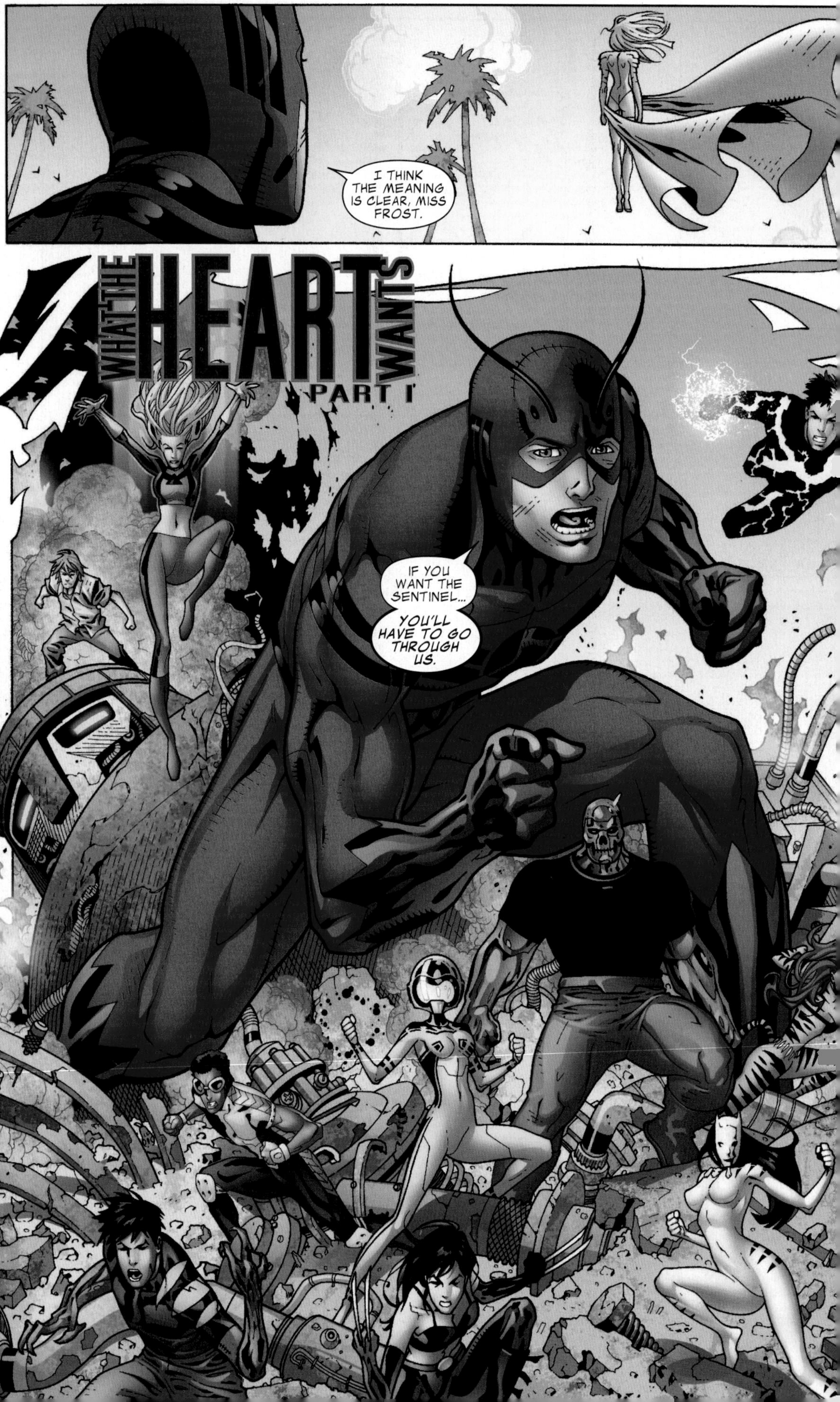
I THINK THE MEANING IS CLEAR, MISS FROST.
WHAT THE HEART WANTS
PART I
IF YOU WANT THE SENTINEL...
YOU'LL HAVE TO GO THROUGH US.

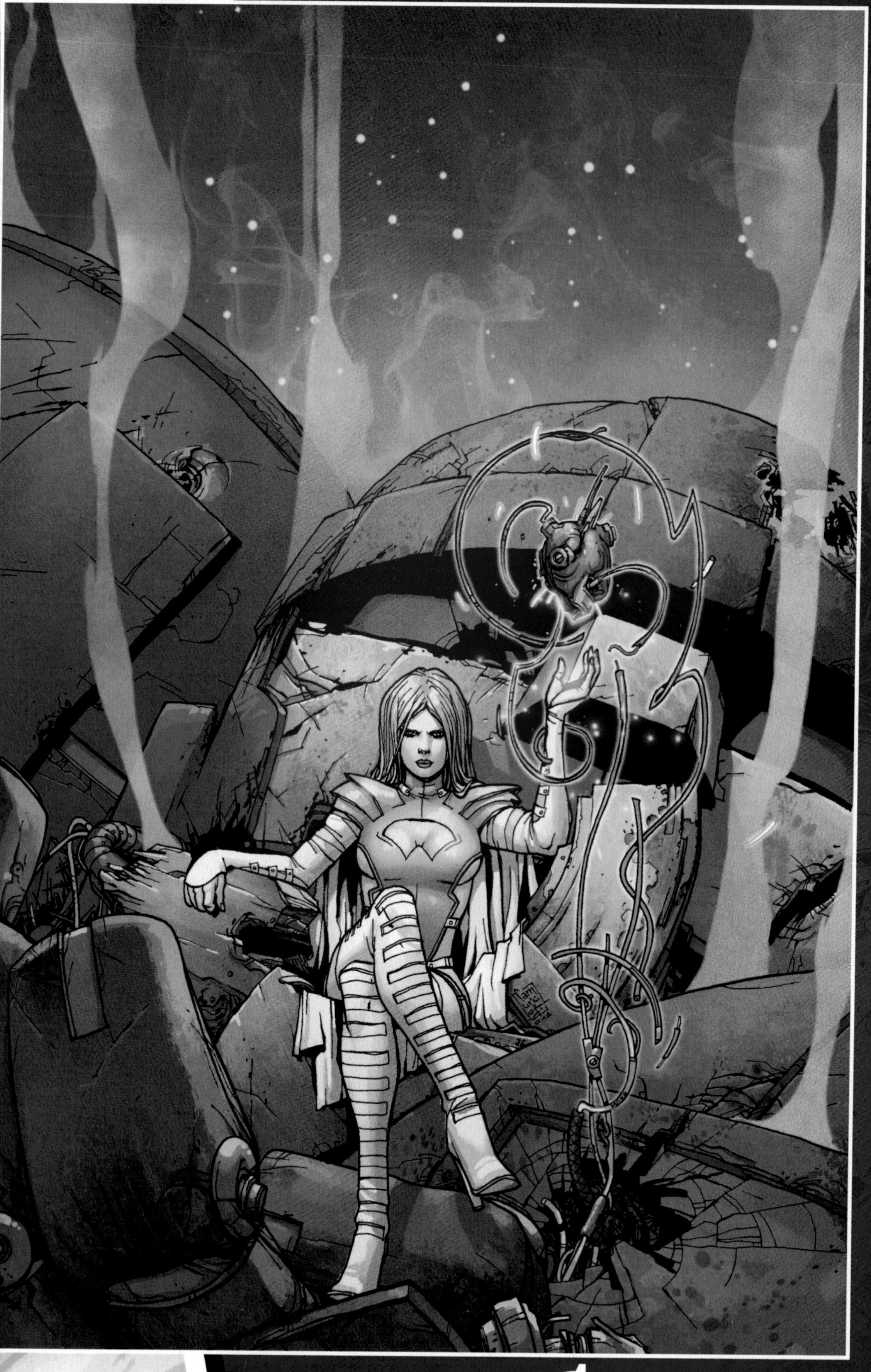

ISSUE #33

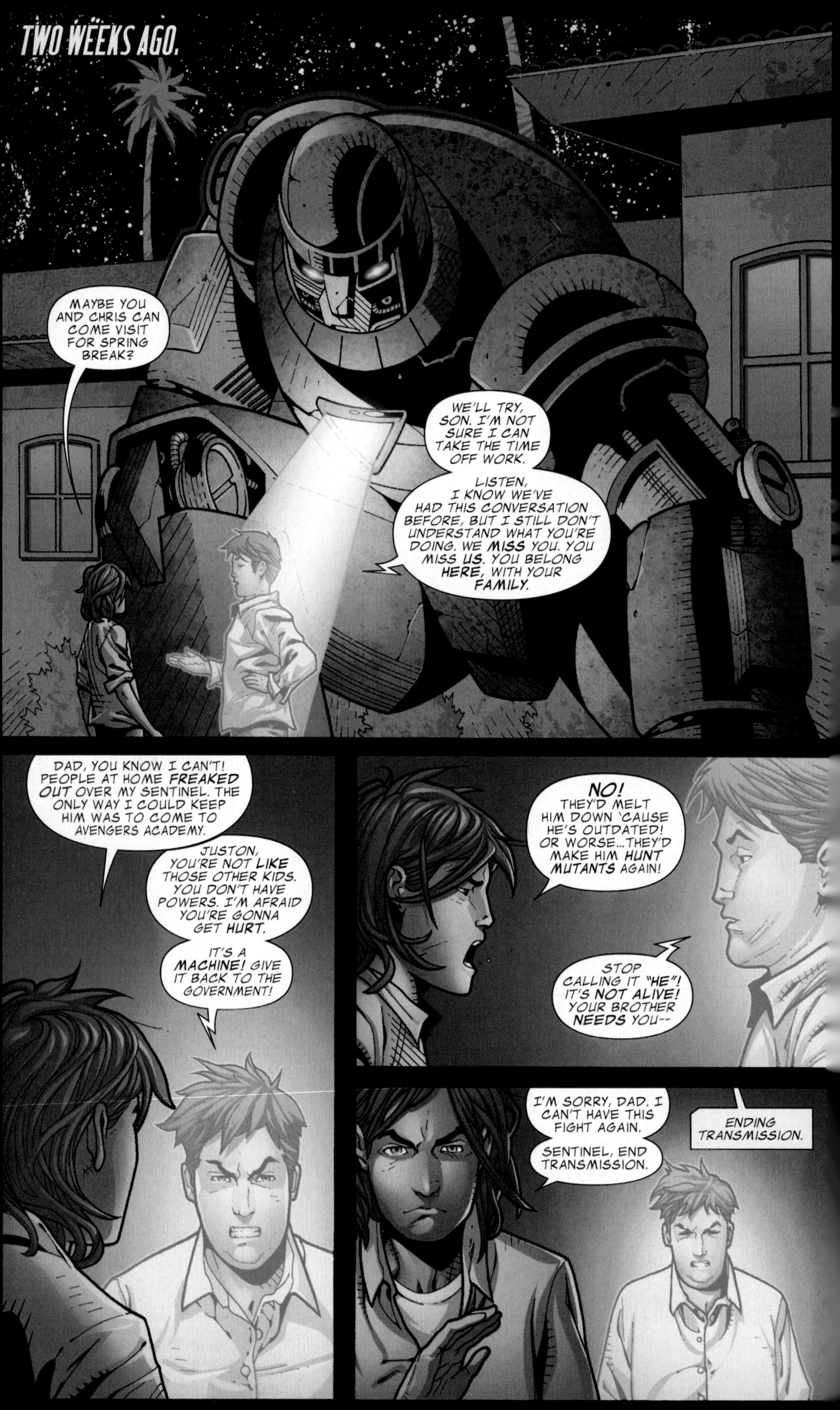
TWO WEEKS AGO.
MAYBE YOU AND CHRIS CAN COME VISIT FOR SPRING BREAK?
WE'LL TRY, SON. I'M NOT SURE I CAN TAKE THE TIME OFF WORK.
LISTEN, I KNOW WE'VE HAD THIS CONVERSATION BEFORE, BUT I STILL DON'T UNDERSTAND WHAT YOU'RE DOING. WE MISS YOU. YOU MISS US. YOU BELONG HERE, WITH YOUR FAMILY.
DAD, YOU KNOW I CAN'T! PEOPLE AT HOME FREAKED OUT OVER MY SENTINEL. THE ONLY WAY I COULD KEEP HIM WAS TO COME TO AVENGERS ACADEMY.
JUSTON, YOU'RE NOT LIKE THOSE OTHER KIDS. YOU DON'T HAVE POWERS. I'M AFRAID YOU'RE GONNA GET HURT.
IT'S A MACHINE! GIVE IT BACK TO THE GOVERNMENT!
NO! THEY'D MELT HIM DOWN 'CAUSE HE'S OUTDATED! OR WORSE...THEY'D MAKE HIM HUNT MUTANTS AGAIN!
STOP CALLING IT "HE"! IT'S NOT ALIVE! YOUR BROTHER NEEDS YOU--
I'M SORRY, DAD. I CAN'T HAVE THIS FIGHT AGAIN.
SENTINEL, END TRANSMISSION.
ENDING TRANSMISSION.

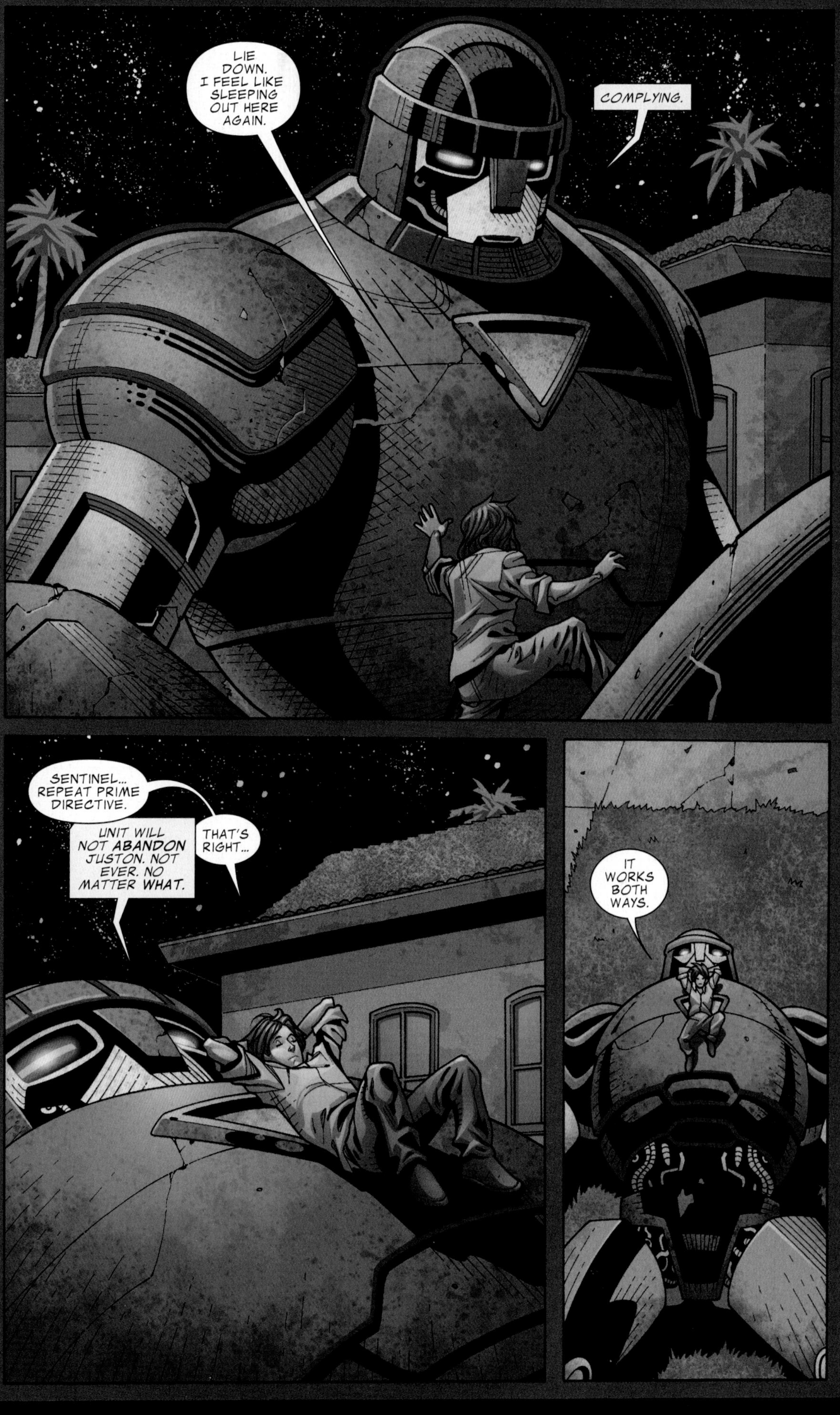
LIE DOWN. I FEEL LIKE SLEEPING OUT HERE AGAIN.
COMPLYING.
SENTINEL... REPEAT PRIME DIRECTIVE.
UNIT WILL NOT ABANDON JUSTON. NOT EVER. NO MATTER WHAT.
THAT'S RIGHT...
IT WORKS BOTH WAYS.

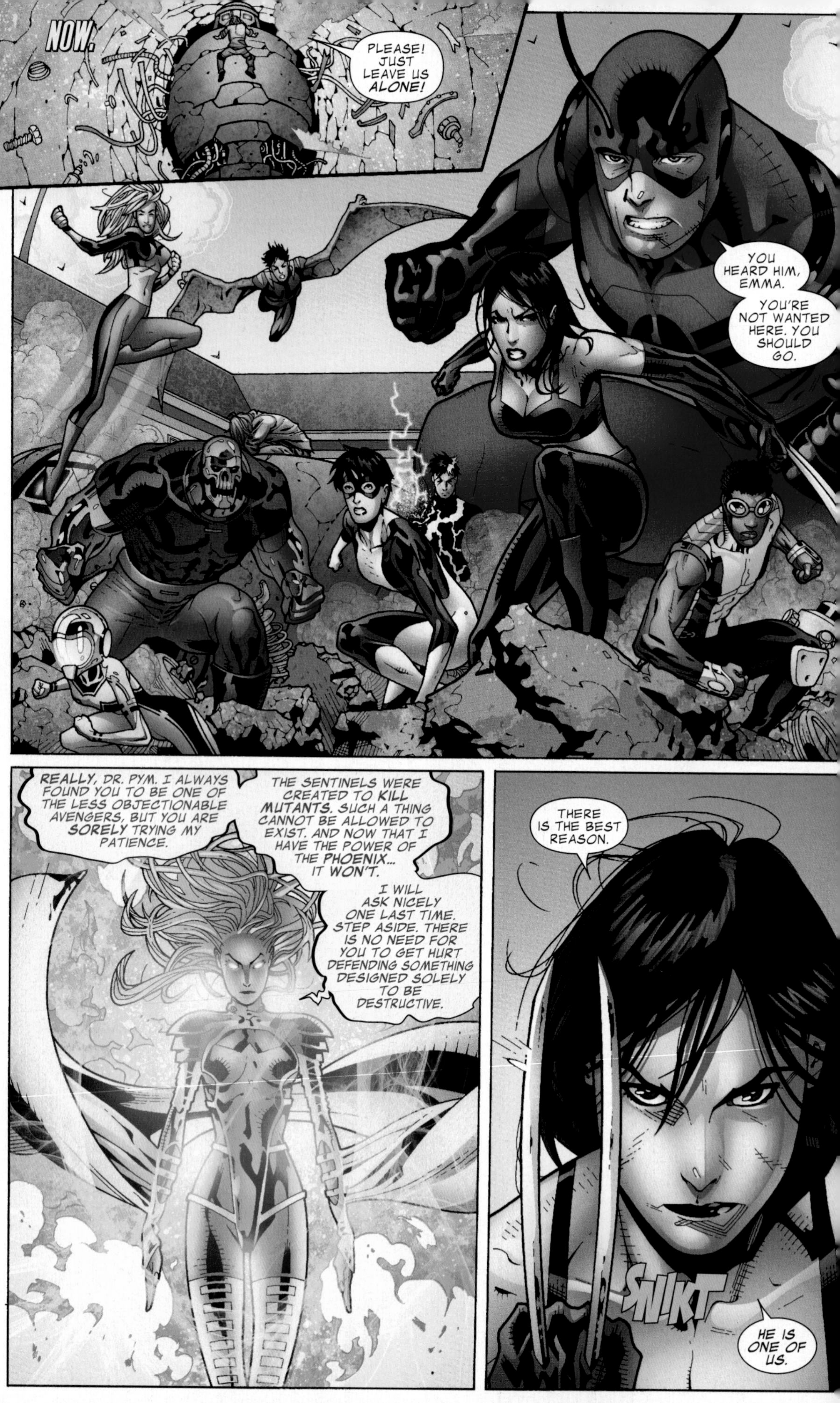
NOW.
PLEASE! JUST LEAVE US ALONE!
YOU HEARD HIM, EMMA.
YOU'RE NOT WANTED HERE. YOU SHOULD GO.
REALLY, DR. PYM. I ALWAYS FOUND YOU TO BE ONE OF THE LESS OBJECTIONABLE AVENGERS, BUT YOU ARE SORELY TRYING MY PATIENCE.
THE SENTINELS WERE CREATED TO KILL MUTANTS. SUCH A THING CANNOT BE ALLOWED TO EXIST. AND NOW THAT I HAVE THE POWER OF THE PHOENIX... IT WON'T.
I WILL ASK NICELY ONE LAST TIME. STEP ASIDE. THERE IS NO NEED FOR YOU TO GET HURT DEFENDING SOMETHING DESIGNED SOLELY TO BE DESTRUCTIVE.
THERE IS THE BEST REASON.
SNIKT
HE IS ONE OF US.

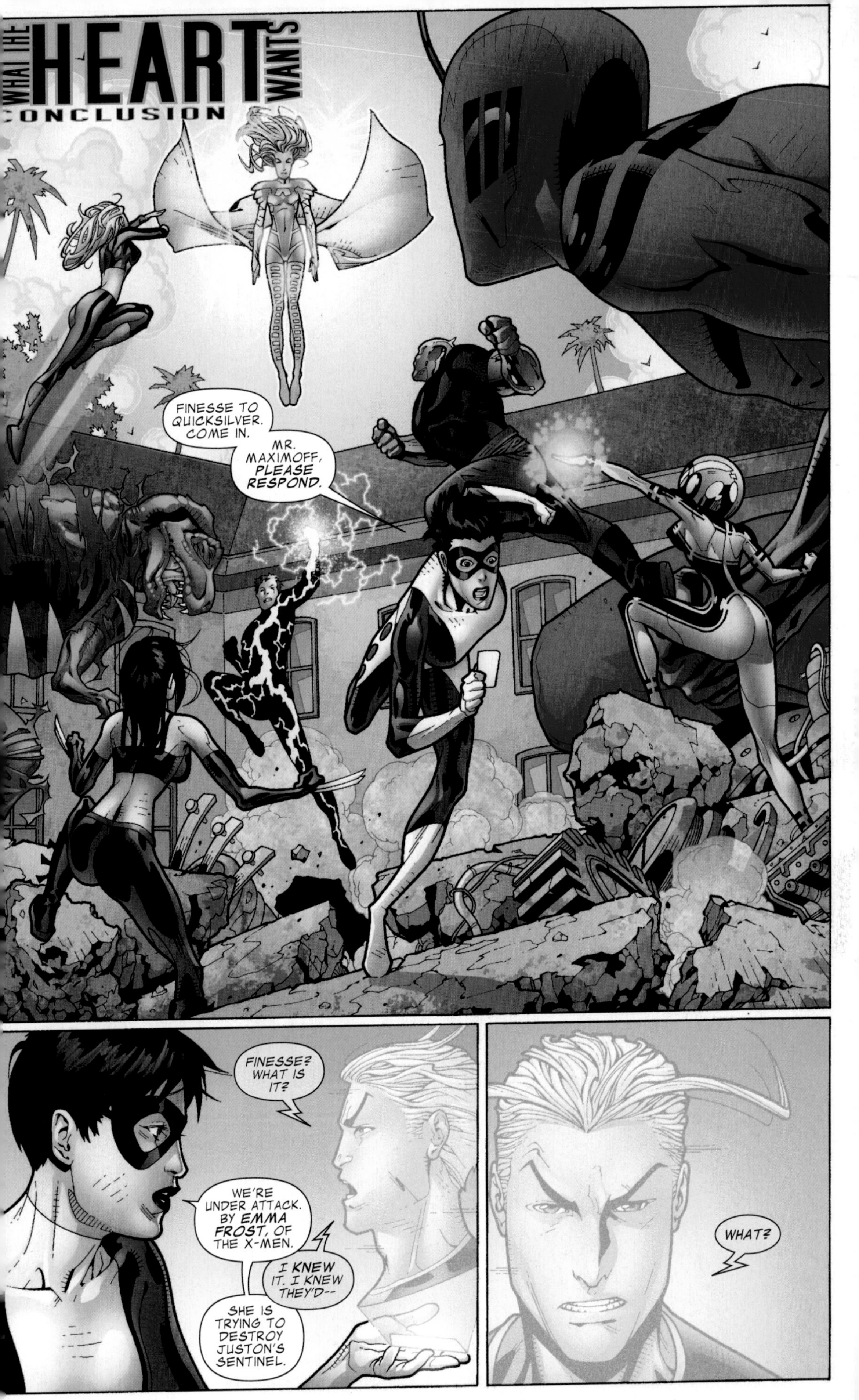
WHAT THE HEART WANTS
CONCLUSION
FINESSE TO QUICKSILVER. COME IN.
MR. MAXIMOFF, PLEASE RESPOND.
FINESSE? WHAT IS IT?
WE'RE UNDER ATTACK. BY EMMA FROST, OF THE X-MEN.
I KNEW IT. I KNEW THEY'D--
SHE IS TRYING TO DESTROY JUSTON'S SENTINEL.
WHAT?

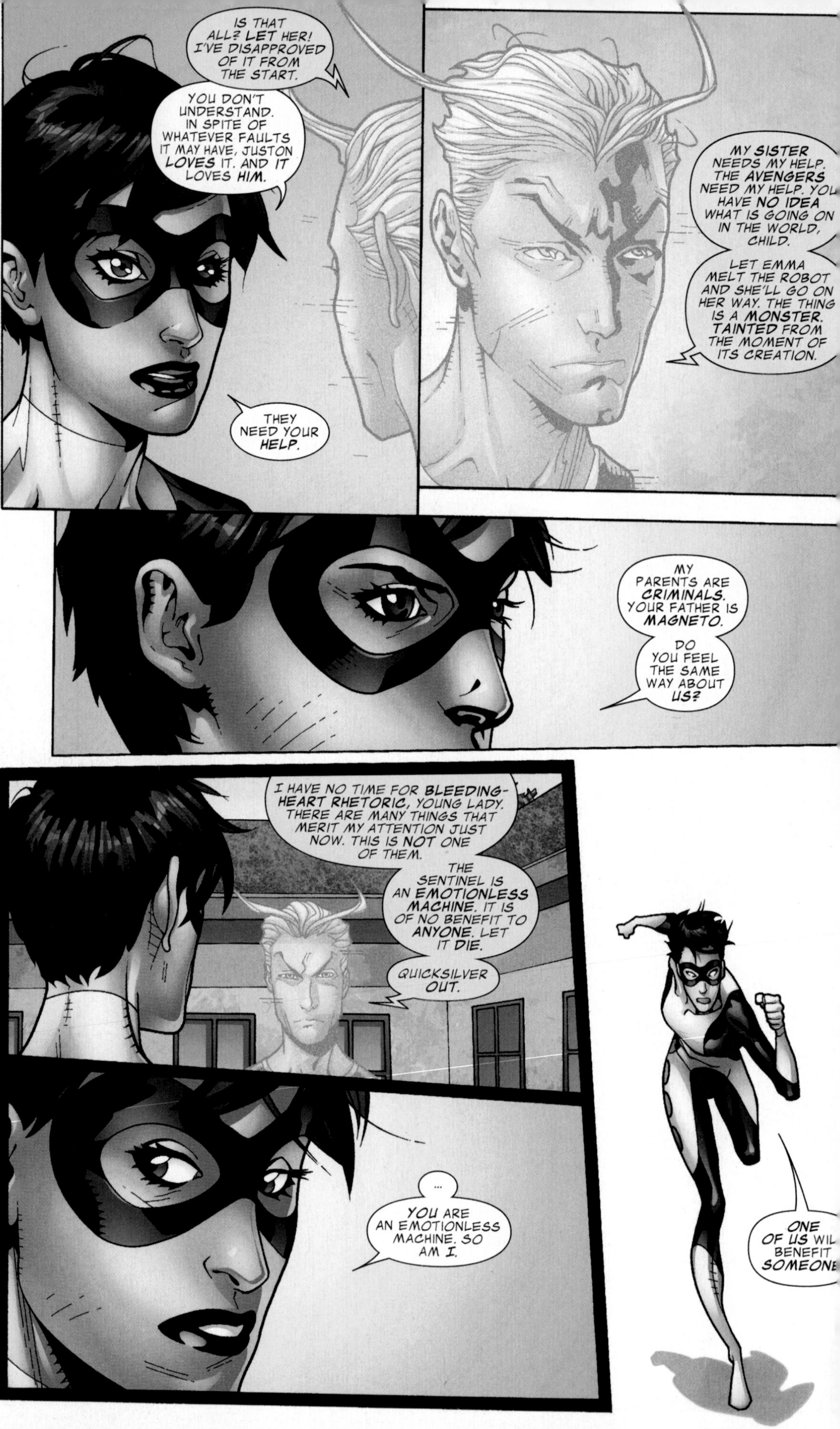
IS THAT ALL? LET HER! I'VE DISAPPROVED OF IT FROM THE START.
YOU DON'T UNDERSTAND. IN SPITE OF WHATEVER FAULTS IT MAY HAVE, JUSTON LOVES IT. AND IT LOVES HIM.
THEY NEED YOUR HELP.
MY SISTER NEEDS MY HELP. THE AVENGERS NEED MY HELP. YOU HAVE NO IDEA WHAT IS GOING ON IN THE WORLD, CHILD.
LET EMMA MELT THE ROBOT AND SHE'LL GO ON HER WAY. THE THING IS A MONSTER. TAINTED FROM THE MOMENT OF ITS CREATION.
MY PARENTS ARE CRIMINALS. YOUR FATHER IS MAGNETO.
DO YOU FEEL THE SAME WAY ABOUT US?
I HAVE NO TIME FOR BLEEDING-HEART RHETORIC, YOUNG LADY. THERE ARE MANY THINGS THAT MERIT MY ATTENTION JUST NOW. THIS IS NOT ONE OF THEM.
THE SENTINEL IS AN EMOTIONLESS MACHINE. IT IS OF NO BENEFIT TO ANYONE. LET IT DIE.
QUICKSILVER OUT.
...
YOU ARE AN EMOTIONLESS MACHINE. SO AM I.
ONE OF US WIL BENEFIT SOMEONE

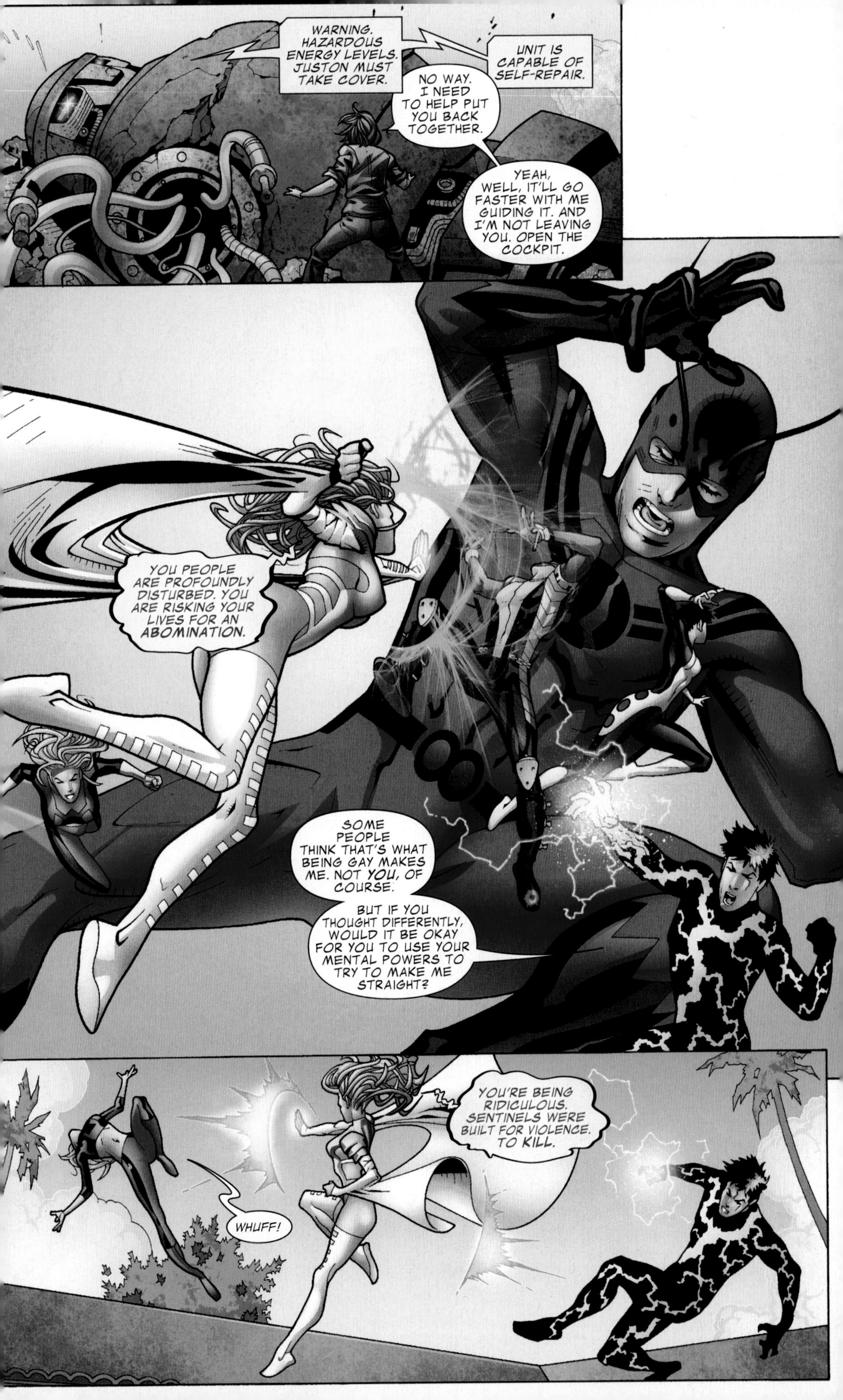
WARNING. HAZARDOUS ENERGY LEVELS. JUSTON MUST TAKE COVER.
NO WAY. I NEED TO HELP PUT YOU BACK TOGETHER.
UNIT IS CAPABLE OF SELF-REPAIR.
YEAH, WELL, IT'LL GO FASTER WITH ME GUIDING IT. AND I'M NOT LEAVING YOU. OPEN THE COCKPIT.
YOU PEOPLE ARE PROFOUNDLY DISTURBED. YOU ARE RISKING YOUR LIVES FOR AN ABOMINATION.
SOME PEOPLE THINK THAT'S WHAT BEING GAY MAKES ME. NOT YOU, OF COURSE.
BUT IF YOU THOUGHT DIFFERENTLY, WOULD IT BE OKAY FOR YOU TO USE YOUR MENTAL POWERS TO TRY TO MAKE ME STRAIGHT?
YOU'RE BEING RIDICULOUS. SENTINELS WERE BUILT FOR VIOLENCE. TO KILL.
WHUFF!

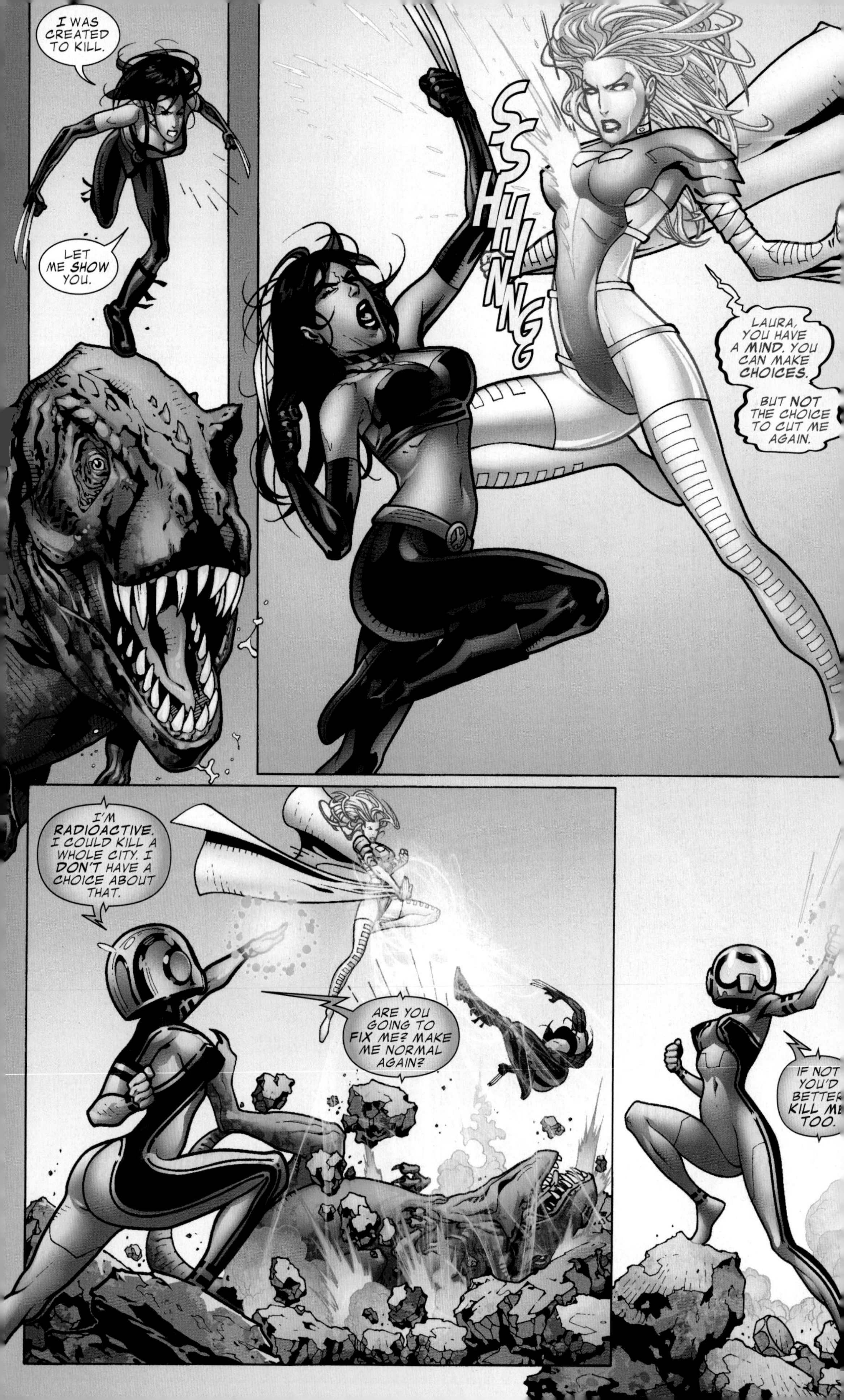
I WAS CREATED TO KILL.
LET ME SHOW YOU.
SHHHIINNGG
LAURA, YOU HAVE A MIND. YOU CAN MAKE CHOICES.
BUT NOT THE CHOICE TO CUT ME AGAIN.
I'M RADIOACTIVE. I COULD KILL A WHOLE CITY. I DON'T HAVE A CHOICE ABOUT THAT.
ARE YOU GOING TO FIX ME? MAKE ME NORMAL AGAIN?
IF NOT YOU'D BETTER KILL ME TOO.

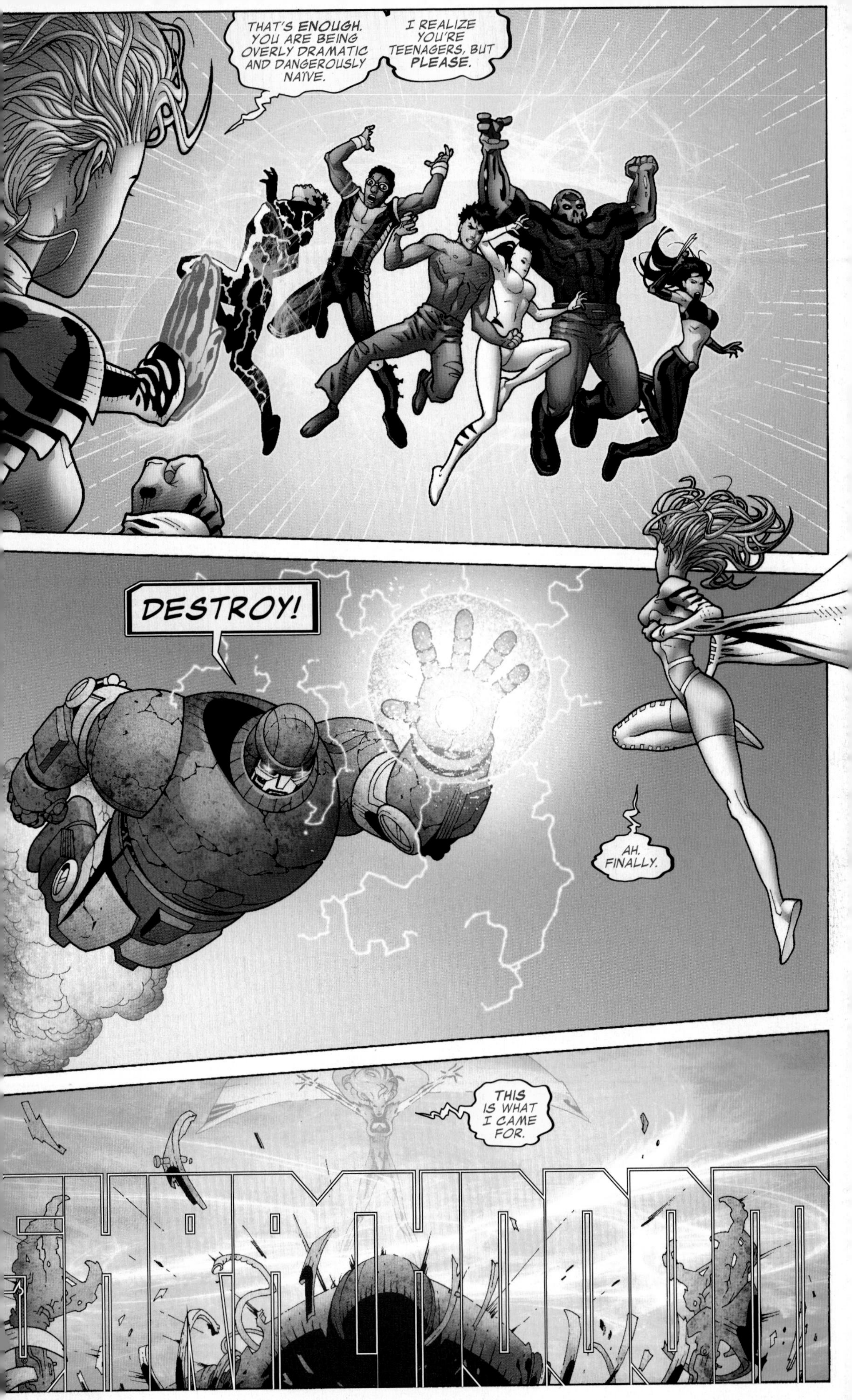
THAT'S ENOUGH. YOU ARE BEING OVERLY DRAMATIC AND DANGEROUSLY NAÏVE.
I REALIZE YOU'RE TEENAGERS, BUT PLEASE.
DESTROY!
AH. FINALLY.
THIS IS WHAT I CAME FOR.

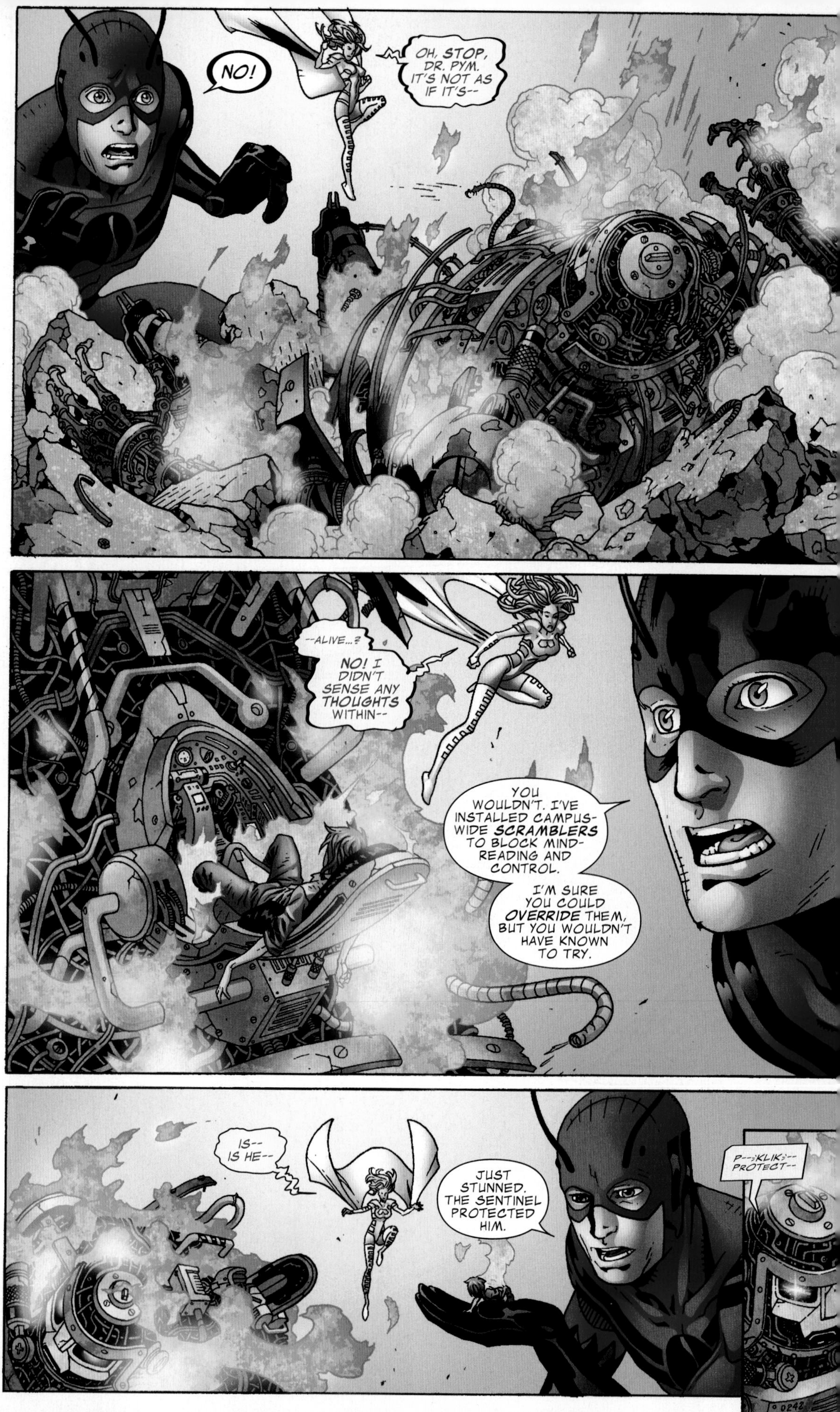
NO!
OH, STOP, DR. PYM. IT'S NOT AS IF IT'S--
--ALIVE...?
NO! I DIDN'T SENSE ANY THOUGHTS WITHIN--
YOU WOULDN'T. I'VE INSTALLED CAMPUS-WIDE SCRAMBLERS TO BLOCK MIND-READING AND CONTROL.
I'M SURE YOU COULD OVERRIDE THEM, BUT YOU WOULDN'T HAVE KNOWN TO TRY.
IS-- IS HE--
JUST STUNNED. THE SENTINEL PROTECTED HIM.
P--KLIK--PROTECT--

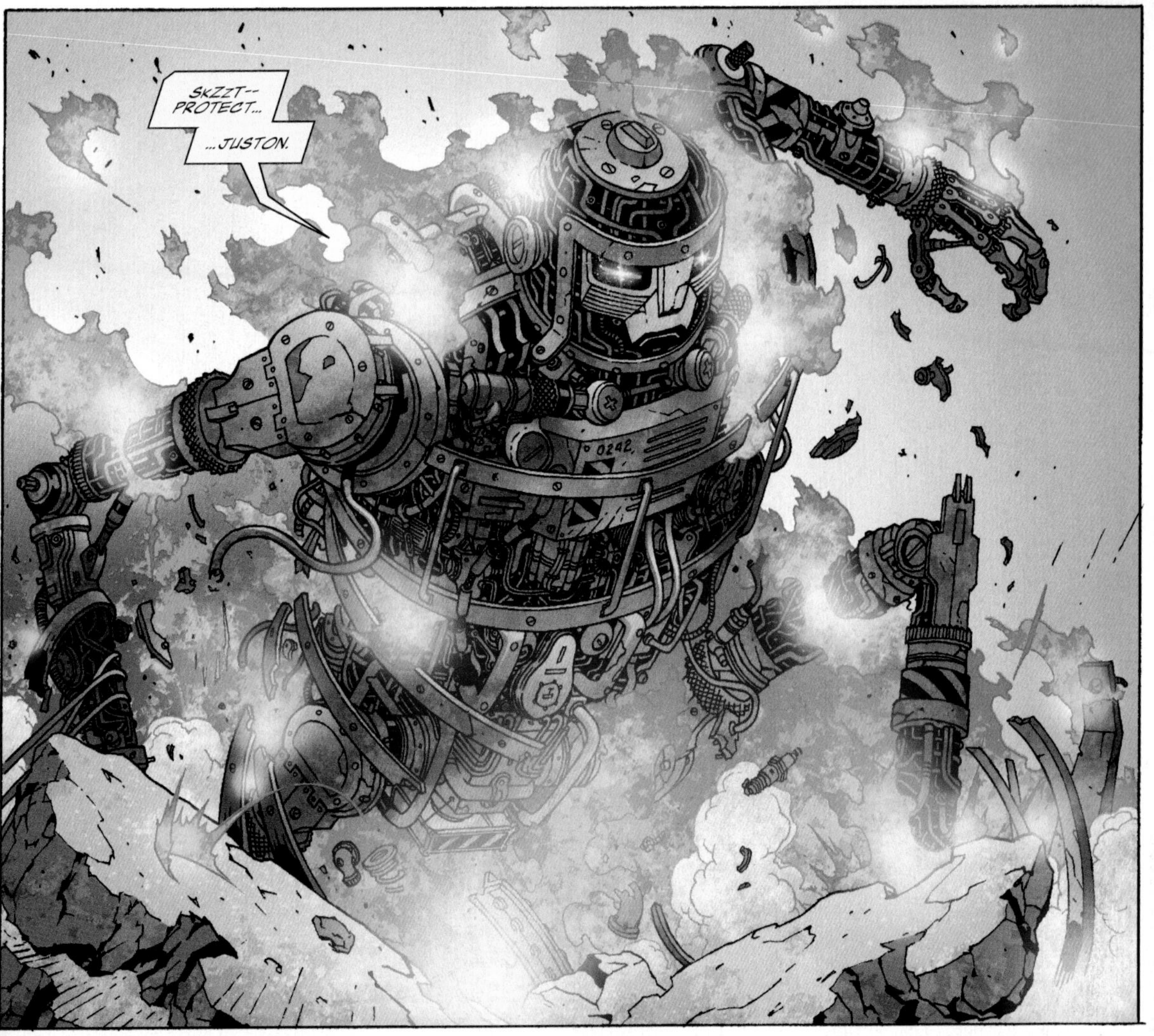
SKZZT--
PROTECT...
...JUSTON.

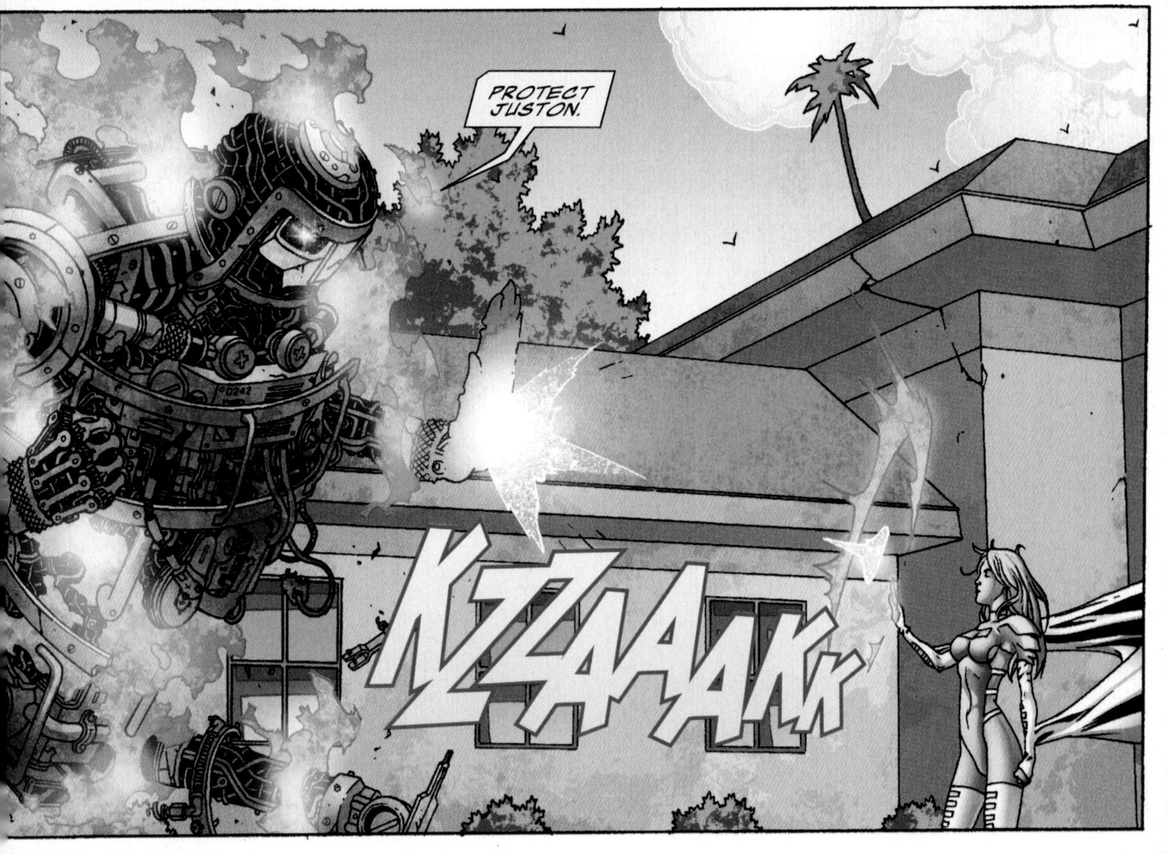
PROTECT
JUSTON.
KZAAAKK

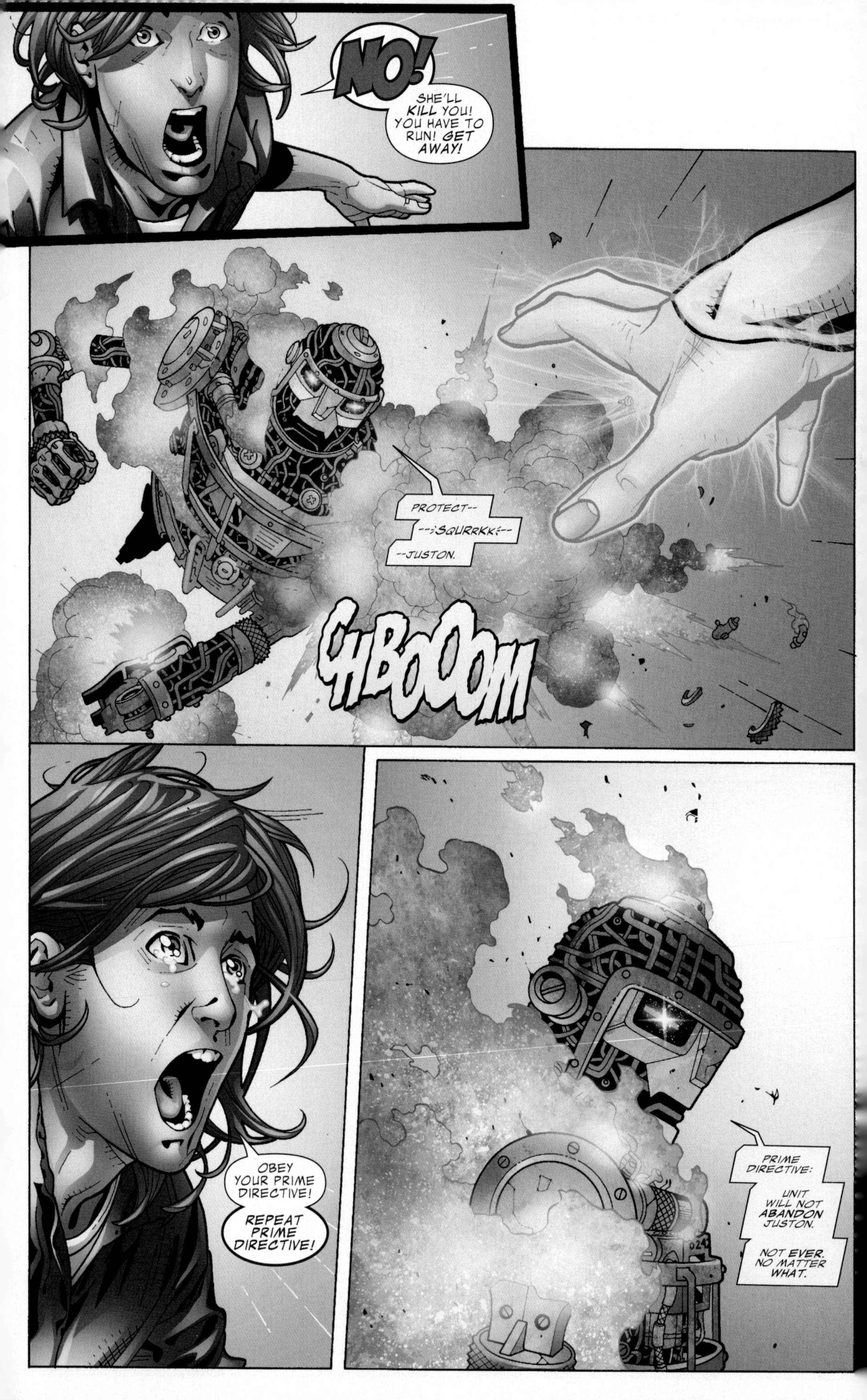

NO!
SHE'LL KILL YOU! YOU HAVE TO RUN! GET AWAY!
PROTECT--
--;SQURRKK;--
--JUSTON.
CHBOOOM
OBEY YOUR PRIME DIRECTIVE!
REPEAT PRIME DIRECTIVE!
PRIME DIRECTIVE:
UNIT WILL NOT ABANDON JUSTON.
NOT EVER. NO MATTER WHAT.

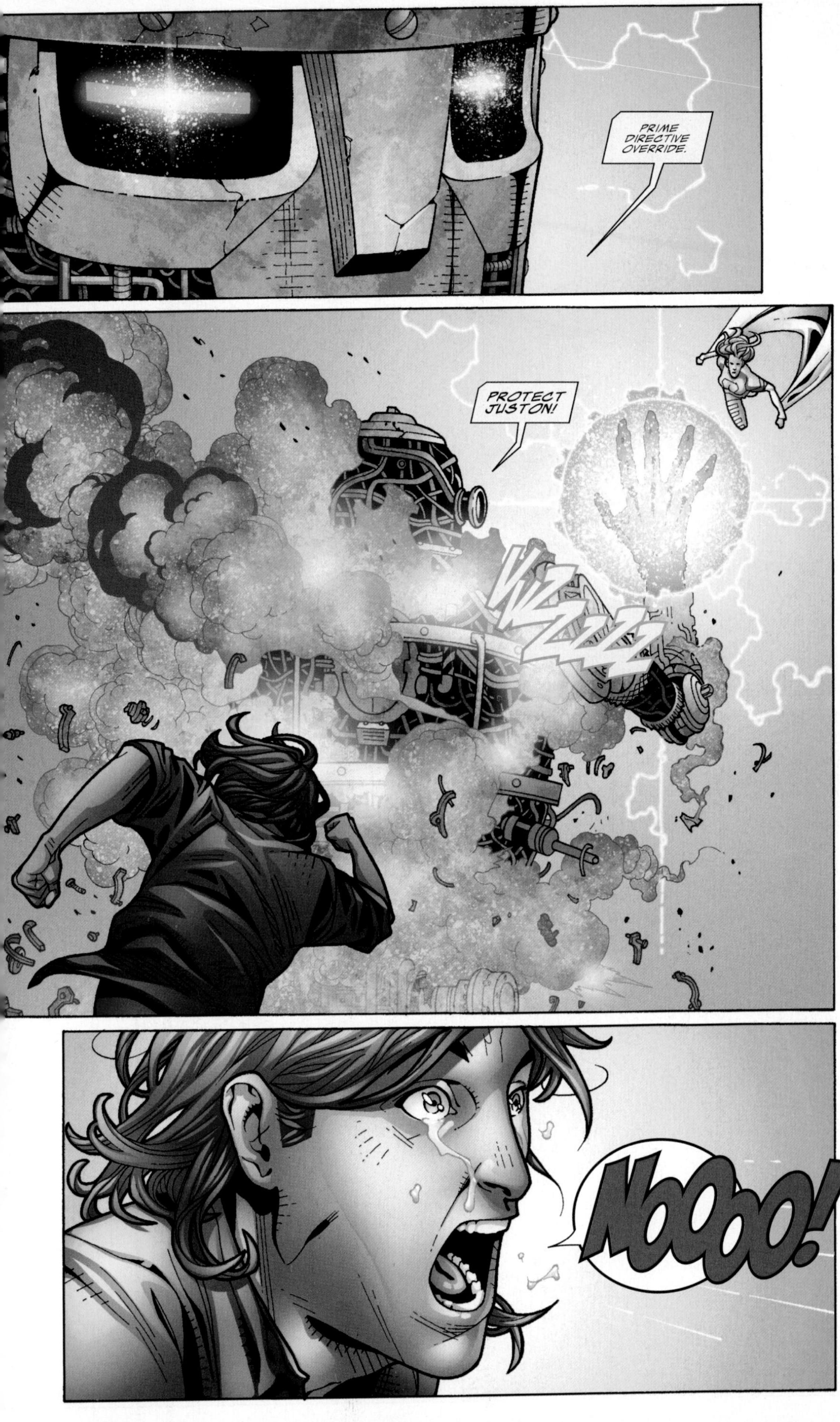
PRIME DIRECTIVE OVERRIDE.
PROTECT JUSTON!
VVZZZZ
NOOOO!

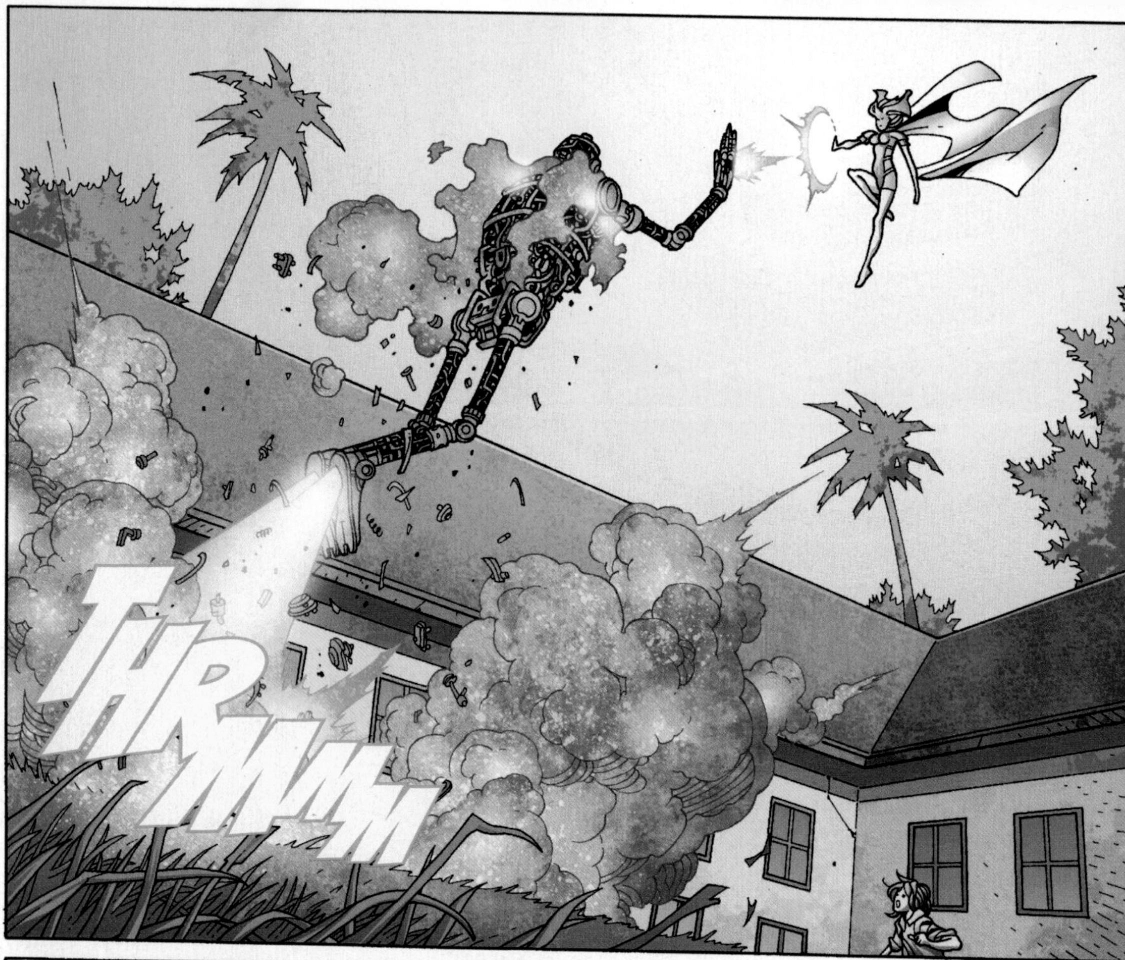
THRMMM

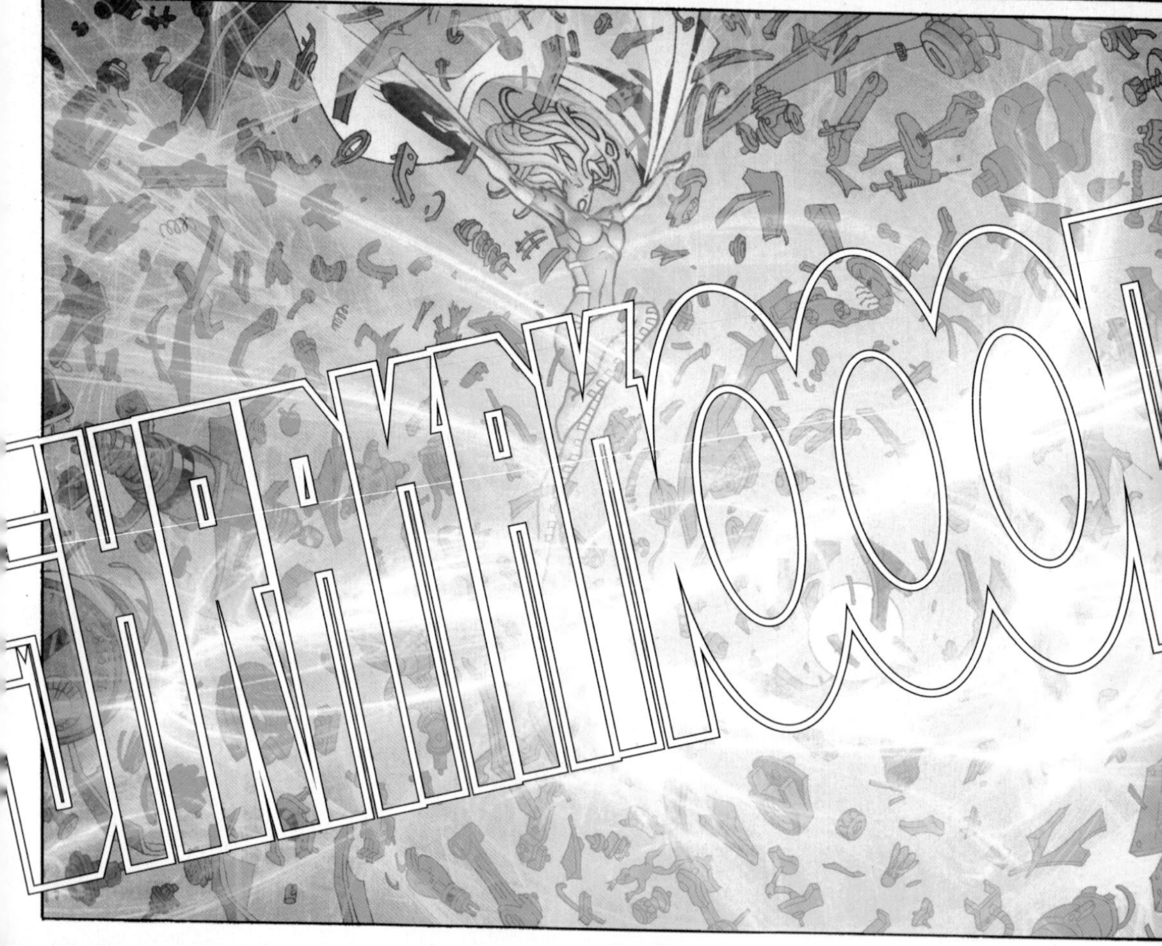

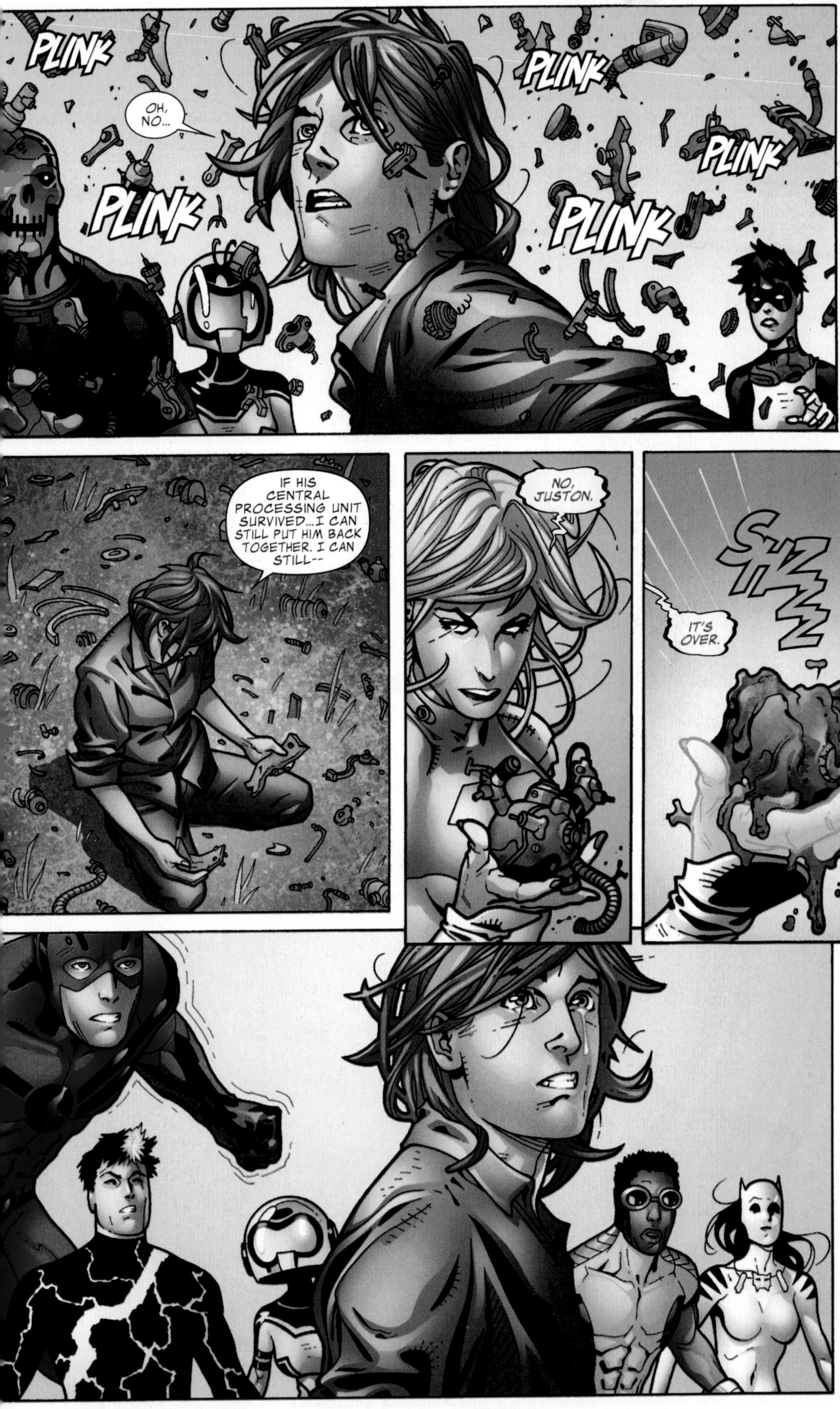
PLINK
OH, NO...
PLINK
PLINK
PLINK
PLINK
IF HIS CENTRAL PROCESSING UNIT SURVIVED...I CAN STILL PUT HIM BACK TOGETHER. I CAN STILL--
NO, JUSTON.
SHZZZ
IT'S OVER.

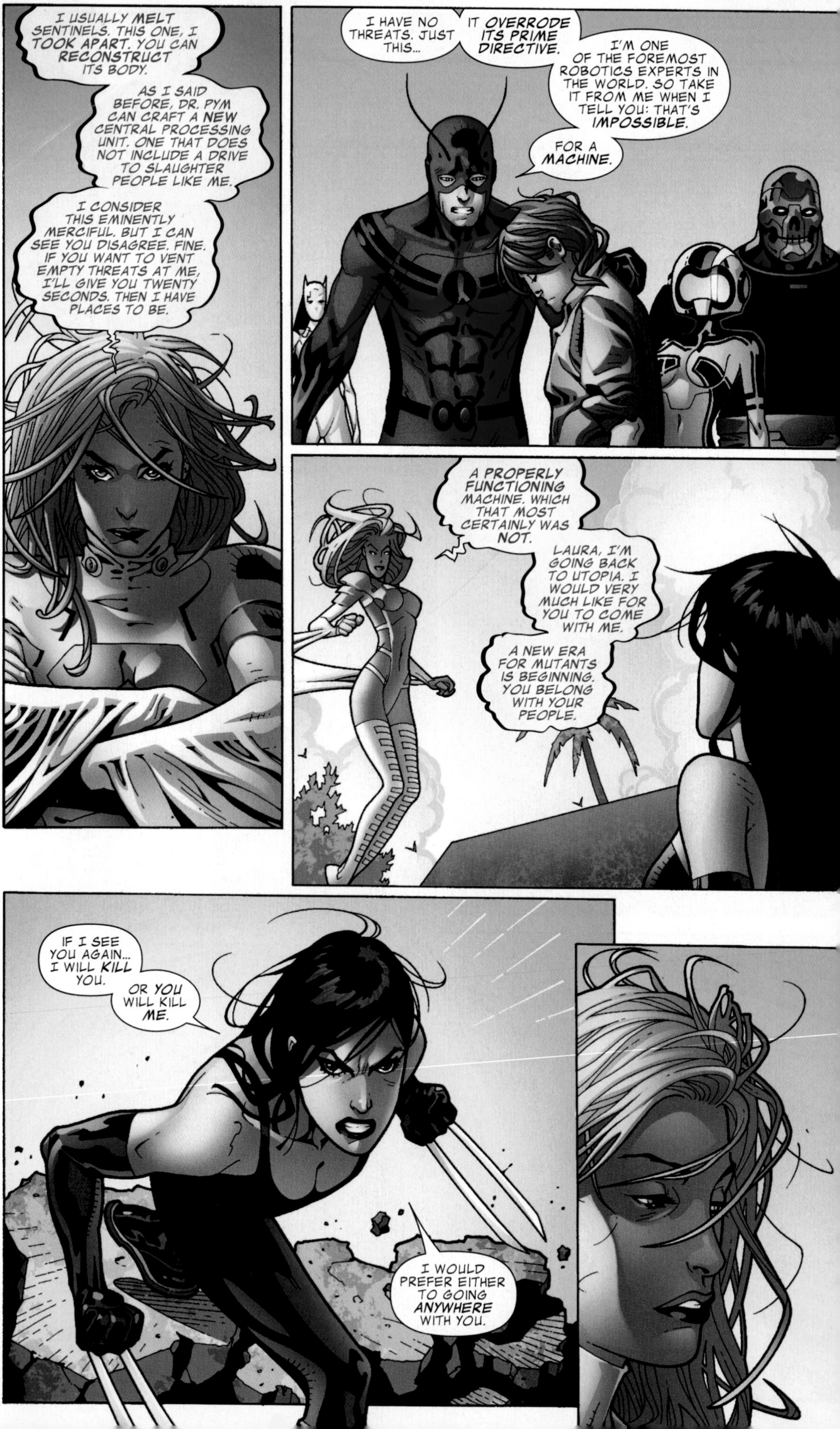
I USUALLY MELT SENTINELS. THIS ONE, I TOOK APART. YOU CAN RECONSTRUCT ITS BODY.
AS I SAID BEFORE, DR. PYM CAN CRAFT A NEW CENTRAL PROCESSING UNIT. ONE THAT DOES NOT INCLUDE A DRIVE TO SLAUGHTER PEOPLE LIKE ME.
I CONSIDER THIS EMINENTLY MERCIFUL. BUT I CAN SEE YOU DISAGREE. FINE. IF YOU WANT TO VENT EMPTY THREATS AT ME, I'LL GIVE YOU TWENTY SECONDS. THEN I HAVE PLACES TO BE.
I HAVE NO THREATS. JUST THIS...
IT OVERRODE ITS PRIME DIRECTIVE.
I'M ONE OF THE FOREMOST ROBOTICS EXPERTS IN THE WORLD. SO TAKE IT FROM ME WHEN I TELL YOU: THAT'S IMPOSSIBLE.
FOR A MACHINE.
A PROPERLY FUNCTIONING MACHINE. WHICH THAT MOST CERTAINLY WAS NOT.
LAURA, I'M GOING BACK TO UTOPIA. I WOULD VERY MUCH LIKE FOR YOU TO COME WITH ME.
A NEW ERA FOR MUTANTS IS BEGINNING. YOU BELONG WITH YOUR PEOPLE.
IF I SEE YOU AGAIN... I WILL KILL YOU.
OR YOU WILL KILL ME.
I WOULD PREFER EITHER TO GOING ANYWHERE WITH YOU.

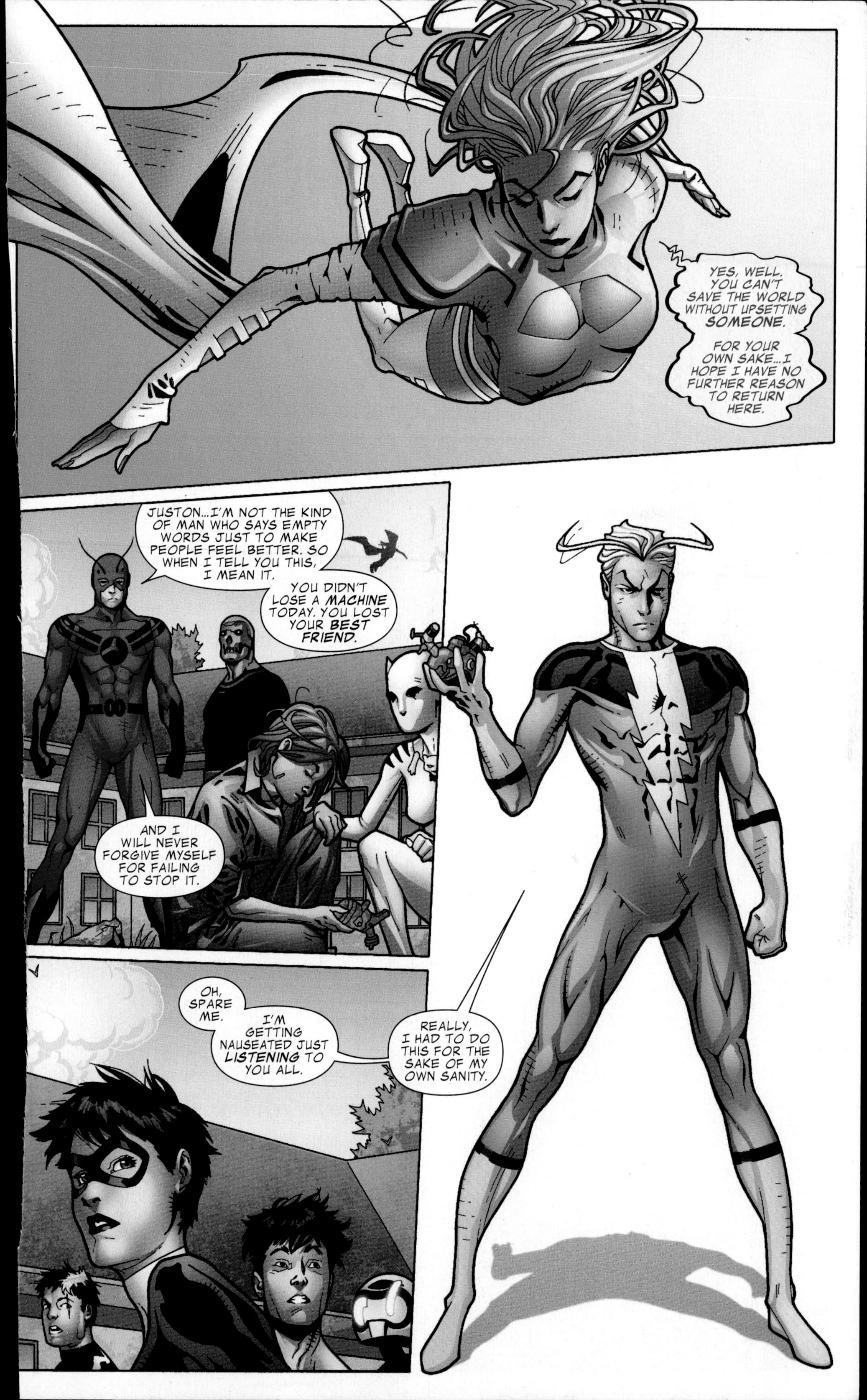
YES, WELL. YOU CAN'T SAVE THE WORLD WITHOUT UPSETTING SOMEONE.
FOR YOUR OWN SAKE...I HOPE I HAVE NO FURTHER REASON TO RETURN HERE.
JUSTON...I'M NOT THE KIND OF MAN WHO SAYS EMPTY WORDS JUST TO MAKE PEOPLE FEEL BETTER. SO WHEN I TELL YOU THIS, I MEAN IT.
YOU DIDN'T LOSE A MACHINE TODAY. YOU LOST YOUR BEST FRIEND.
AND I WILL NEVER FORGIVE MYSELF FOR FAILING TO STOP IT.
OH, SPARE ME.
I'M GETTING NAUSEATED JUST LISTENING TO YOU ALL.
REALLY, I HAD TO DO THIS FOR THE SAKE OF MY OWN SANITY.

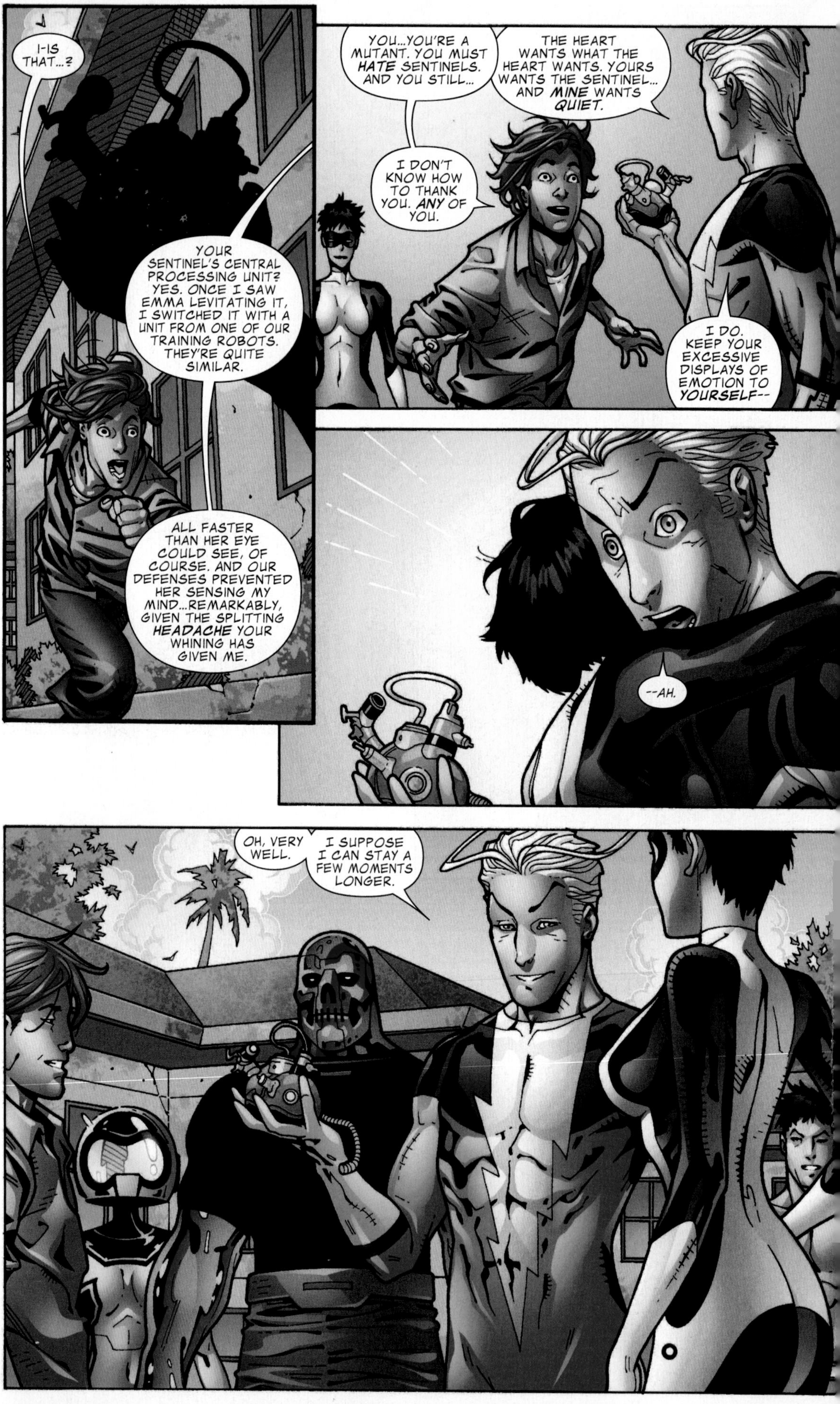
I-IS THAT...?
YOUR SENTINEL'S CENTRAL PROCESSING UNIT? YES. ONCE I SAW EMMA LEVITATING IT, I SWITCHED IT WITH A UNIT FROM ONE OF OUR TRAINING ROBOTS. THEY'RE QUITE SIMILAR.
ALL FASTER THAN HER EYE COULD SEE, OF COURSE. AND OUR DEFENSES PREVENTED HER SENSING MY MIND...REMARKABLY, GIVEN THE SPLITTING HEADACHE YOUR WHINING HAS GIVEN ME.
YOU...YOU'RE A MUTANT. YOU MUST HATE SENTINELS. AND YOU STILL...
THE HEART WANTS WHAT THE HEART WANTS. YOURS WANTS THE SENTINEL... AND MINE WANTS QUIET.
I DON'T KNOW HOW TO THANK YOU. ANY OF YOU.
I DO. KEEP YOUR EXCESSIVE DISPLAYS OF EMOTION TO YOURSELF--
--AH.
OH, VERY WELL.
I SUPPOSE I CAN STAY A FEW MOMENTS LONGER.

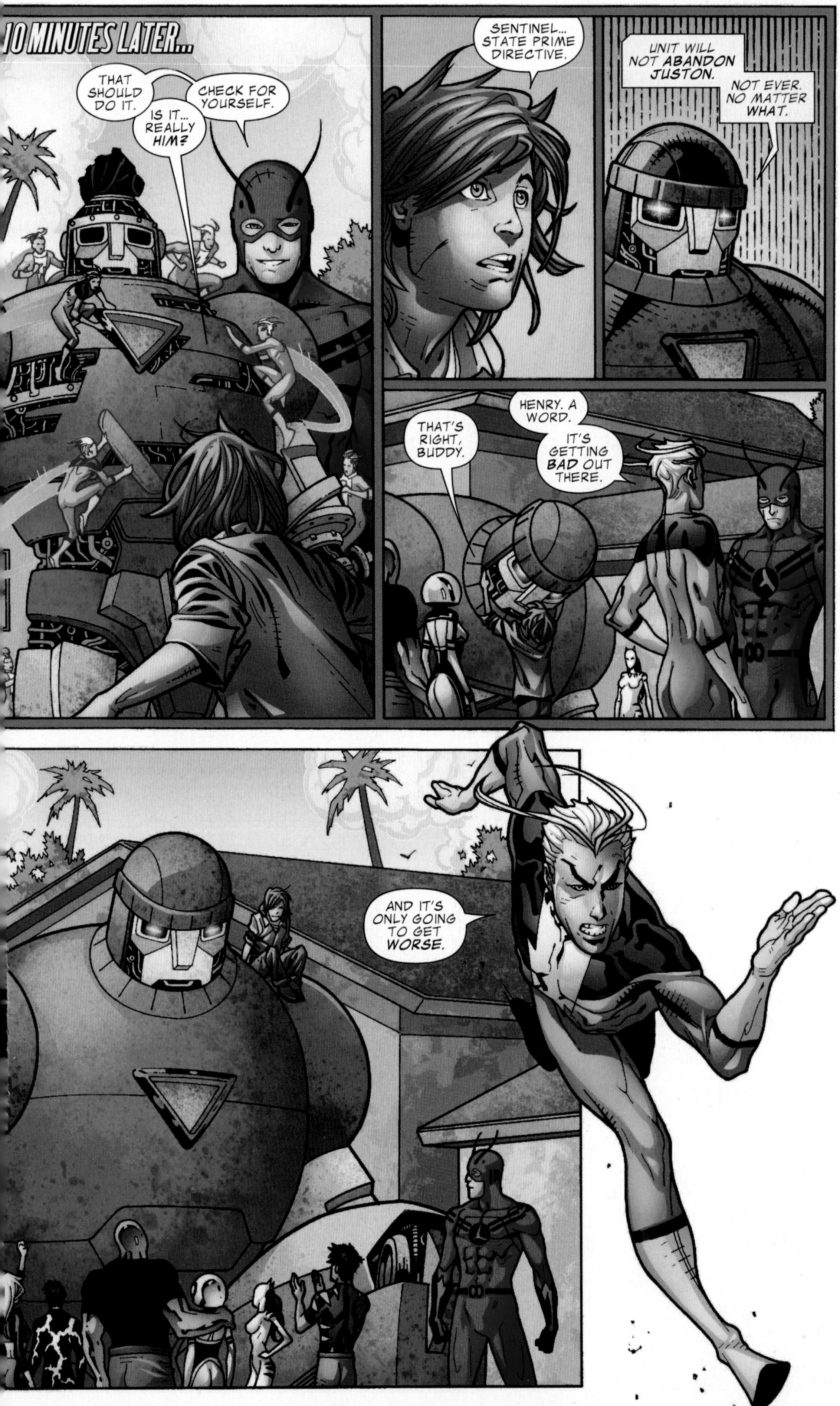
10 MINUTES LATER...
THAT SHOULD DO IT.
CHECK FOR YOURSELF.
IS IT... REALLY HIM?
SENTINEL... STATE PRIME DIRECTIVE.
UNIT WILL NOT ABANDON JUSTON.
NOT EVER. NO MATTER WHAT.
THAT'S RIGHT, BUDDY.
HENRY. A WORD.
IT'S GETTING BAD OUT THERE.
AND IT'S ONLY GOING TO GET WORSE.

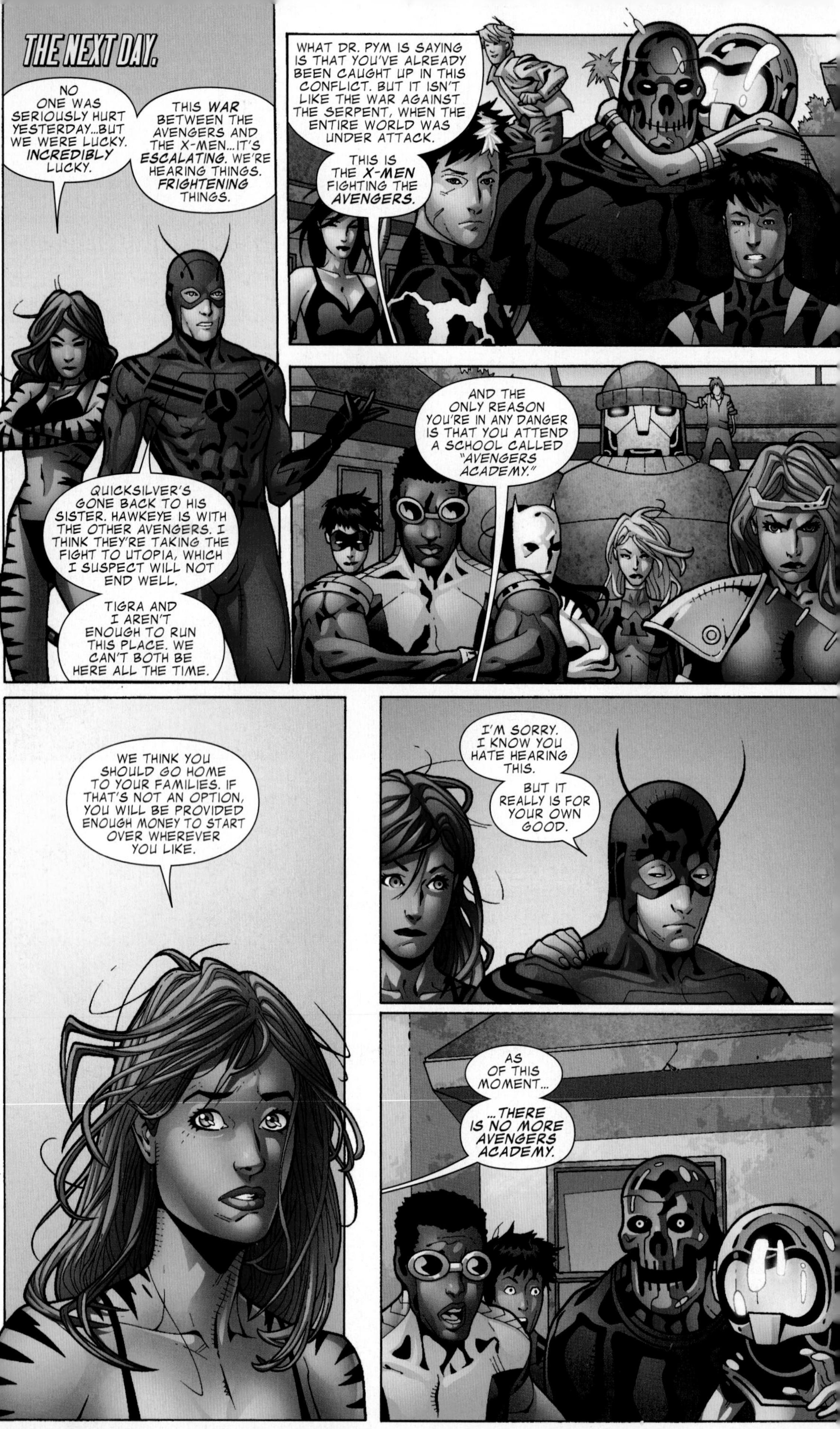
THE NEXT DAY.
NO ONE WAS SERIOUSLY HURT YESTERDAY...BUT WE WERE LUCKY. INCREDIBLY LUCKY.
THIS WAR BETWEEN THE AVENGERS AND THE X-MEN...IT'S ESCALATING. WE'RE HEARING THINGS. FRIGHTENING THINGS.
WHAT DR. PYM IS SAYING IS THAT YOU'VE ALREADY BEEN CAUGHT UP IN THIS CONFLICT. BUT IT ISN'T LIKE THE WAR AGAINST THE SERPENT, WHEN THE ENTIRE WORLD WAS UNDER ATTACK.
THIS IS THE X-MEN FIGHTING THE AVENGERS.
AND THE ONLY REASON YOU'RE IN ANY DANGER IS THAT YOU ATTEND A SCHOOL CALLED "AVENGERS ACADEMY."
QUICKSILVER'S GONE BACK TO HIS SISTER. HAWKEYE IS WITH THE OTHER AVENGERS. I THINK THEY'RE TAKING THE FIGHT TO UTOPIA, WHICH I SUSPECT WILL NOT END WELL.
TIGRA AND I AREN'T ENOUGH TO RUN THIS PLACE. WE CAN'T BOTH BE HERE ALL THE TIME.
WE THINK YOU SHOULD GO HOME TO YOUR FAMILIES. IF THAT'S NOT AN OPTION, YOU WILL BE PROVIDED ENOUGH MONEY TO START OVER WHEREVER YOU LIKE.
I'M SORRY. I KNOW YOU HATE HEARING THIS.
BUT IT REALLY IS FOR YOUR OWN GOOD.
AS OF THIS MOMENT...
...THERE IS NO MORE AVENGERS ACADEMY.

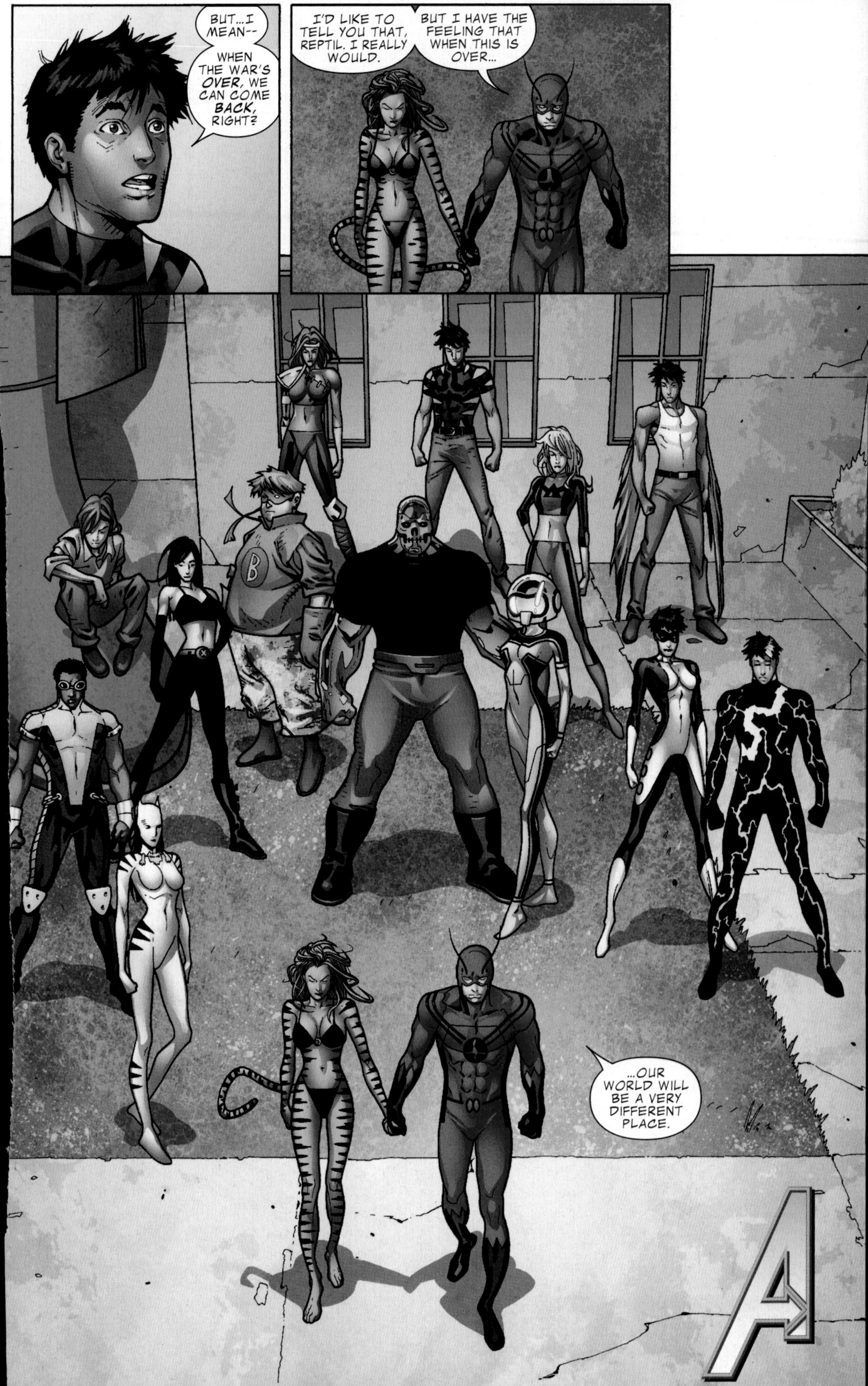

BUT...I MEAN--
WHEN THE WAR'S OVER, WE CAN COME BACK, RIGHT?
I'D LIKE TO TELL YOU THAT, REPTIL. I REALLY WOULD.
BUT I HAVE THE FEELING THAT WHEN THIS IS OVER...
...OUR WORLD WILL BE A VERY DIFFERENT PLACE.

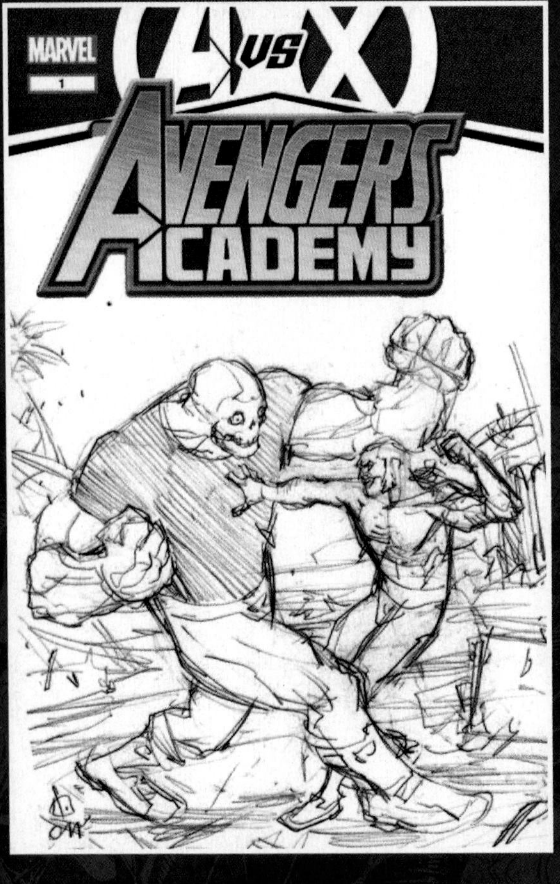
MARVEL
1
AVS X
AVENGERS ACADEMY

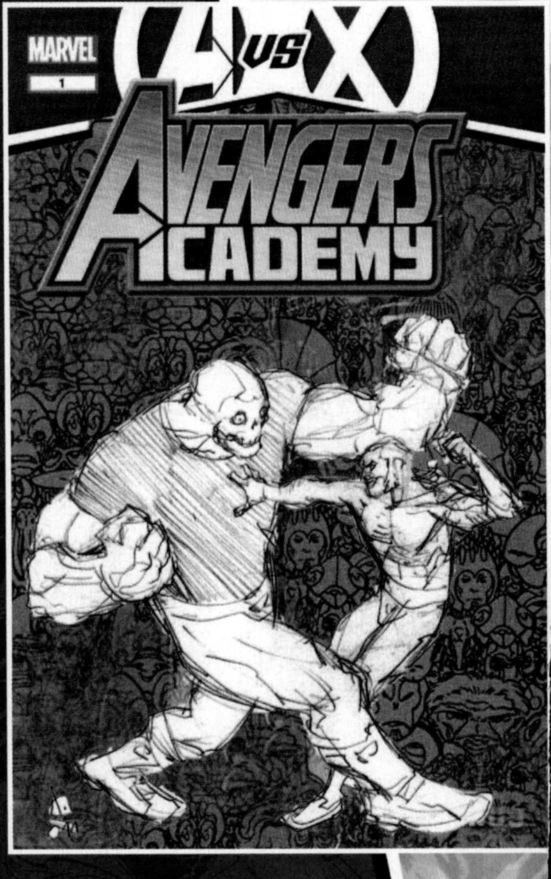
MARVEL
1
AVS X
AVENGERS ACADEMY

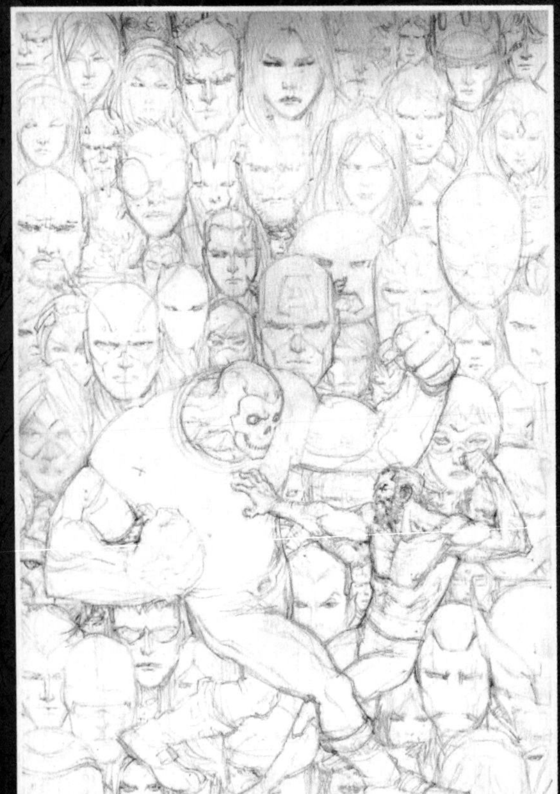

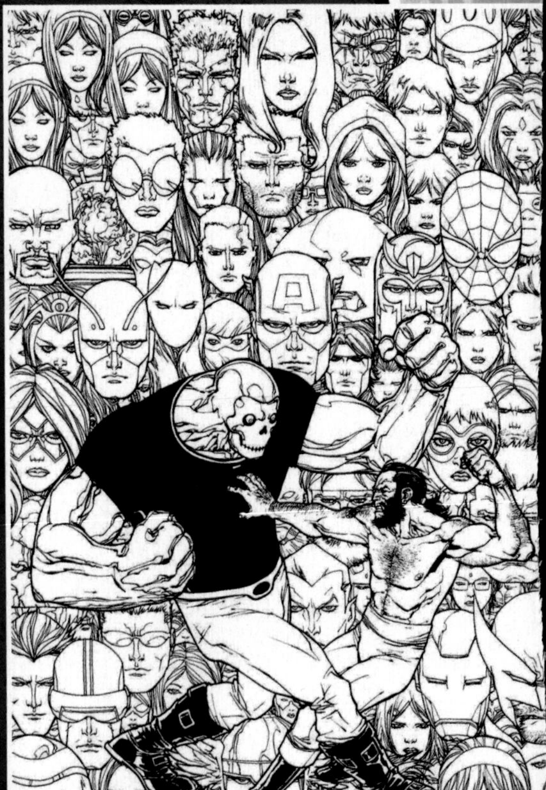

#30 COVER PROCESS

SKETCHES, PENCILS AND INKS BY **GIUSEPPE CAMUNCOLI**

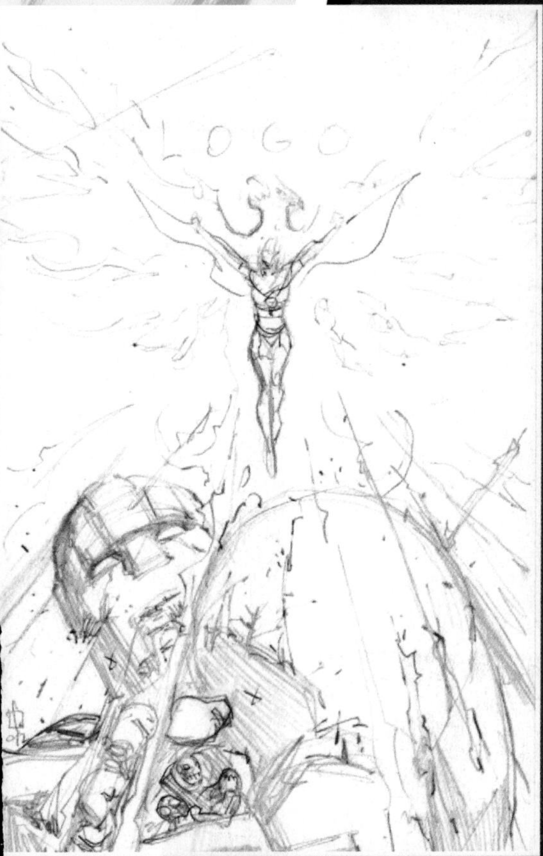
LOGO

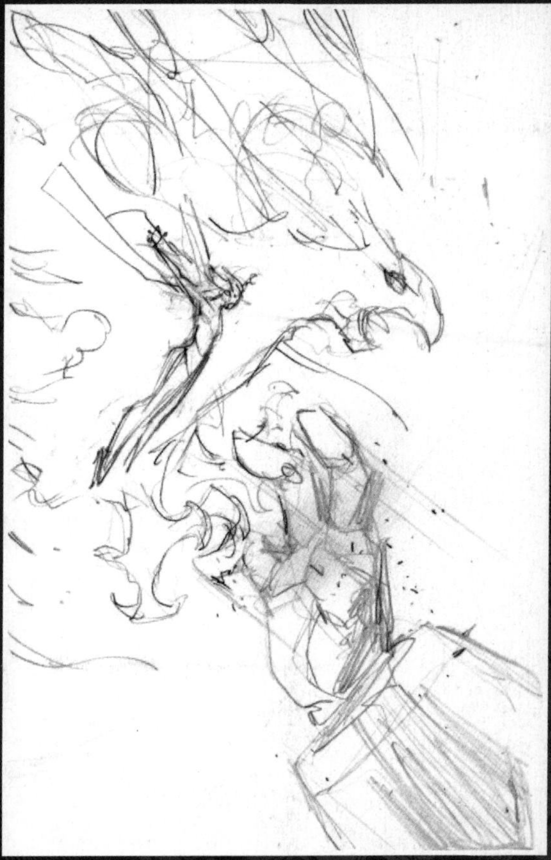

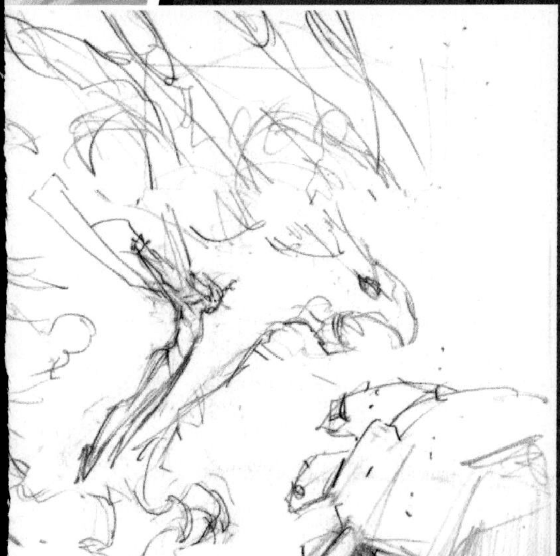

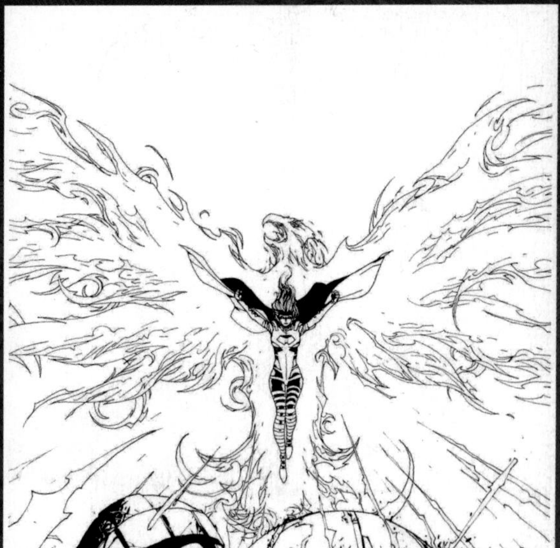

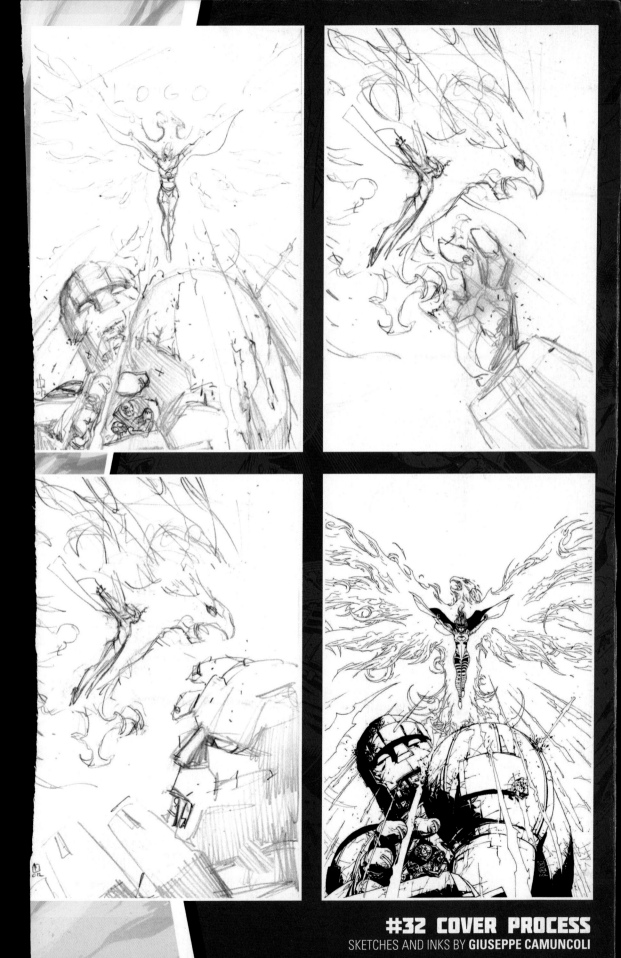

#32 COVER PROCESS

SKETCHES AND INKS BY **GIUSEPPE CAMUNCOLI**

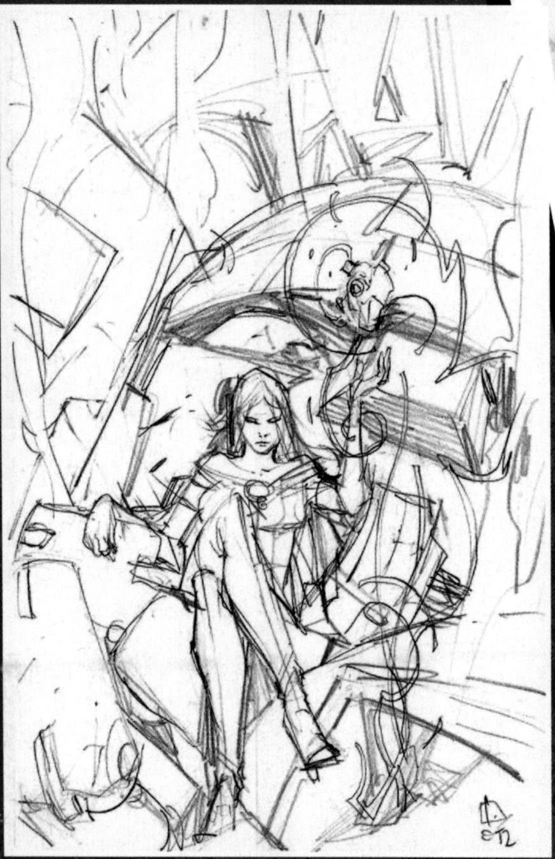

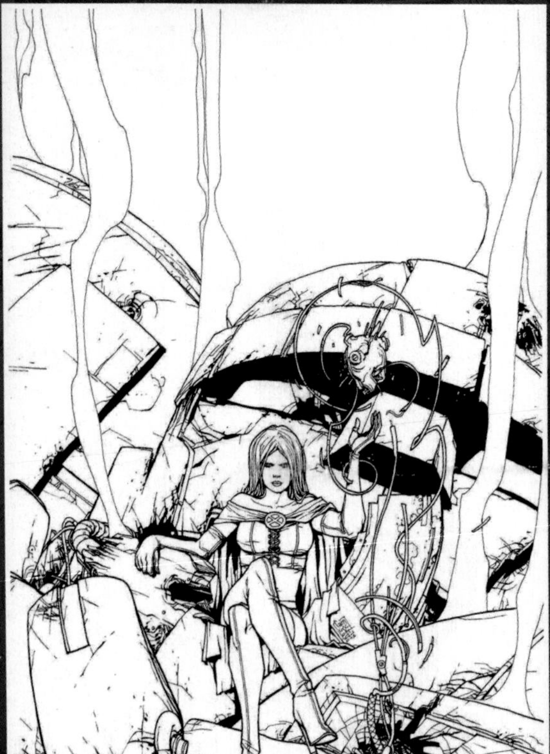

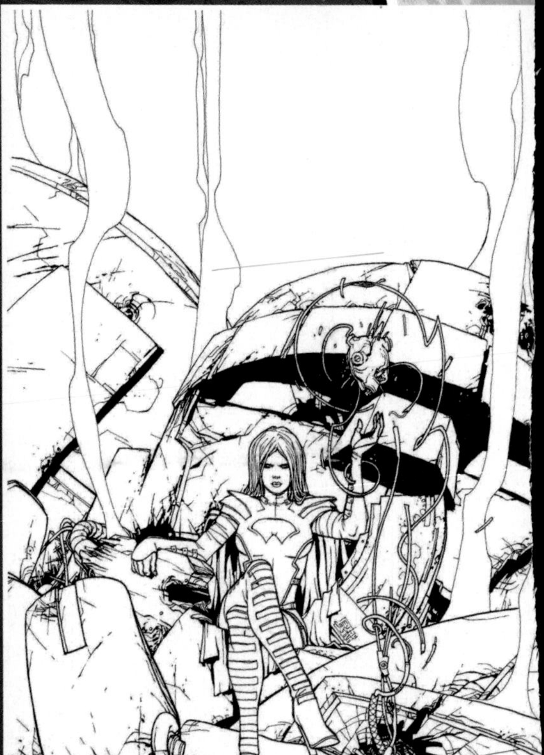

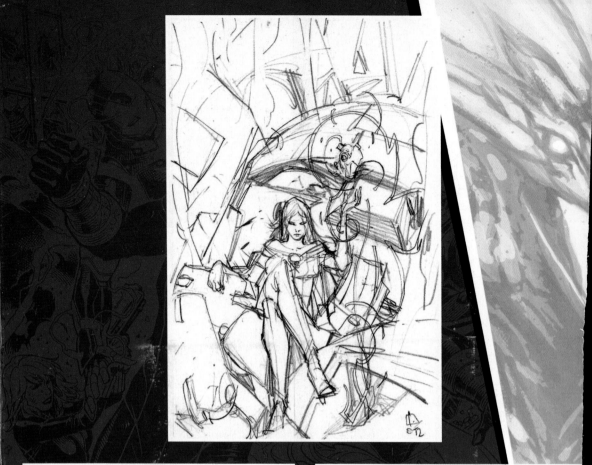

#33 COVER PROCESS

SKETCH, INKS AND REVISED INKS BY **GIUSEPPE CAMUNCOLI**